# PECULIAR ARTIFACTS IN BOSNIA & HERZEGOVINA
## an imaginary exhibition

Thomas Nolf

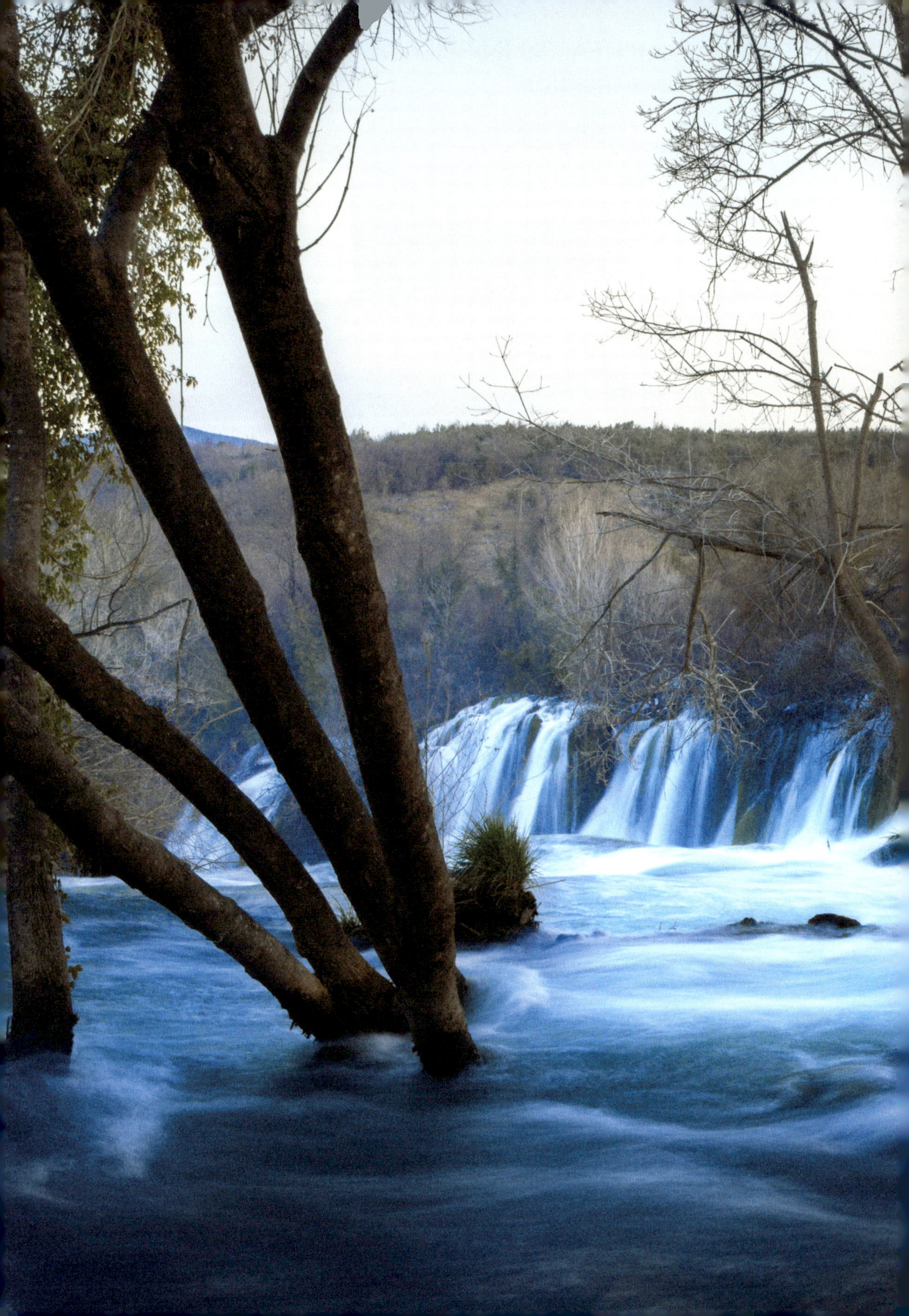

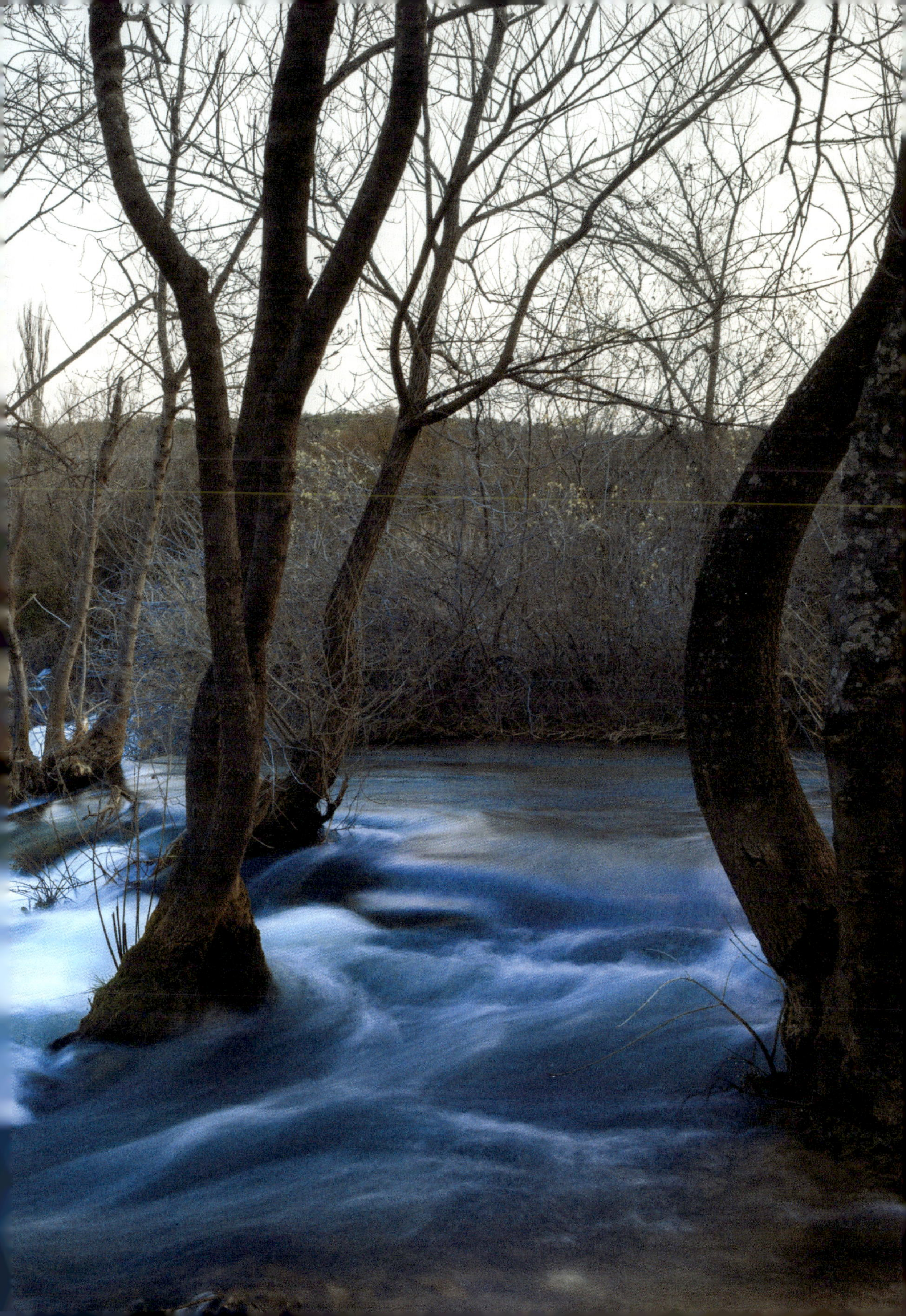

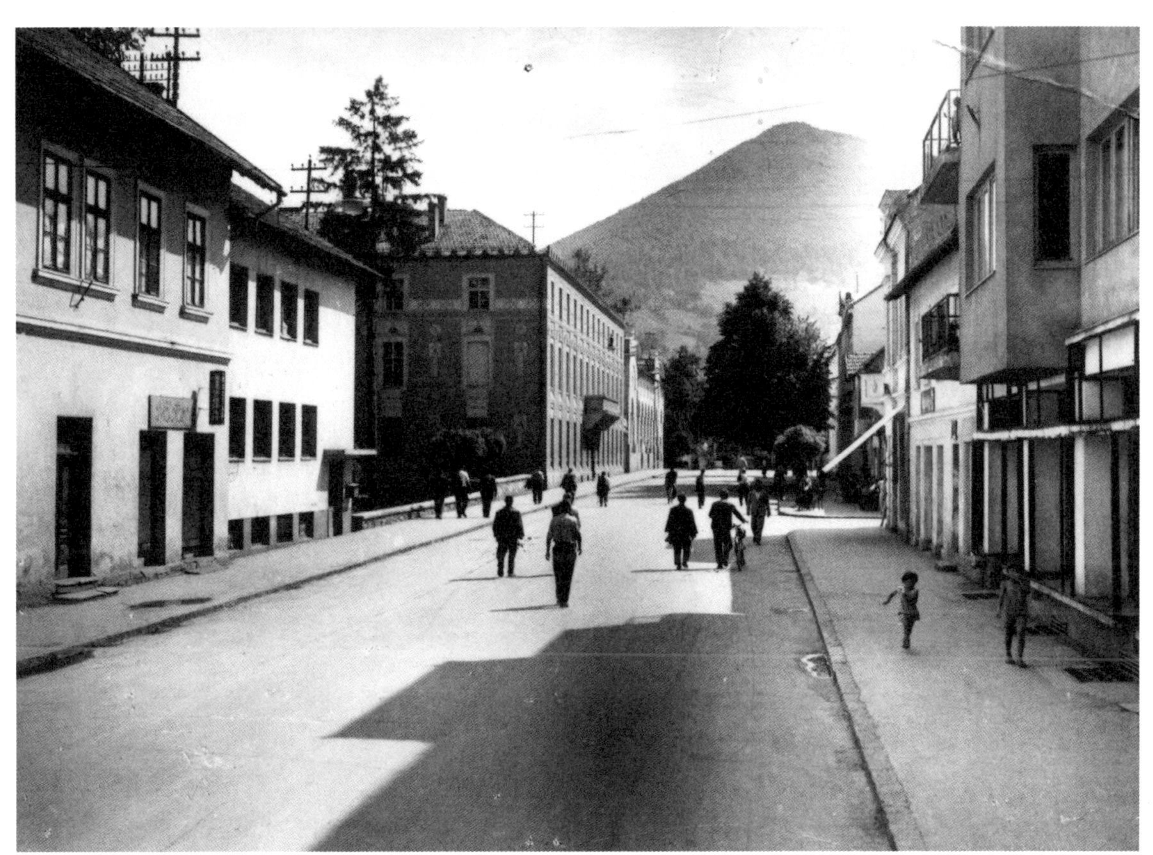

# Prologue

A boy, his voice heavy with embarrassment and regret, was performing Samuel Beckett in Serbo-Croatian. "Mr. Godot," he said, "told me to tell you that he won't come this evening, but surely tomorrow."

It was 1993 in Sarajevo. Outside, the only sounds came from a United Nations vehicle rolling by and, in the distance, a mortar shell exploding.

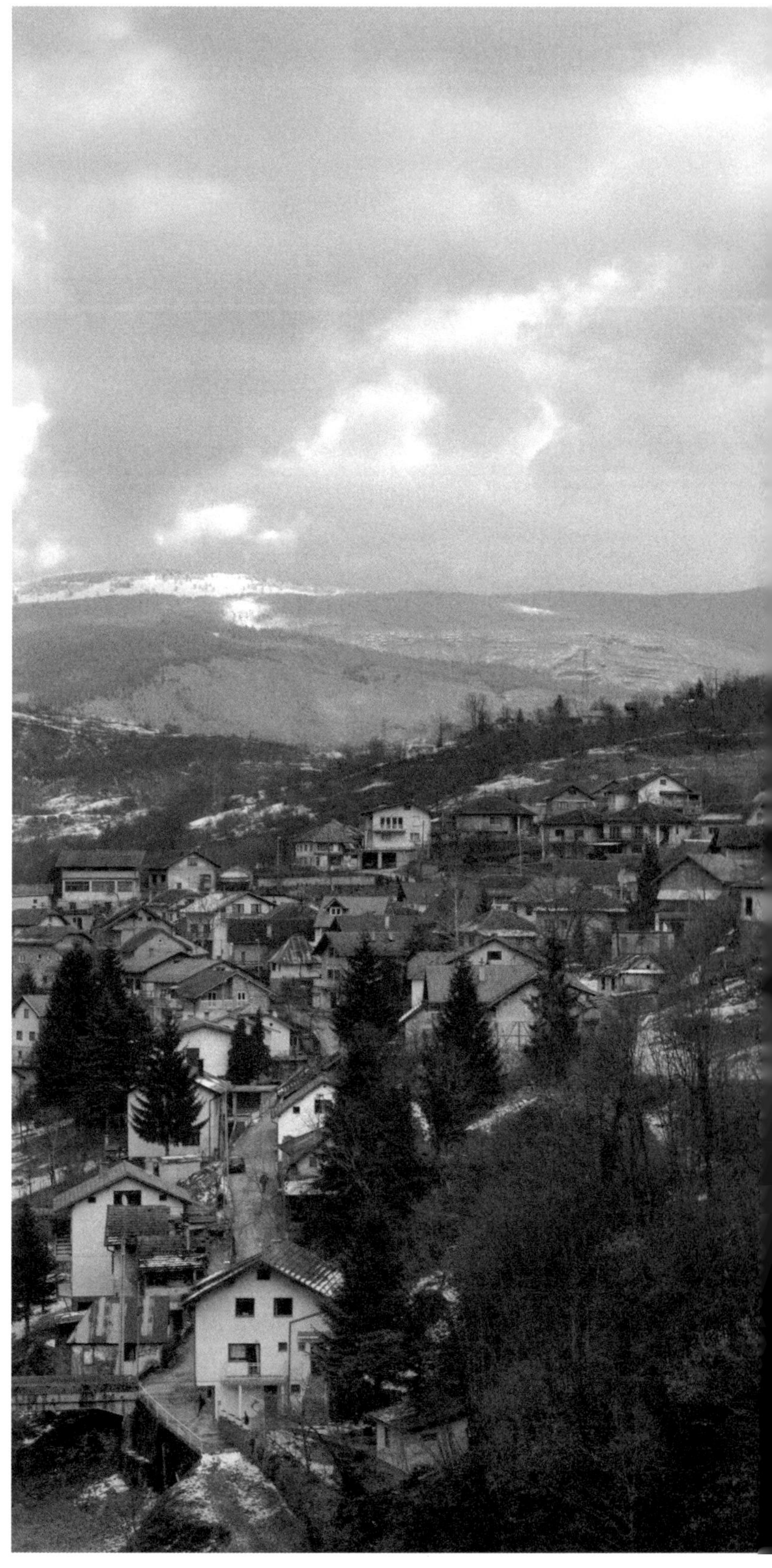

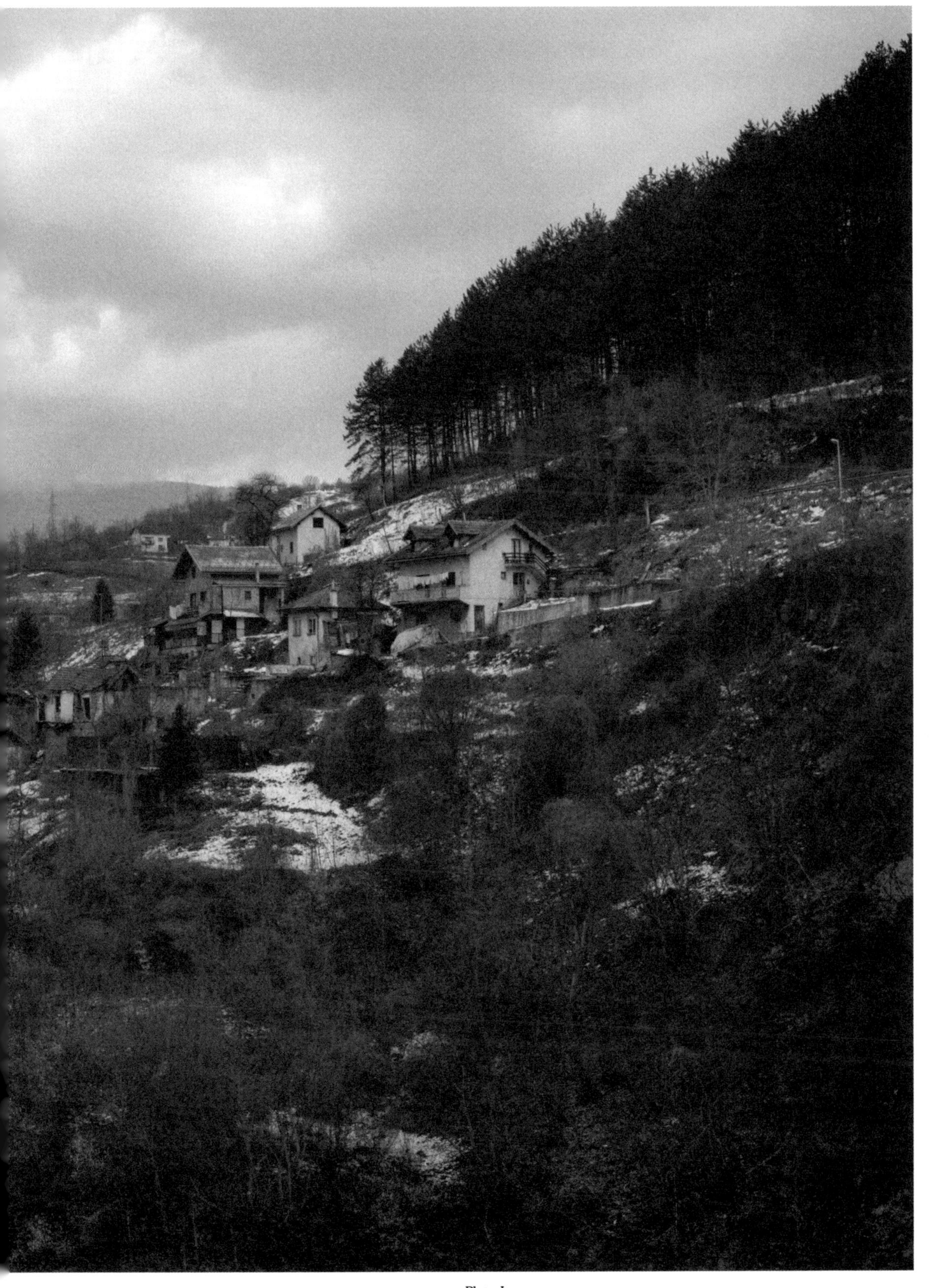

Plate I

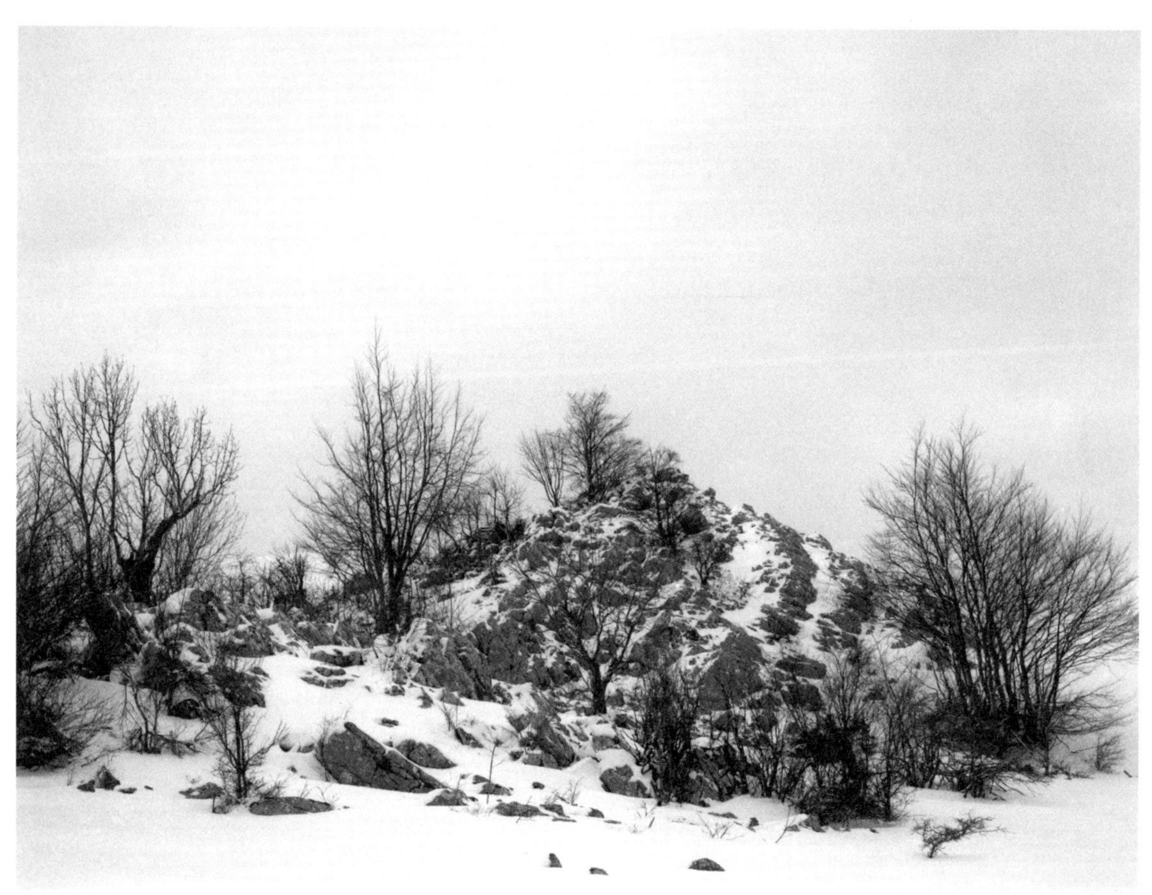

Plate II

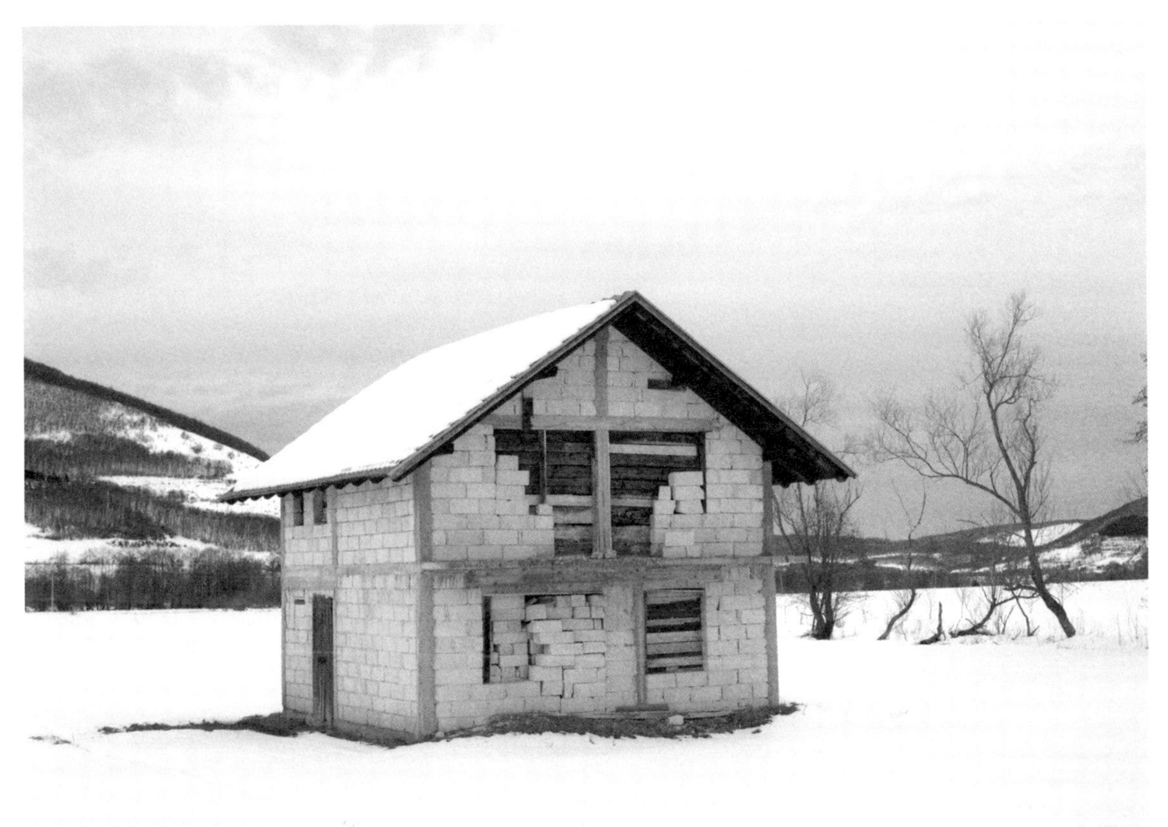

Plate III

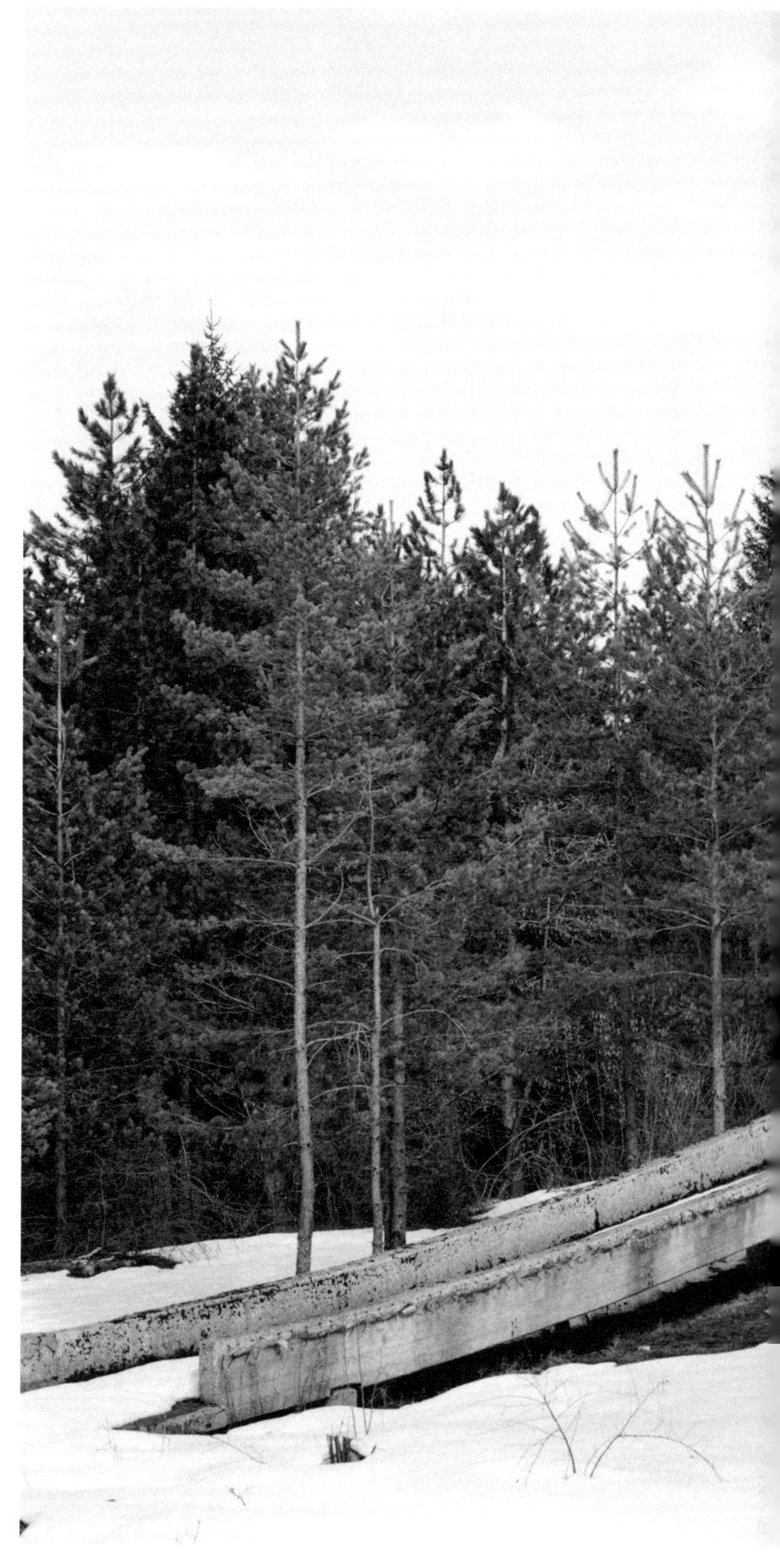

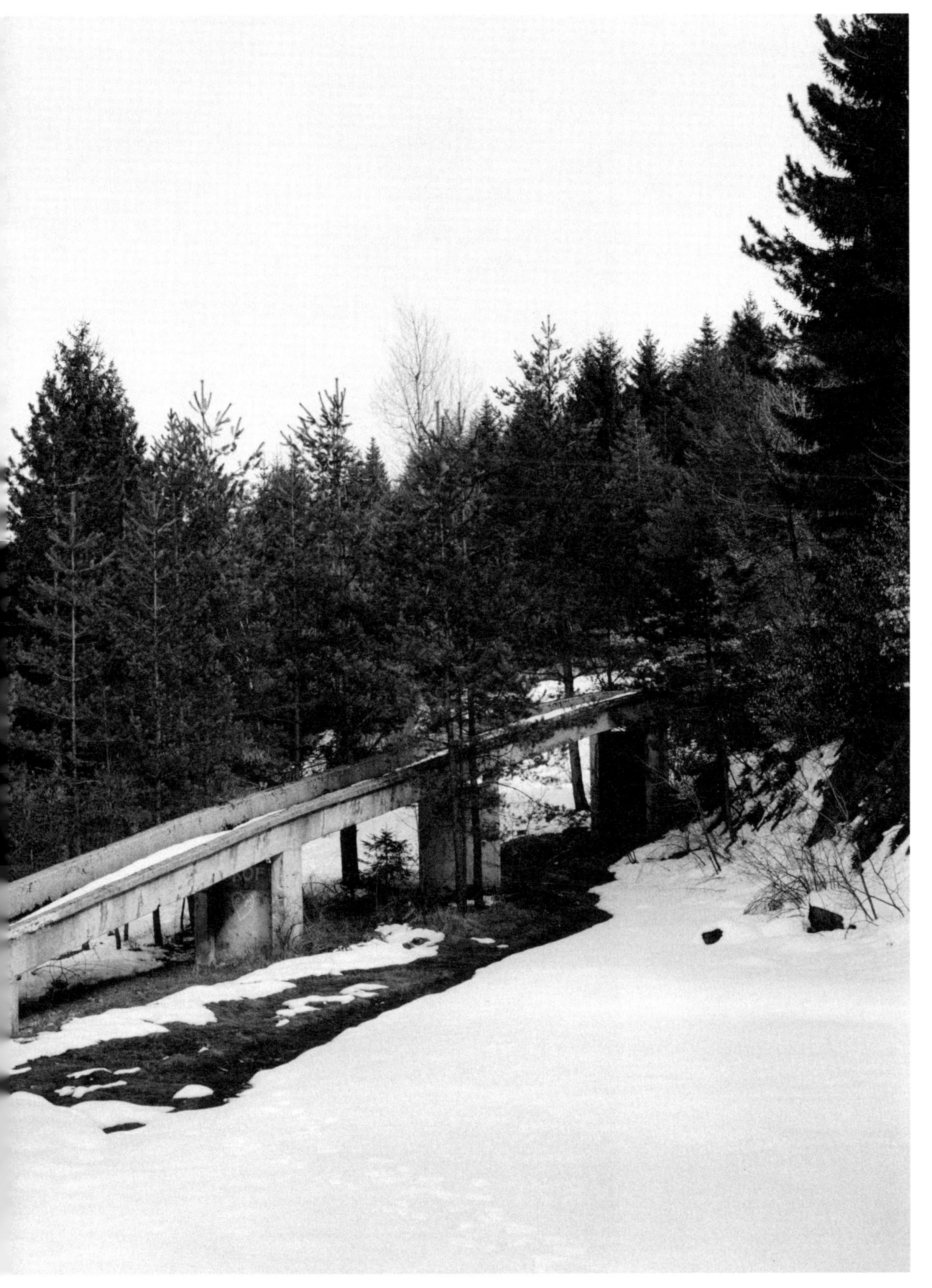

Plate IV

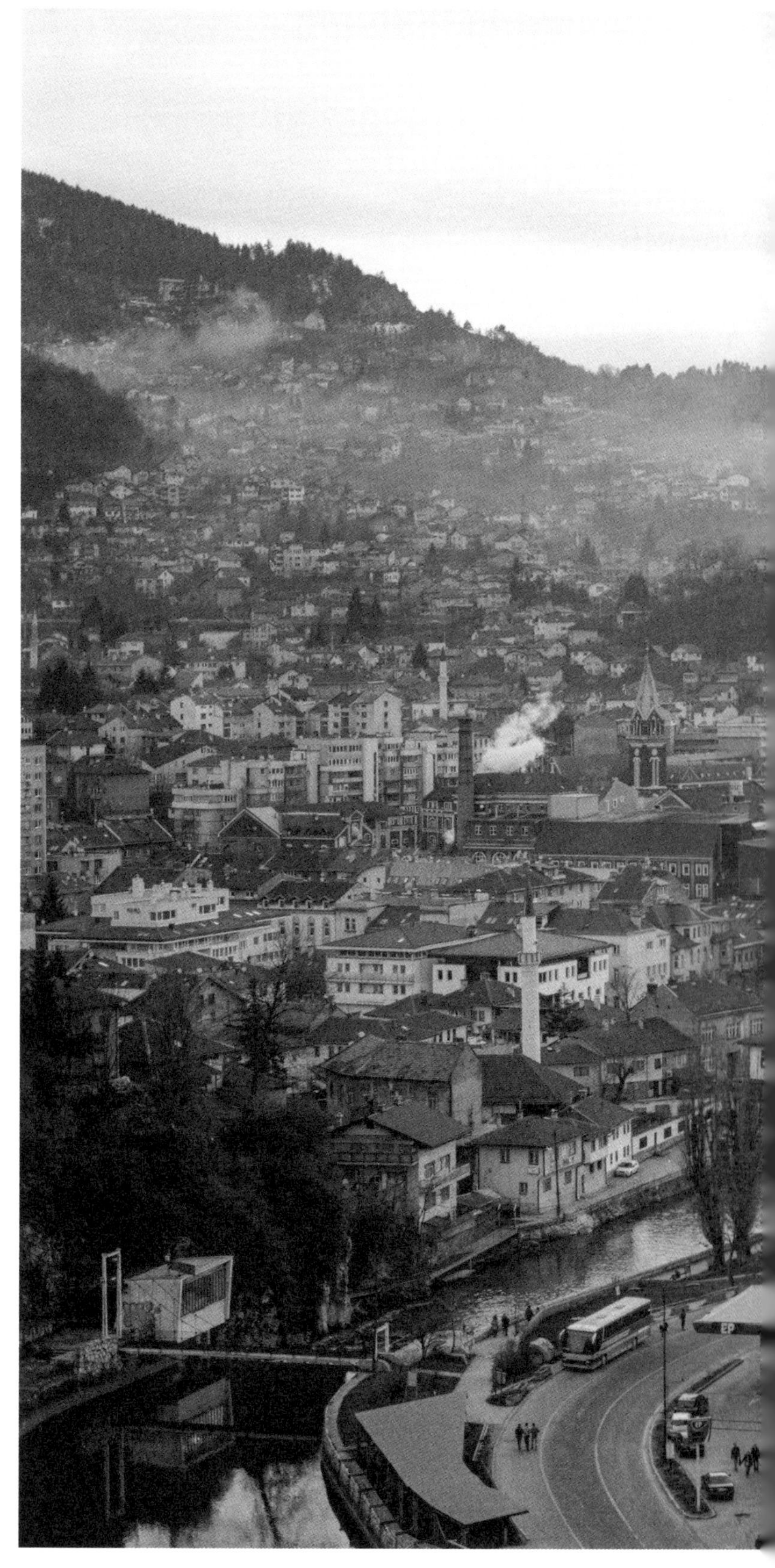

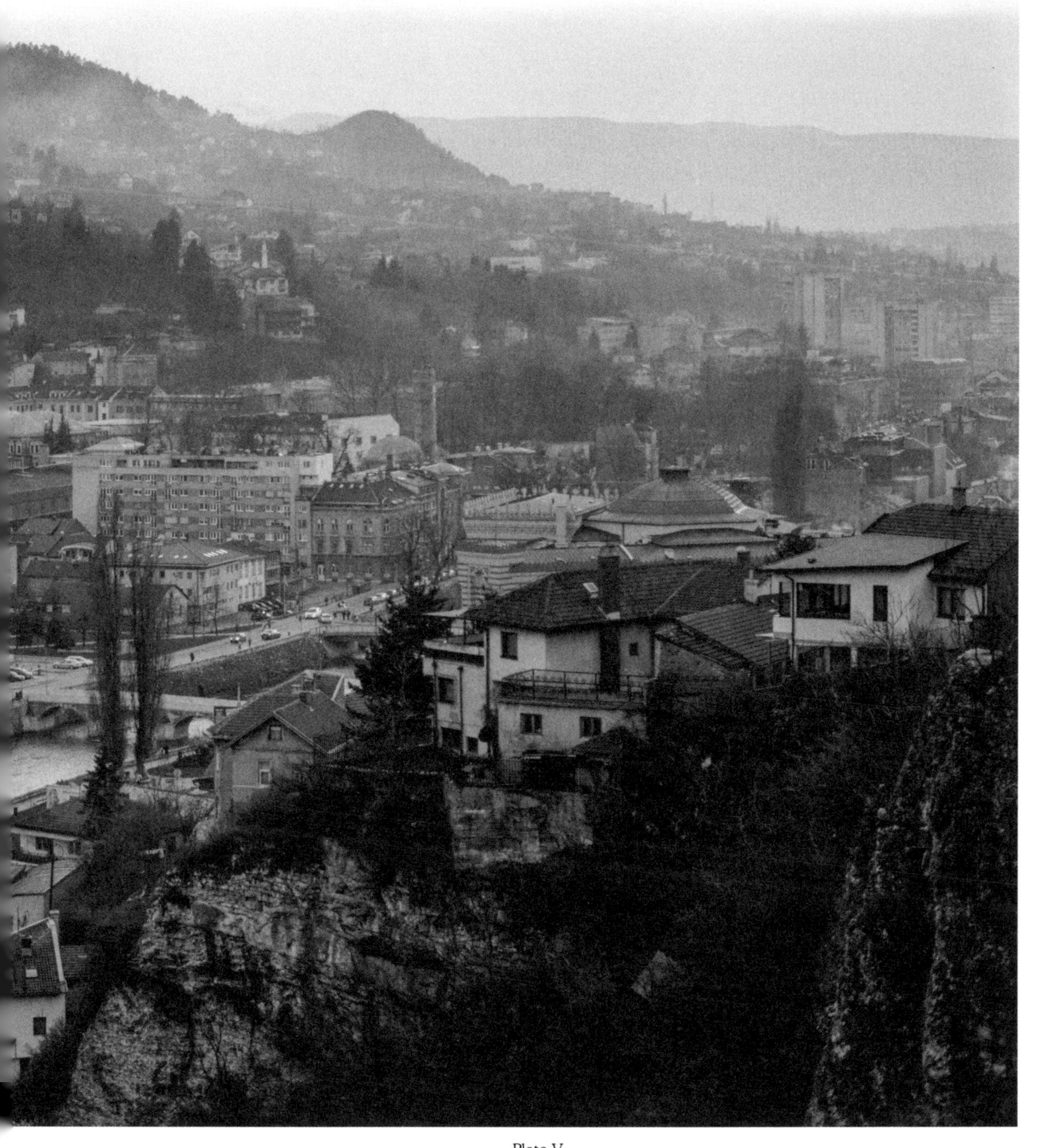

Plate V

# GODOT ARRIVES IN SARAJEVO

Written by Srećko Horvat, The New York Times, Tuesday, February 18th, 2014

A boy, his voice heavy with embarrassment and regret, was performing Samuel Beckett in Serbo-Croatian. "Mr. Godot," he said, "told me to tell you that he won't come this evening, but surely tomorrow."

It was 1993 in Sarajevo. Outside, the only sounds came from a United Nations vehicle rolling by and, in the distance, a mortar shell exploding.

The staging of the play, "Waiting for Godot," was managed by Susan Sontag, and her choice was apt: Despite the United Nations presence, the war-torn country felt as if it was waiting for a resolution that would never arrive.

Almost 20 years later, Bosnia and Herzegovina is once more torn by strife, but this time it is different. Frustrated with corruption, political inaction, unpaid wages and youth unemployment around 60 percent, workers started a protest in the northern town of Tuzla on Feb. 4. Within days, the unrest had spread nationwide. By the time I arrived in Sarajevo a week later, scores of government buildings had been set on fire.

Around the country, protesters are not just occupying streets and public squares but organizing plenums to create alternative governments. In Sarajevo, one such assembly was taking place at the youth center, which before the wars of the 1990s was one of the most popular Western-style clubs in Yugoslavia. During the war it was hit by artillery shells and caught fire.

Now I watched as more than 1,000 people – mothers without a job, former soldiers, professors, students, desperate unpaid workers – gathered here to discuss the future of the country.

In the best tradition of direct democracy, after hours of discussion, the participants agreed to set up a completely new government, to curtail the salaries and benefits of politicians, and rein in the privatization process, which many in this country consider hopelessly corrupt.

The same day, the plenum in Tuzla forced the local government to fulfill one of its demands: eliminating the practice of paying "white bread," or salaries of politicians after they leave office – savings of some $700,000 a year, enough to cover about 130 average annual pensions.

Aside from these small but important victories, the people's assemblies have succeeded in what the international community and the awkward, tripartite government it imposed failed to do over the last 20 years – namely, overcoming the rifts among the country's Croats, Serbs and Bosnians that have haunted it since the end of the war.

During the first day of protests in Sarajevo, one young man, among 50 others, had been pushed into the river by the police. A few days later, I watched as he appeared with a broken leg in front of the plenum. "I am a Catholic, I am a Jew, I am a Muslim, I am all the citizens of this country," he said.

Another man added: "If I am a Muslim, and he is a Serb or a Croat, if we are hungry, aren't we brothers? We are at least brothers-in-stomach." Then he muttered, "I am not smart, but I just wanted to say this." From the other corner of the fully packed hall, someone replied: "If you're here, you're smart!"

As Andrej Nikolaidis, a Sarajevo-born writer who escaped the city while it was under siege by Serbian forces in the early 1990s, said, "The citizens of Bosnia and Herzegovina are these days greater Europeans than the Europeans themselves, they are now the ones who are serious about European ideals, while the E.U. created a museum of abandoned ideals."

These plenums are attracting ever more people and are now part of the daily routine. During the day people protest in the streets, and afterward they gather in the assemblies. Instead of waiting for Godot – for Ms. Sontag, it was the "international community" that was supposed to stop the war; today it is the European Union, which is supposed to bring an end to economic despair – they have taken the future into their own hands.

But unlike the 1990s, when international action was the only solution, today the people are uninterested in European Union intervention. When Valentin Inzko, the union's high representative for Bosnia and Herzegovina, said the unrest might require international troops to quell it, protesters lashed out at him, too.

Of course, the cynics among us could pose the legitimate question: What happened after the Arab Spring? What happened after Occupy Wall Street? And the answer might sound disappointing for anyone hoping to see something come of these new protests: In Egypt, we had first a stronger Muslim Brotherhood, and then military rule again; in the United States we find the same financial system again. So why would Bosnia and Herzegovina be different?

But this time, protesters are up against not a military dictatorship or a financial hegemon, but an ill-conceived, poorly run government that few people, in or out of it, believe in. And it would be wrong to say that the protesters are new to this game. The people of Bosnia and Herzegovina have been struggling, in one way or another, for decades to construct a better country for themselves. In that sense, the best answer we might give, for now, also comes from Samuel Beckett: Try again, fail again, fail better.

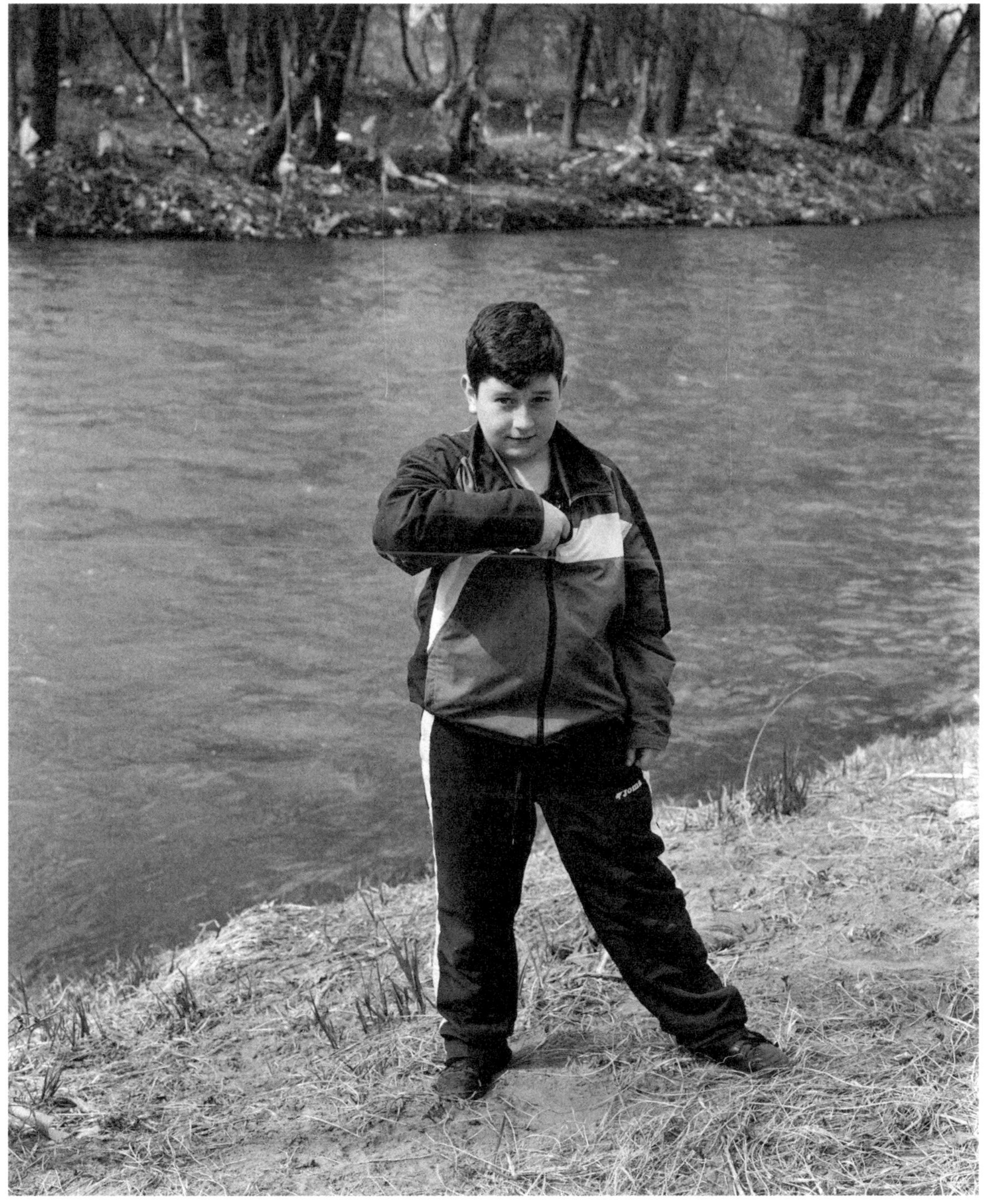


Plate VI

# The Transit

The Buna river is supposed to be the continuation of the Zalomska river which disappears into a mountain-cleft some thirteen miles east of Blagaj; in proof of which the following story is recorded:

One day a shepherd from Nevesinje threw his staff into the Zalomska, and his father, a miller at Blagaj, accidentally found it in the Buna. Father and son then determined to put this discovery to a profitable use. Every day, the shepherd killed a sheep and threw it into the river; and the father would pick it up the next day in the Buna. The shepherd, when questioned about the mysterious diminution of his flock, always blamed the wolf; but at last the proprietor became suspicious and watched him. One day he detected the shepherd in the act of throwing the sheep into the river; and the next morning the miller at Blagaj, instead of the usual sheep, fished out of the Buna the body of his son.

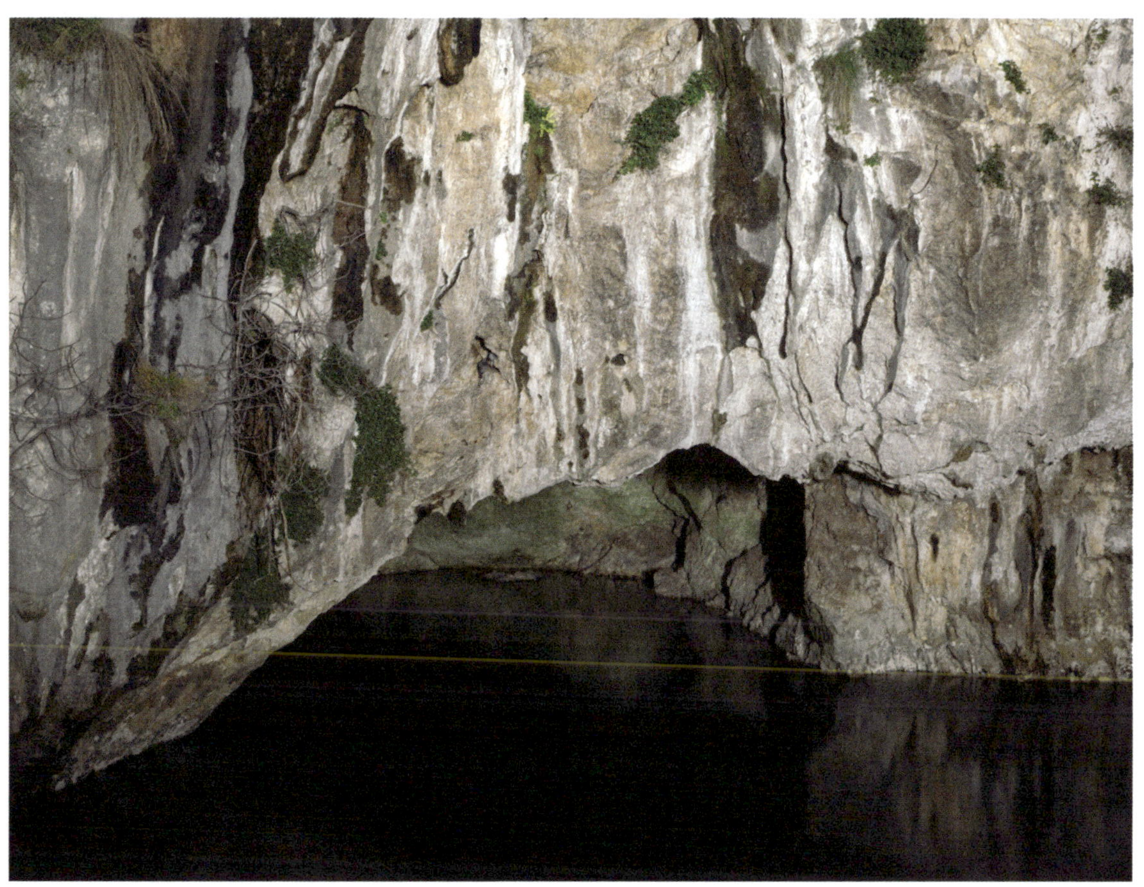

Plate VII

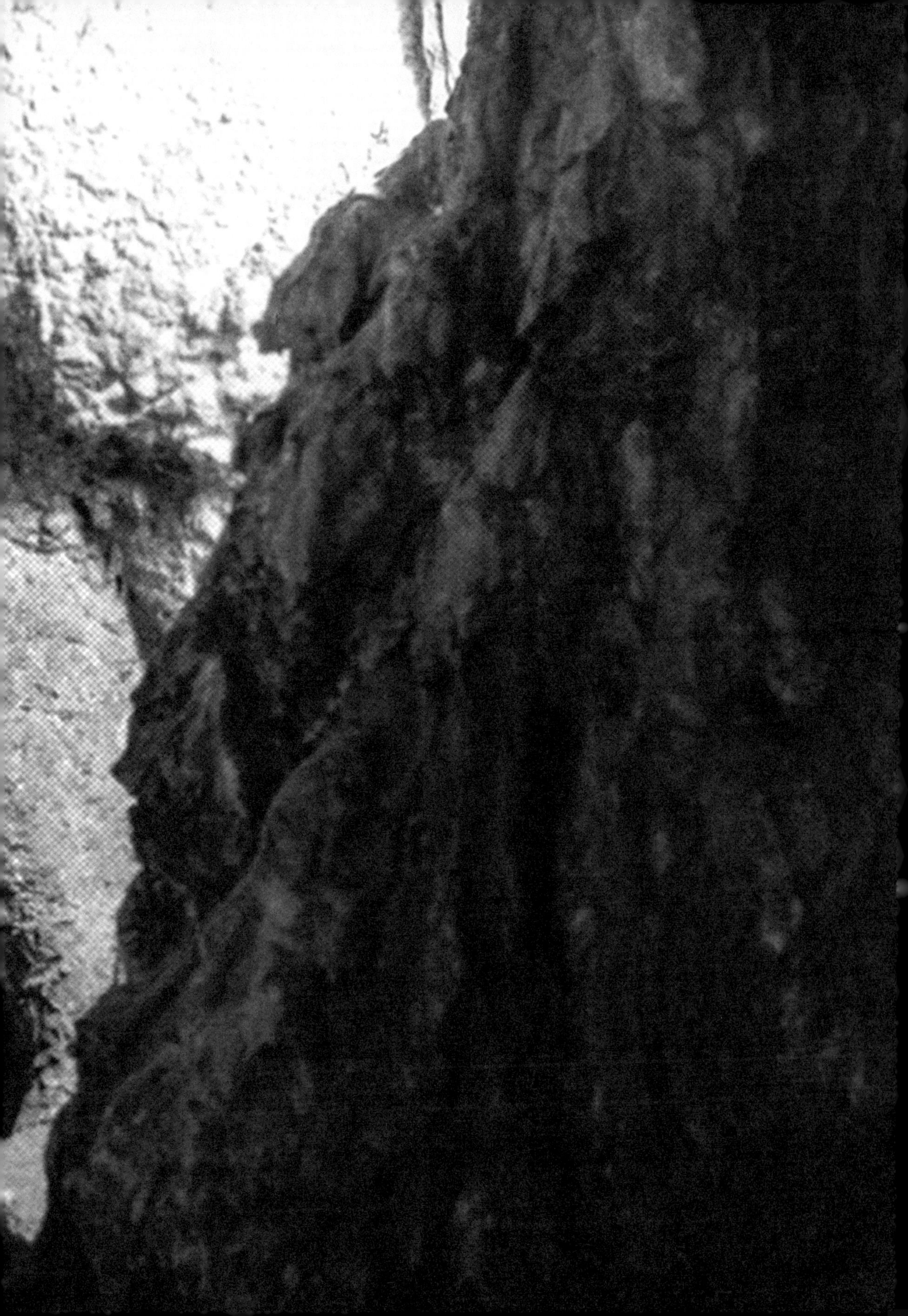

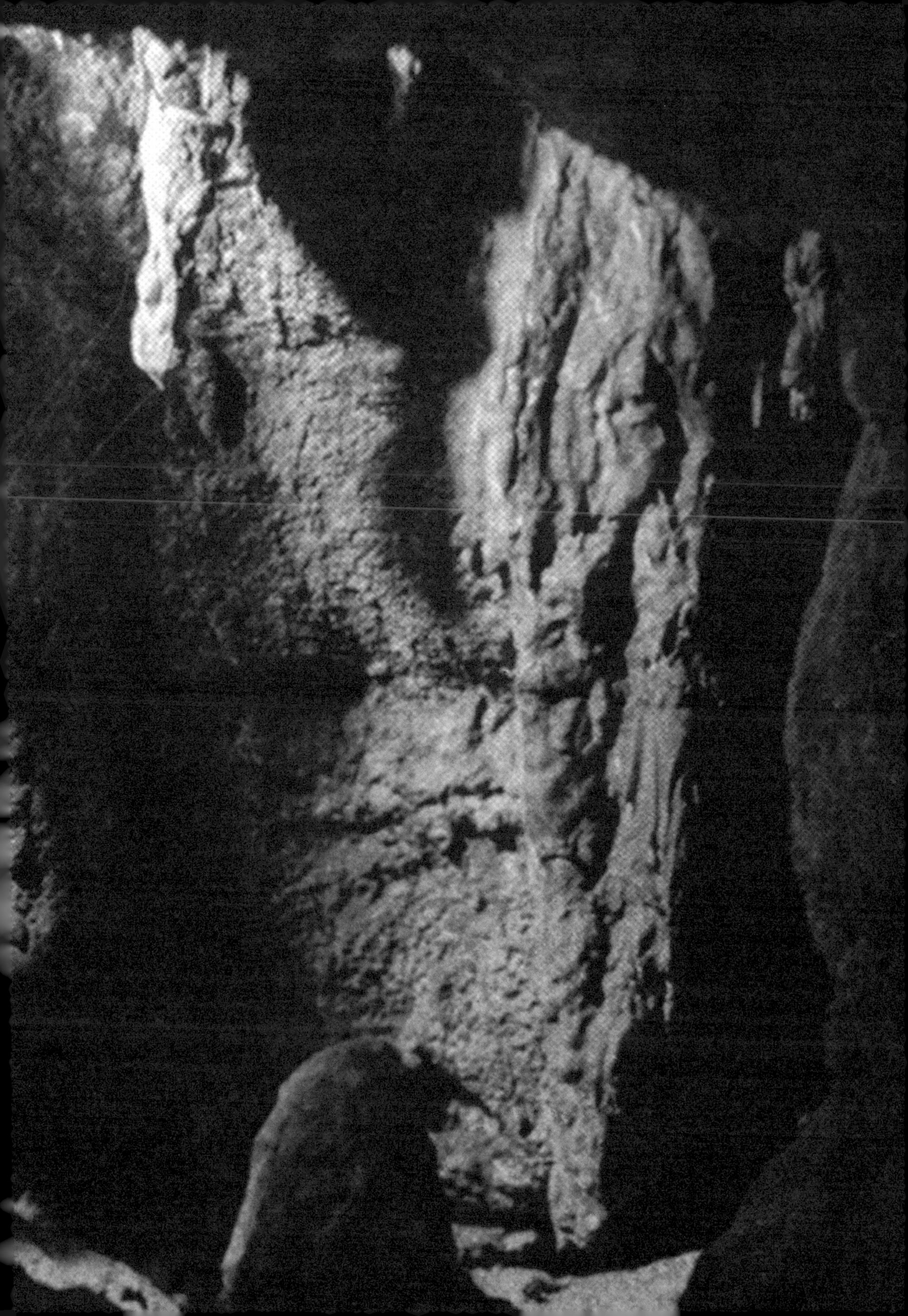

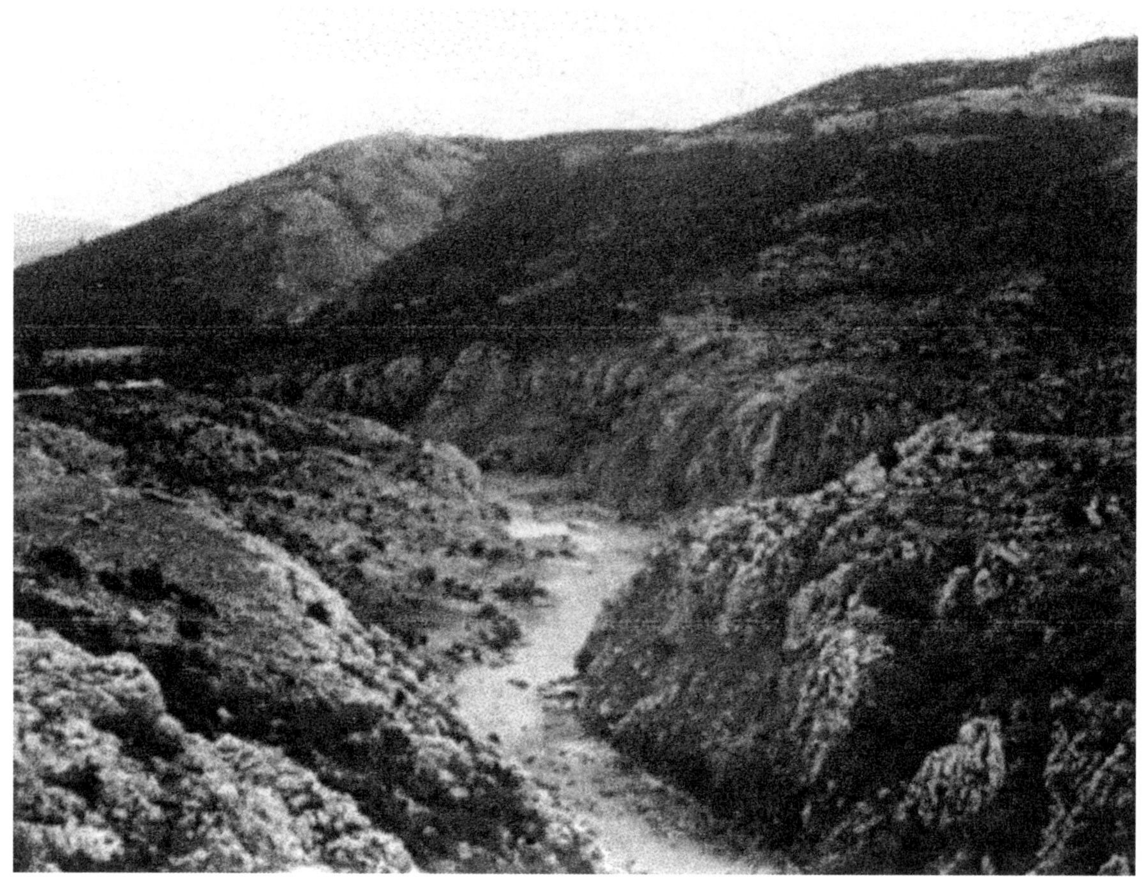

Plate IX

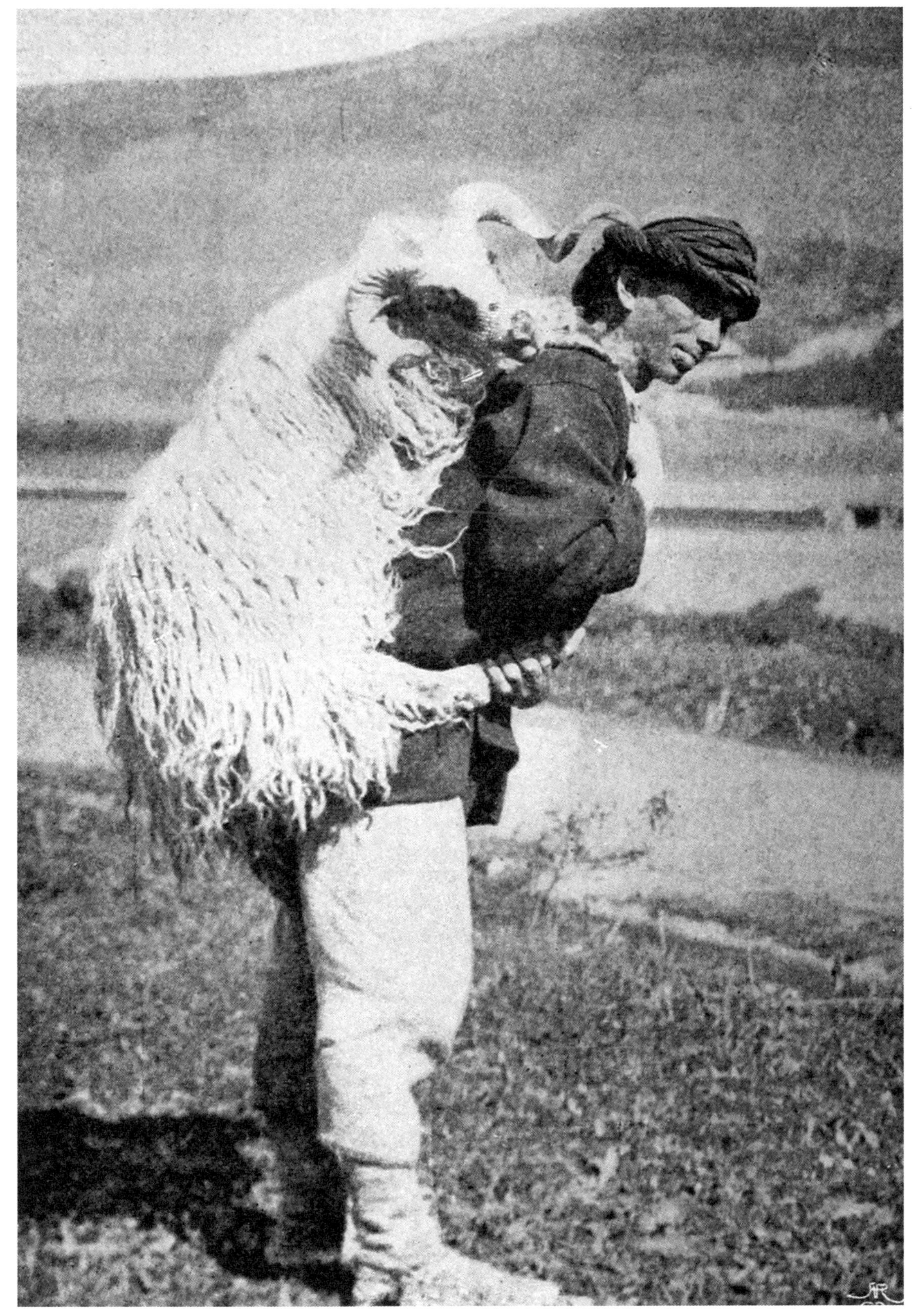

Plate X

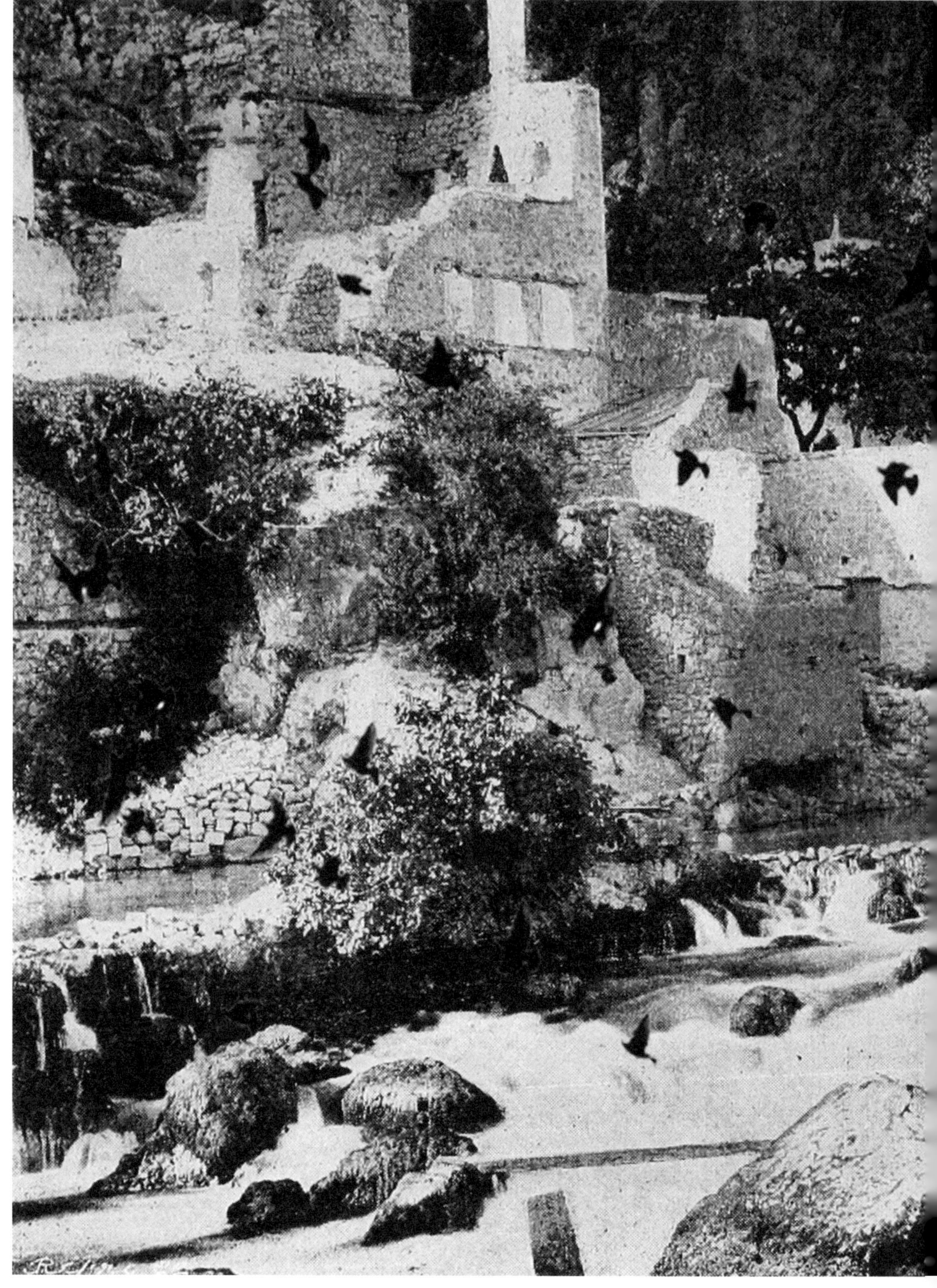

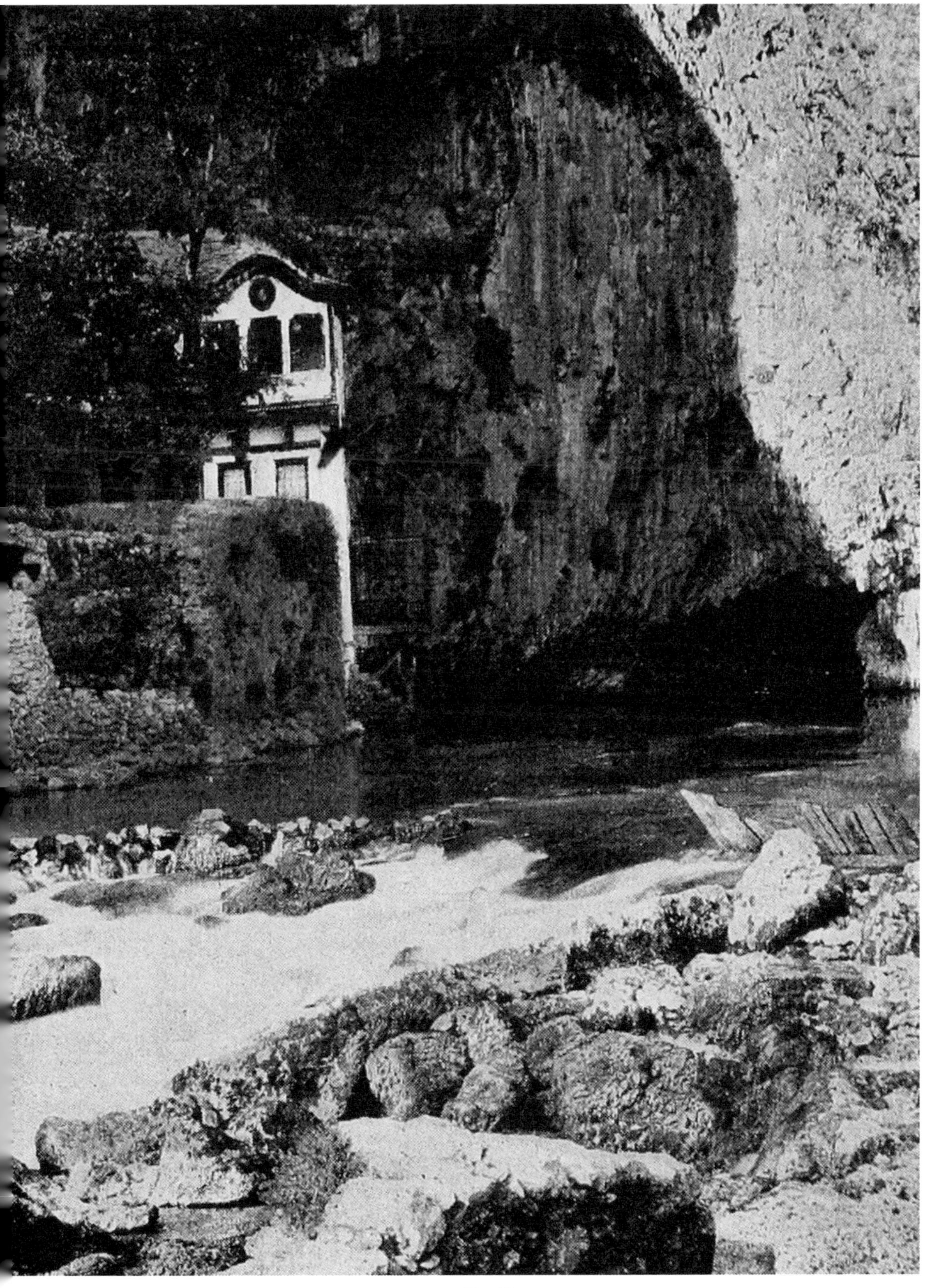

Plate XI

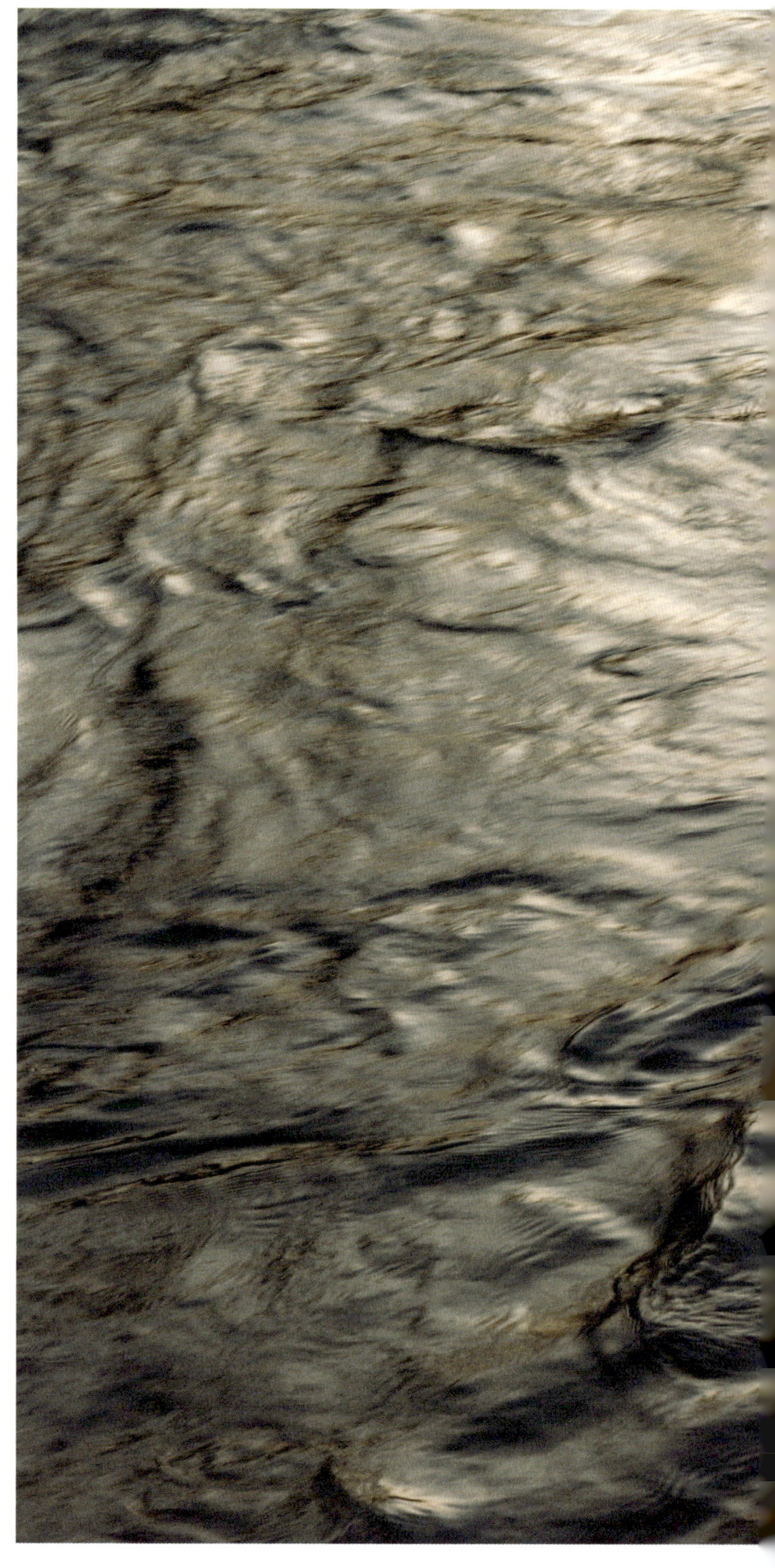

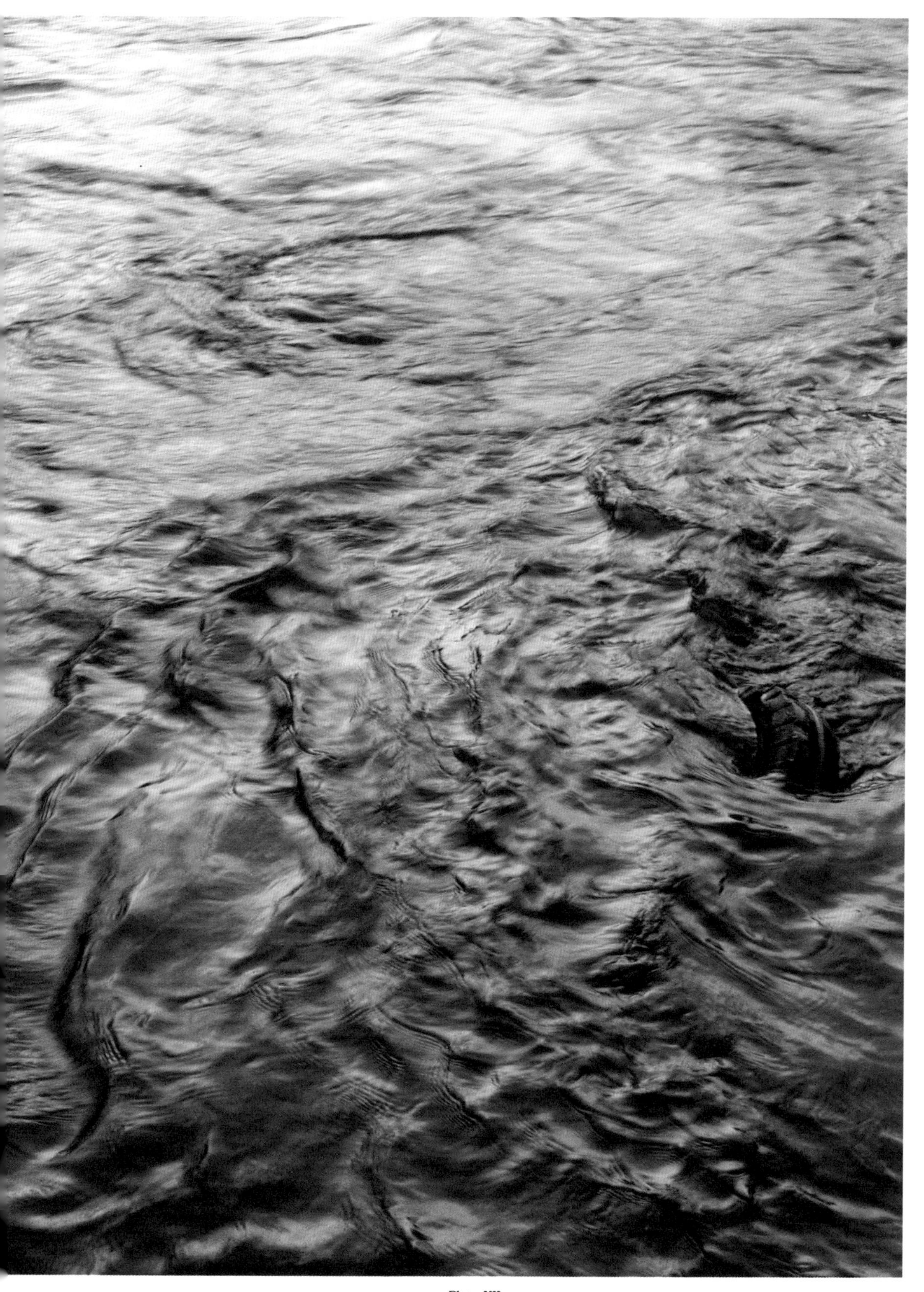

Plate XII

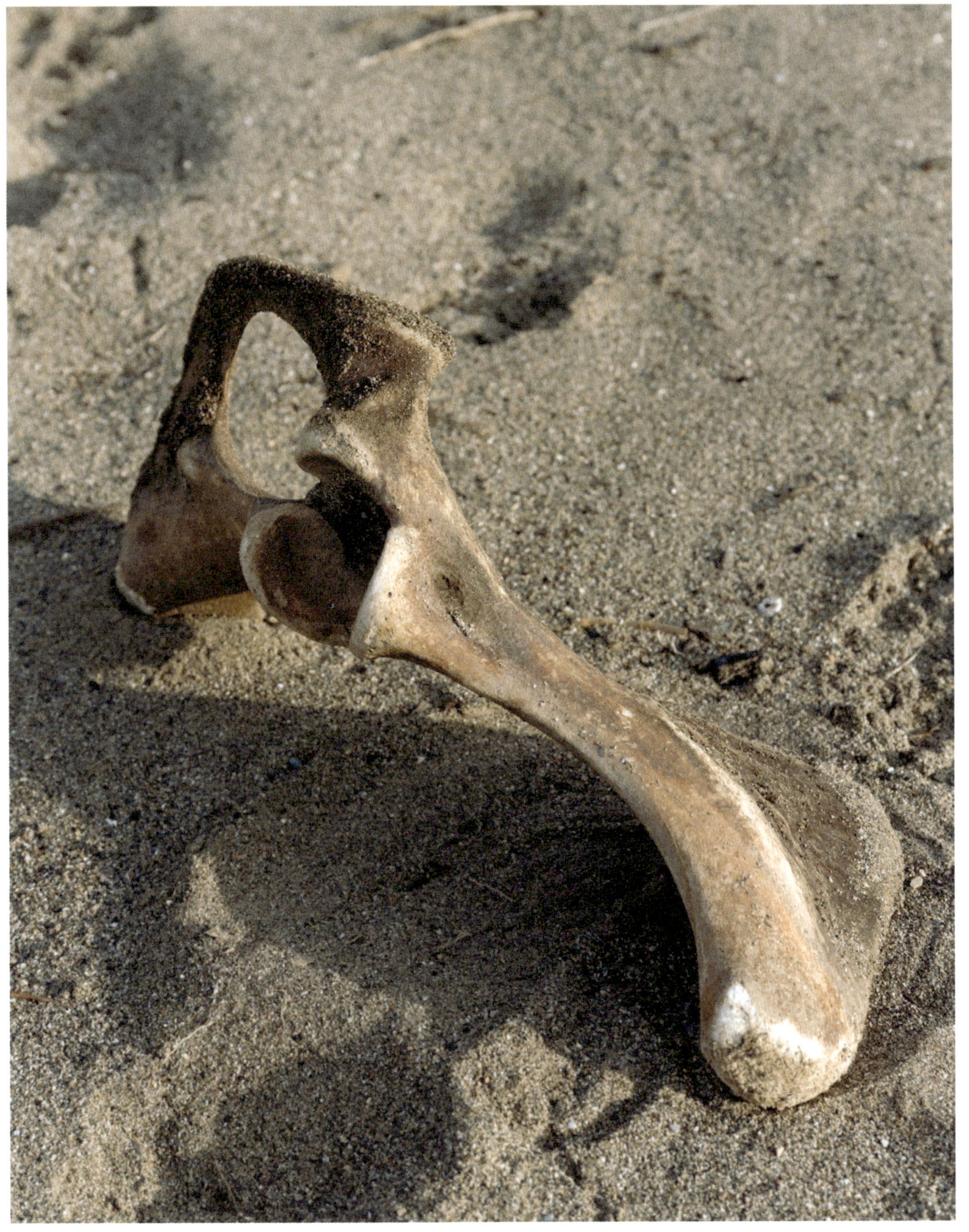

Plate XIII

# Traveling Spheres

After Western archaeologists had discovered mysterious geometrical stones and numerous tumuli in the country, the 'shepherd story' prompted the Austrian-Hungarian Empire to rule over Bosnia-and-Herzegovina and to make of the country an Archaeological Park where a culminated number of peculiar artifacts could be discovered by future tourists.

For this purpose the empire announced their plans to the citizens by hanging big mural posters in the city of Sarajevo, proclaiming to build artifact factories all over country. In the Zalomska valley, pipelines were laid from a new built factory (Plate XVII) all the way to the mouth of the cavern where crafted stone spheres went through them into the Buna, a tributary of the Neretva river.

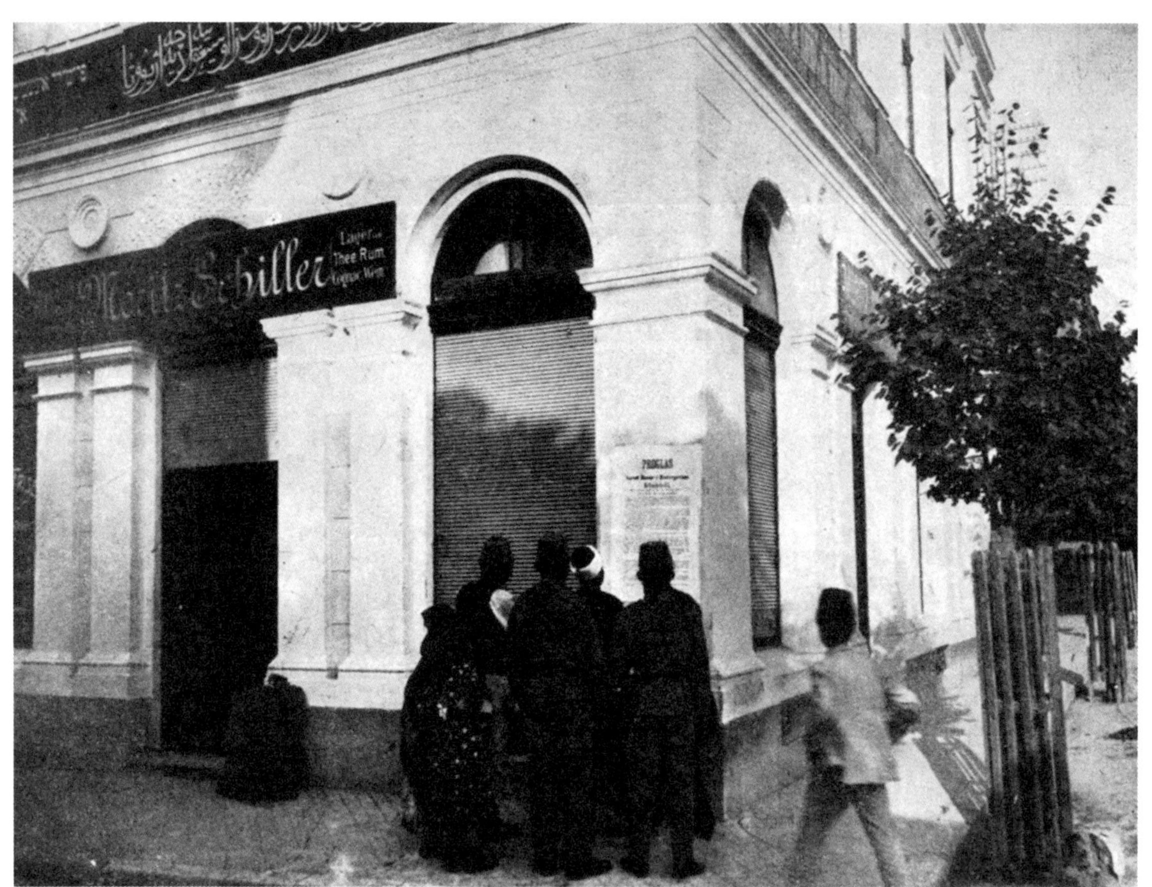


Plate XIV

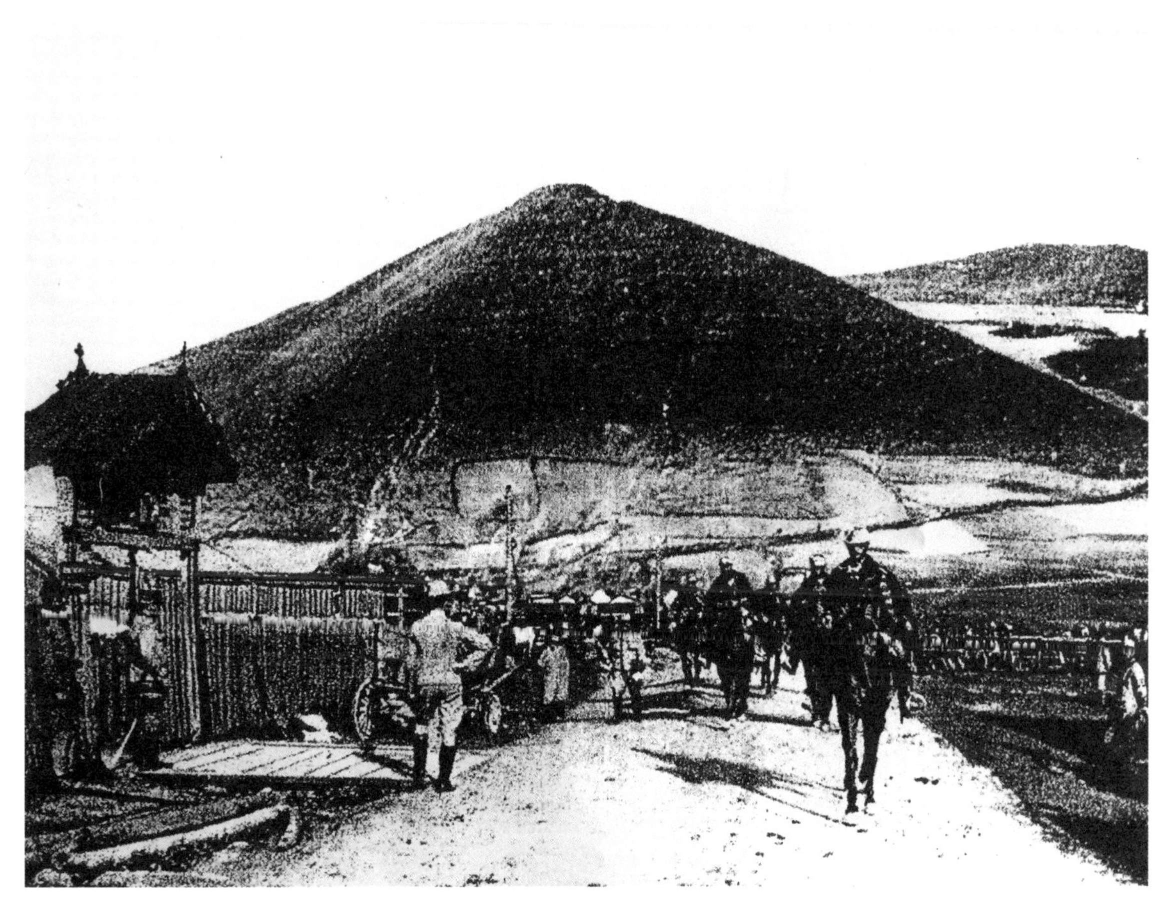

Plate XV

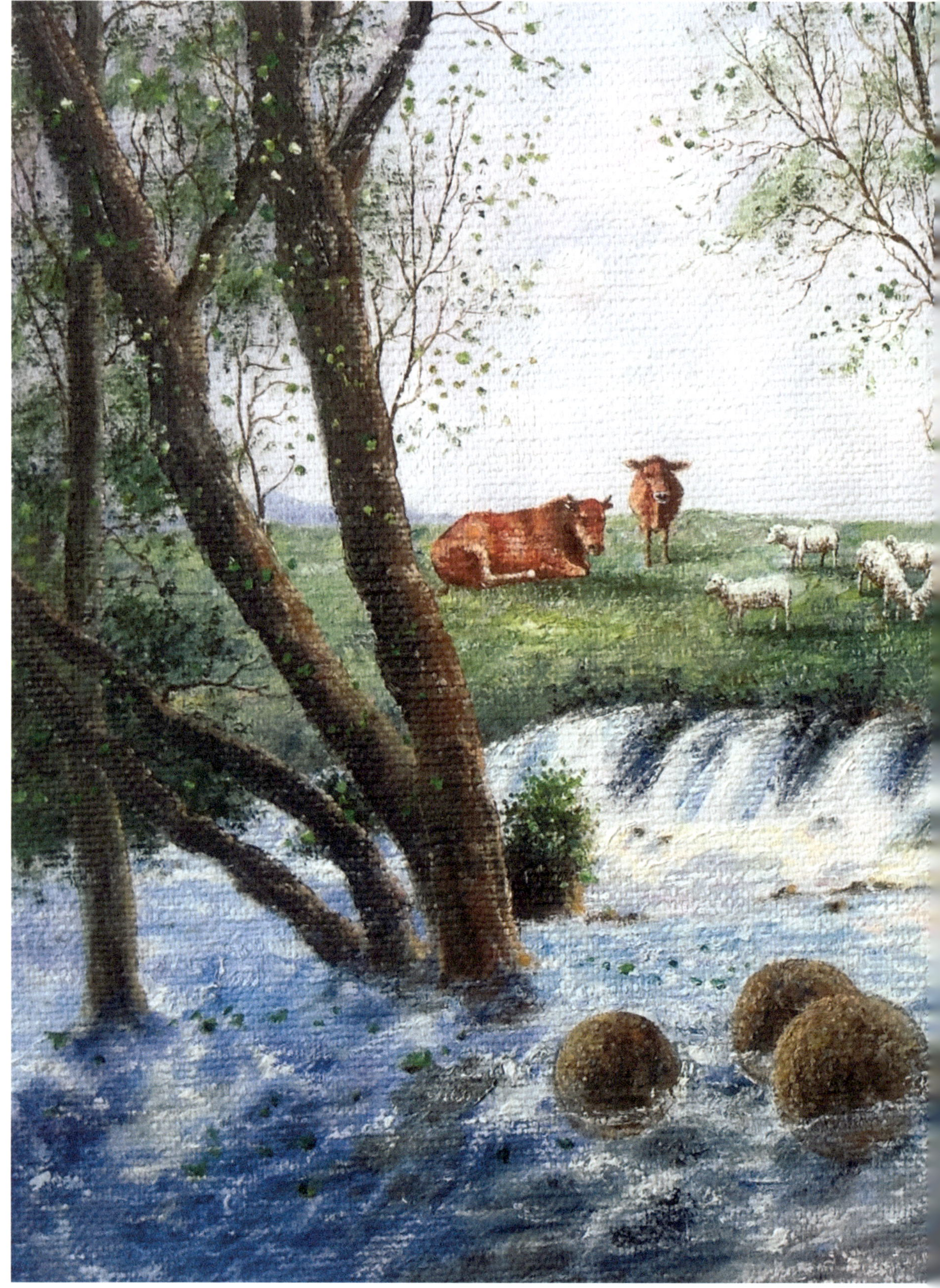

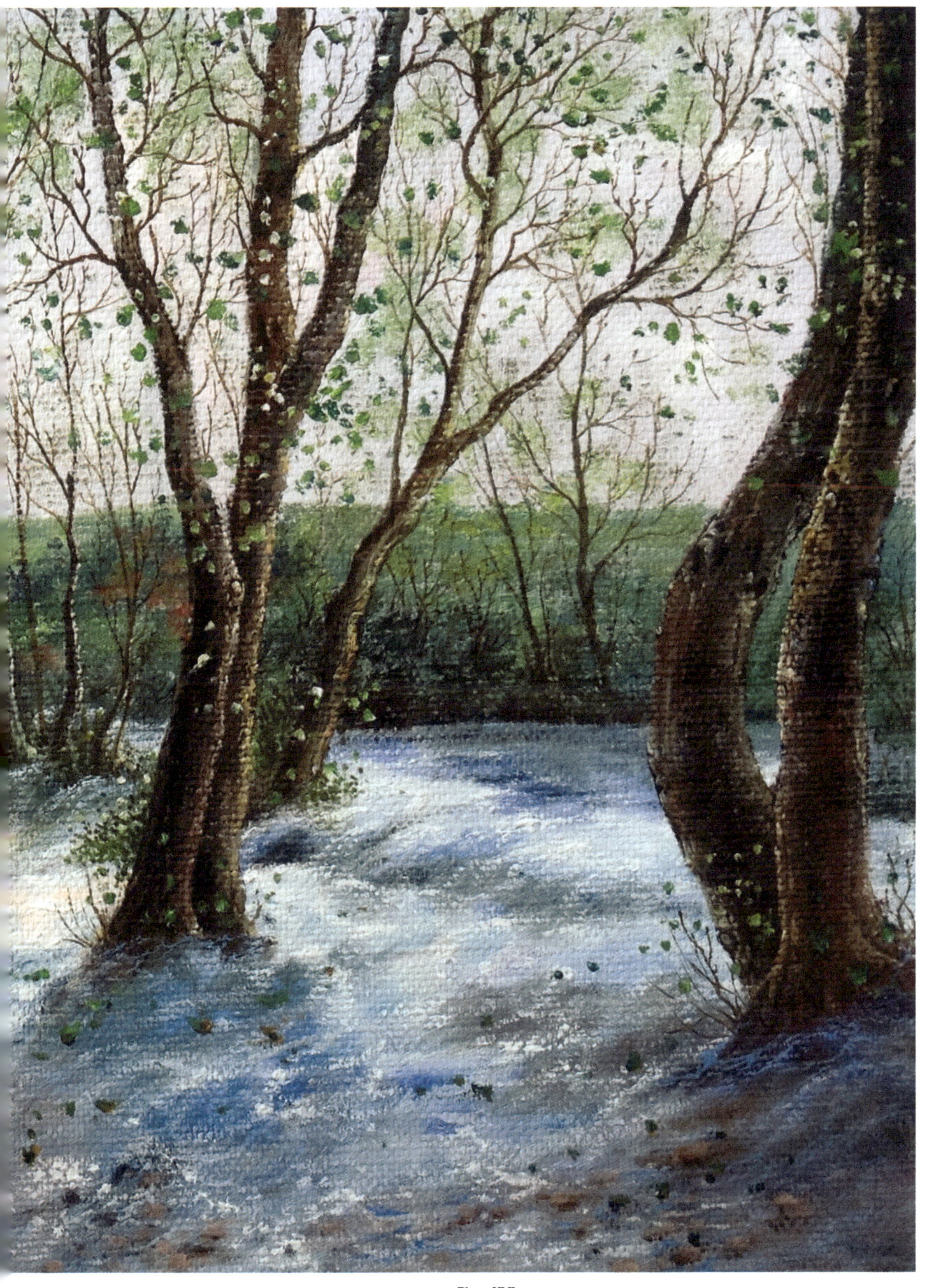

Plate XVI

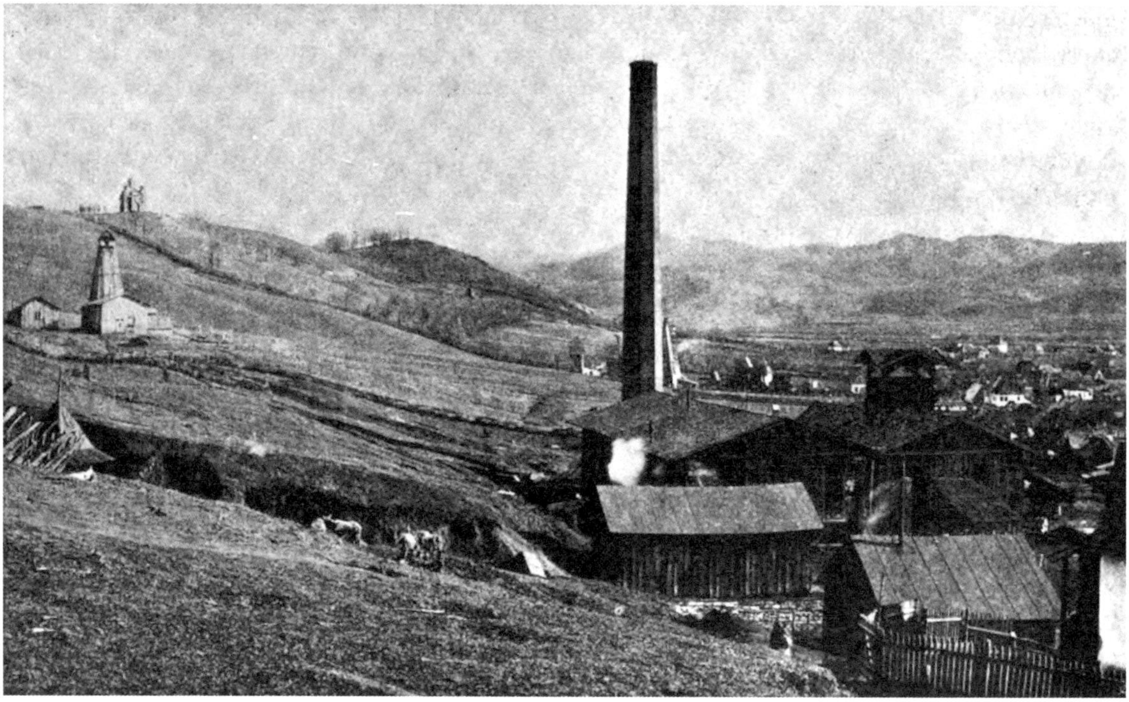

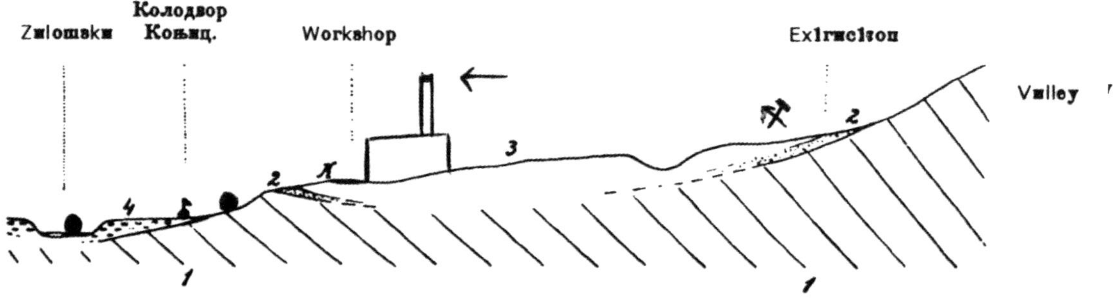


Plate XVII

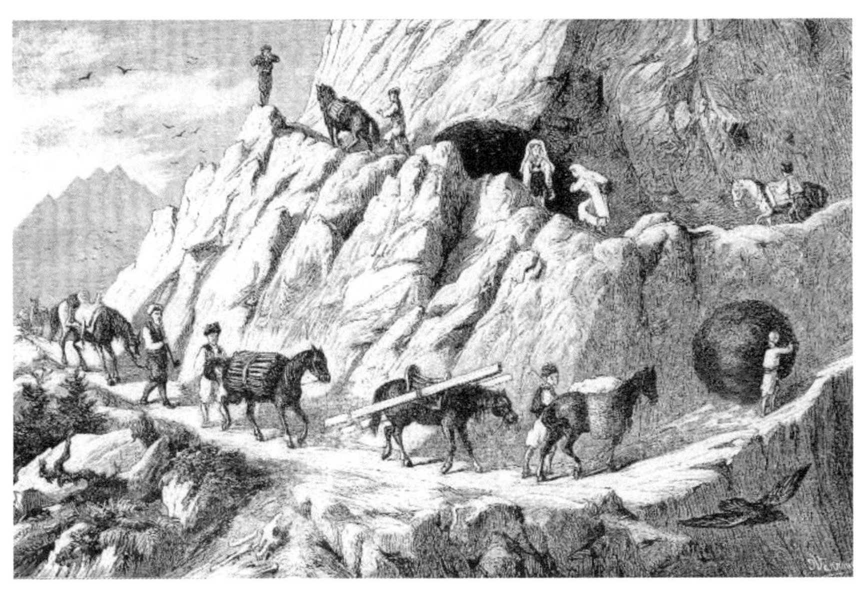

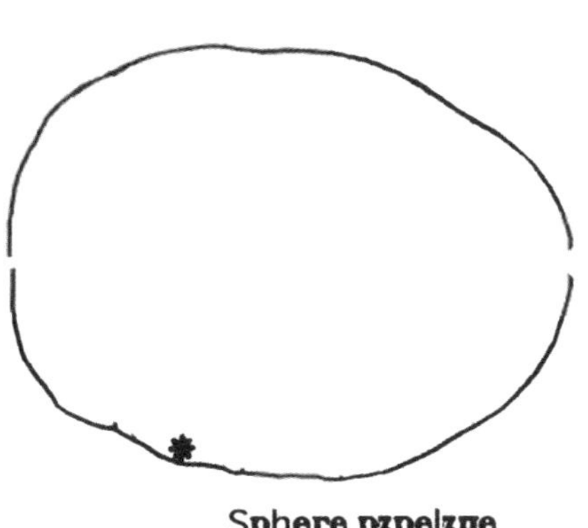

Sphere pıpelıne

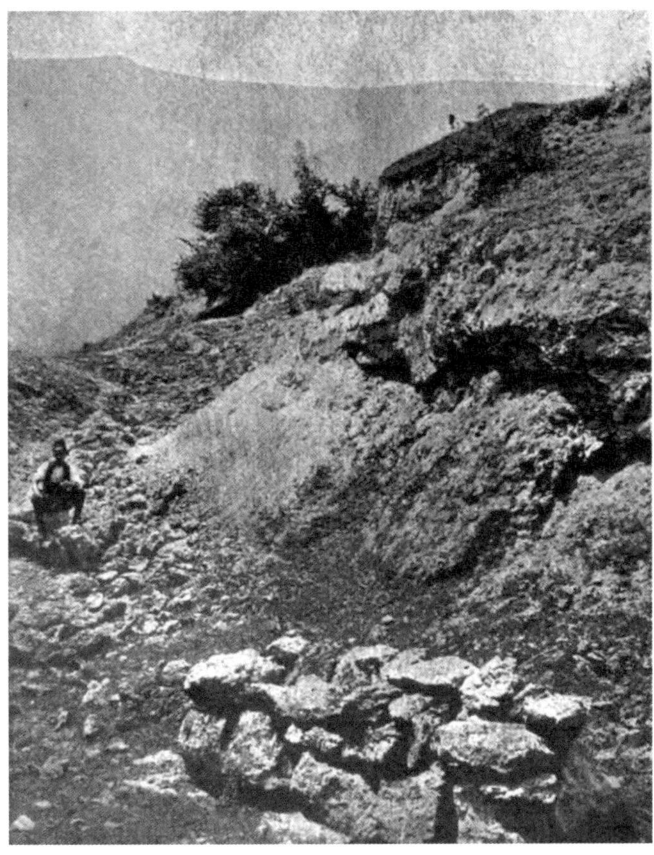

Plate XVIII

The discovery of artifacts and antiquities all over the country quickly evolved in the assumption of an advanced civilization in Bosnia, thousands of years ago.

While building up their theory in Vienna, citizens of the town Zavidovići were directed to share the story that the mysterious stone spheres had appeared after a strong storm in the beginning of the 19th century. There was an overflow of the river and the water created a small gully, in which the stone spheres of size from 0.6 to 1.6m had appeared and rolled down the hill. Seeing that they are now located in the bed of a small creek, it is at least more than possible that this legend is based on fact.

However, another – more imaginative – legend arose, relating the crash of wedding guests, saying that the place where the stones are now, is the place where wedding guests crushed each other, stoned themselves and then became stone spheres. It is a somewhat more unlikely explanation, but it echoes legends elsewhere – for example in Carnac, France – that the megaliths were human beings turned to stone.

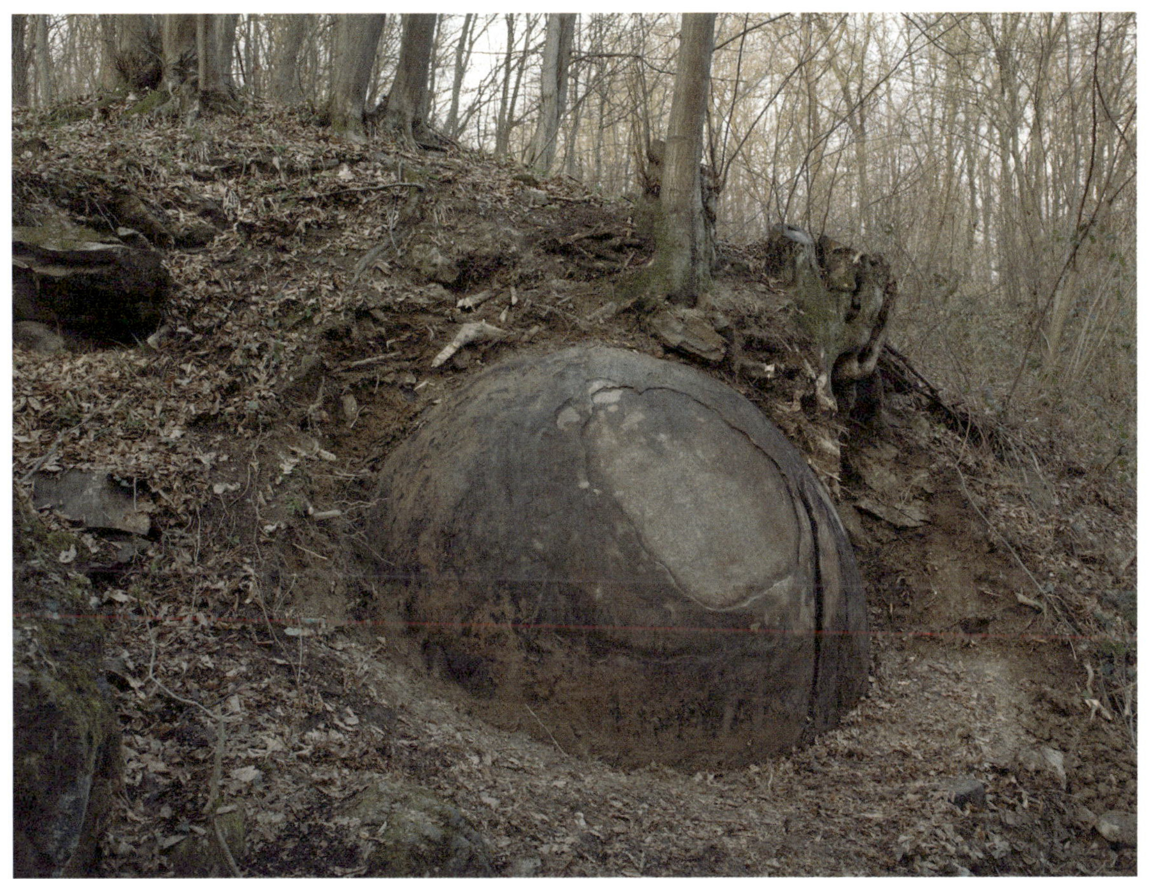

Plate XIX

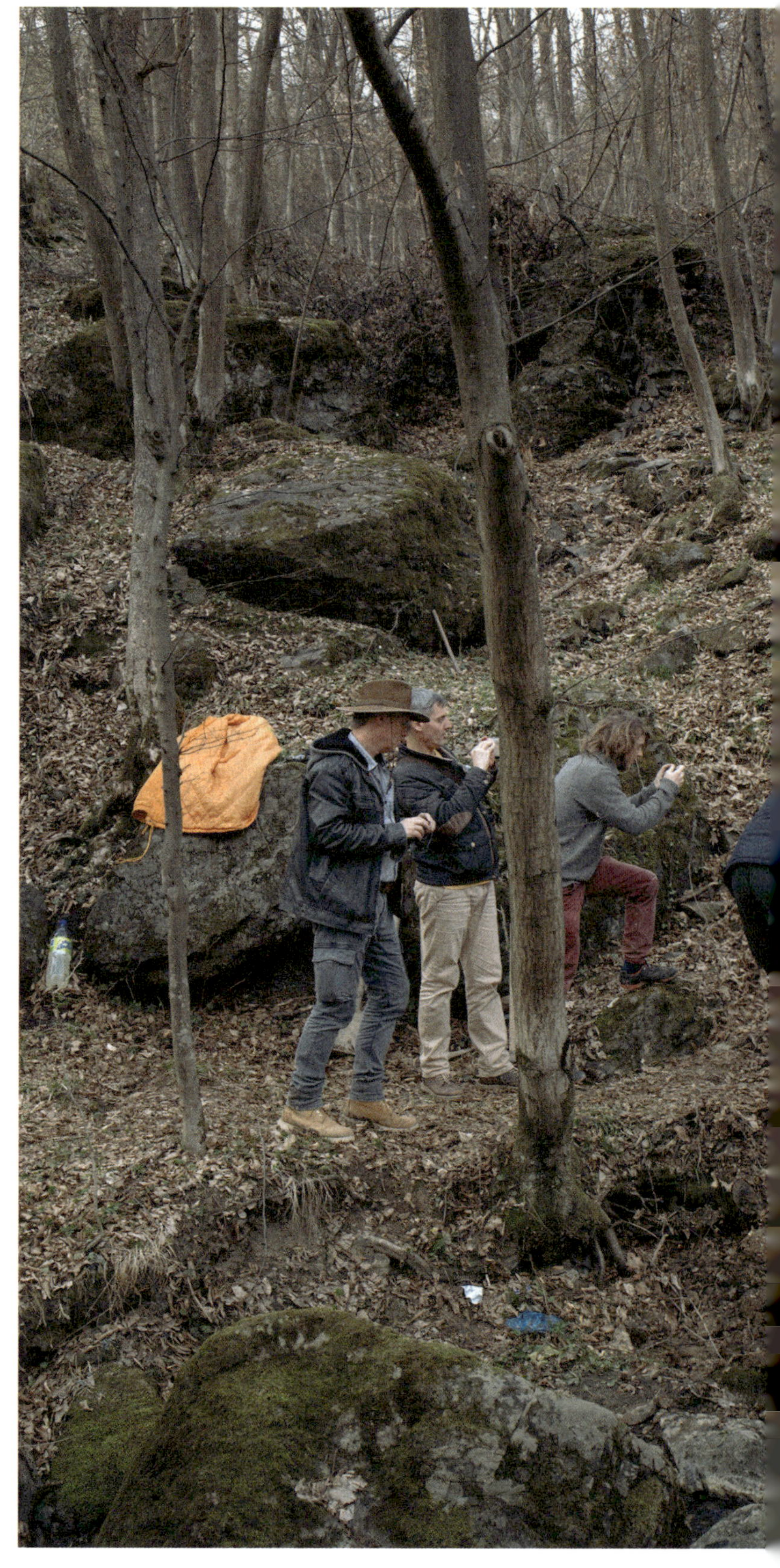

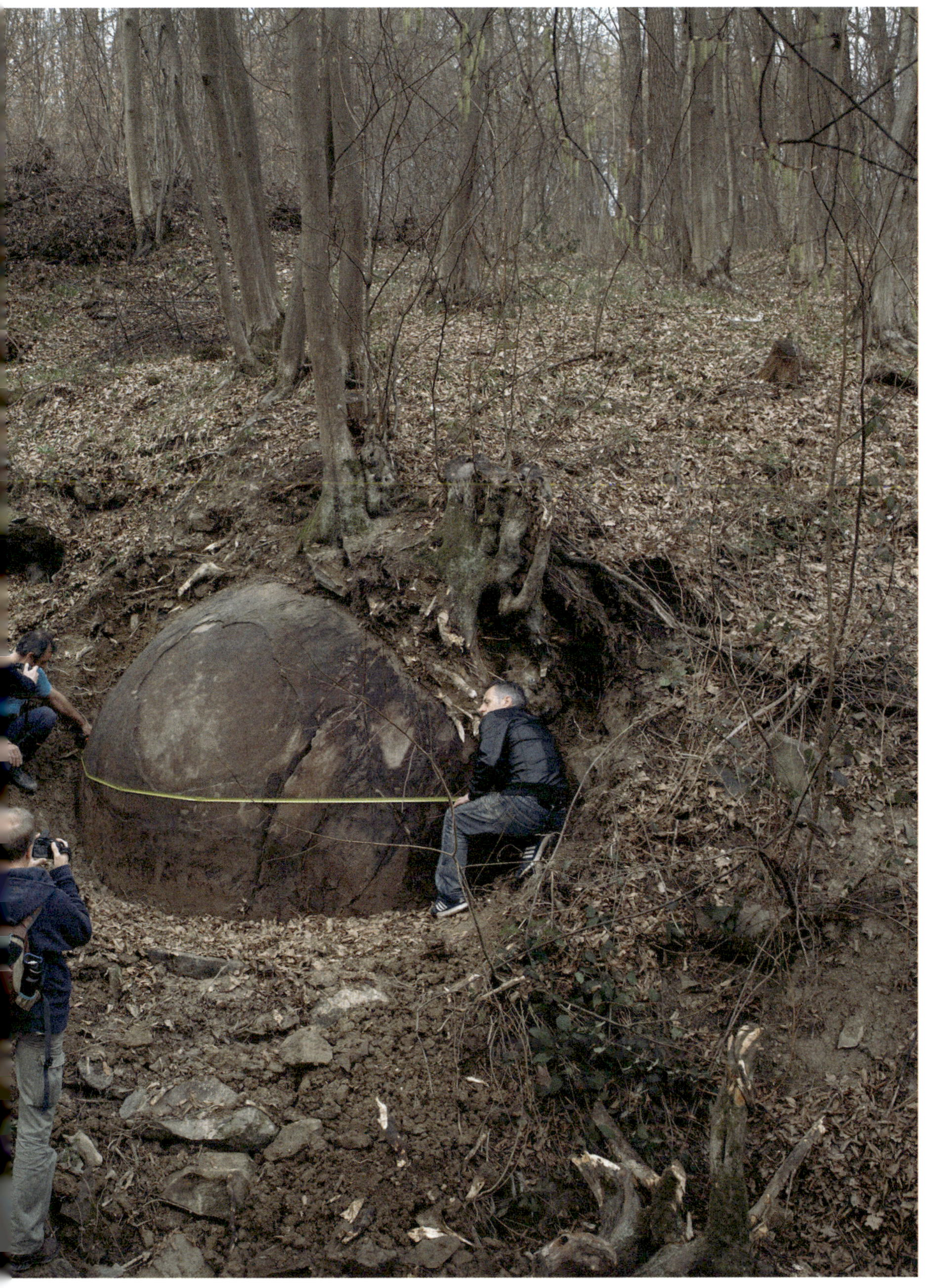

Plate XX

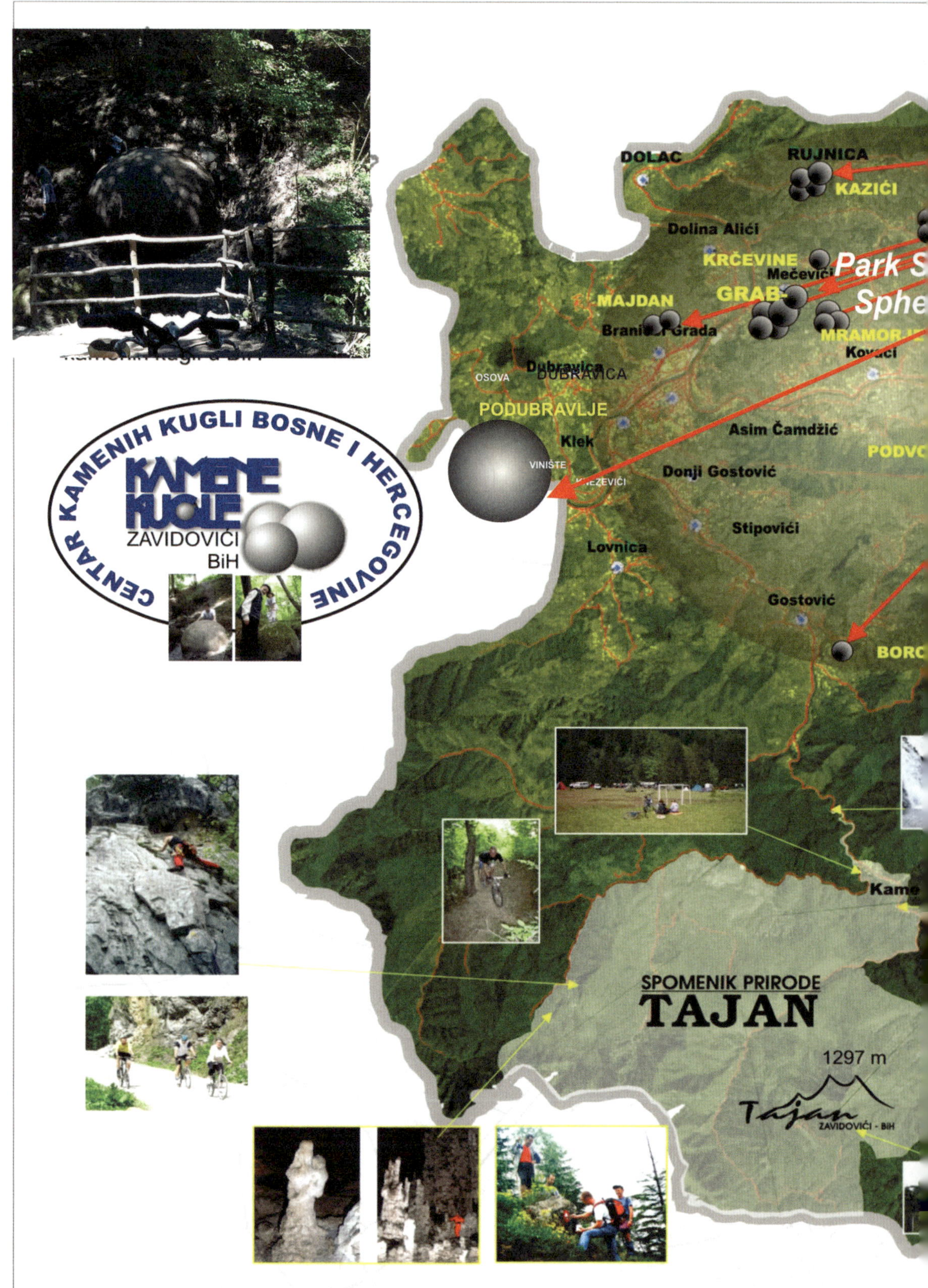
DOLAC
RUJNICA
KAZIĆI
Dolina Alići
KRČEVINE
Mečevići
Park S
Sphe
MAJDAN
GRAB-
MRAMORJE
Kovači
OSOVA
Dubravica
DUBRAVICA
PODUBRAVLJE
Klek
VINIŠTE
Asim Čamdžić
PODVC
Donji Gostović
Stipovići
Lovnica
Gostović
BORC
CENTAR KAMENIH KUGLI BOSNE I HERCEGOVINE
KAMENE KUGLE
ZAVIDOVIĆI
BiH
Kame
SPOMENIK PRIRODE
TAJAN
1297 m
Tajan
ZAVIDOVIĆI - BIH

CENTAR KAMENIH KUGLI BOSNE I HERCEGOVINE
KAMENE KUGLE
ZAVIDOVIĆI
BiH
KONAK
KUVELJ-LAZ
ŠIĆI
STOG
TRIVIĆI
Vozuća
Ribnica

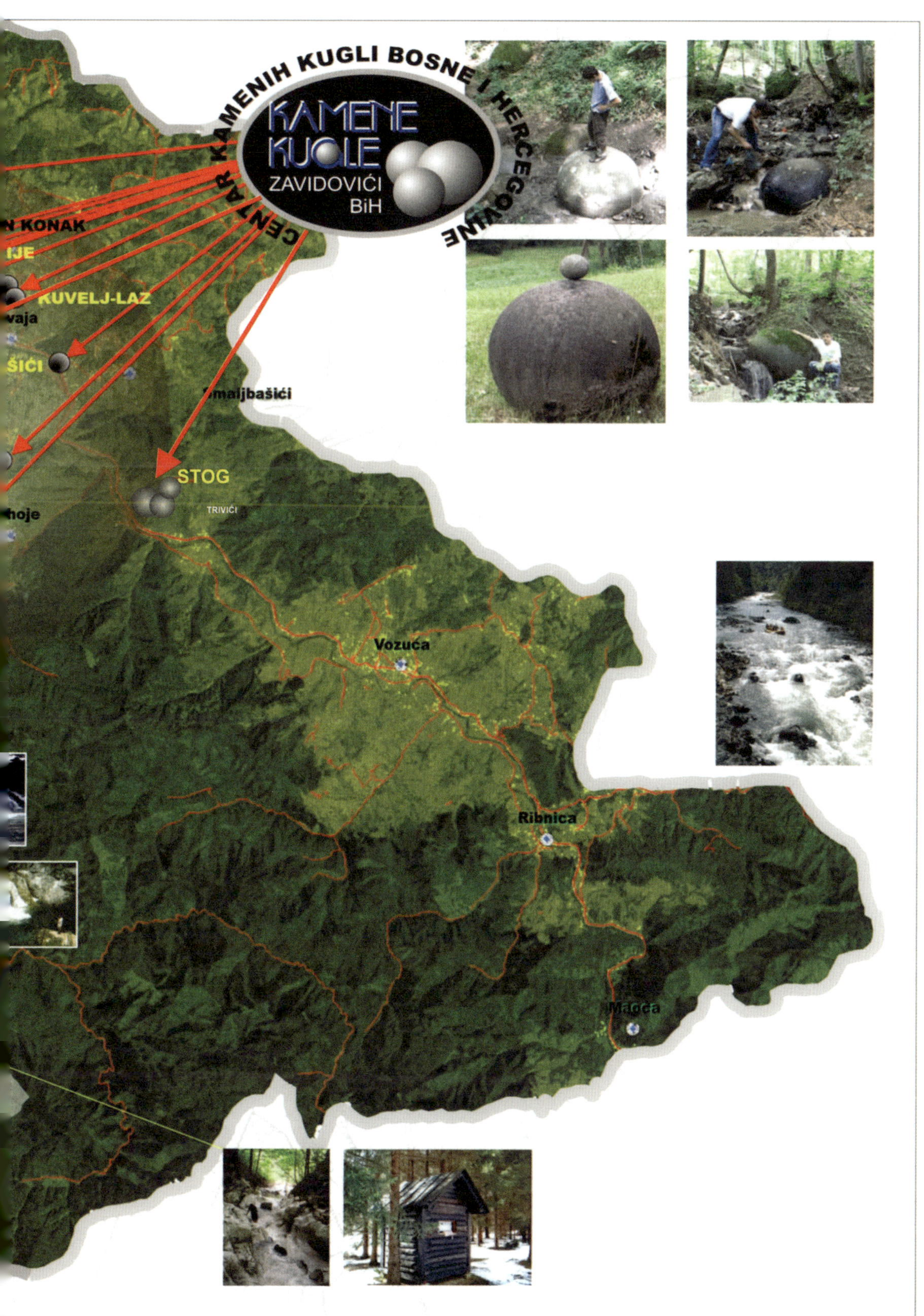

Plate XXI

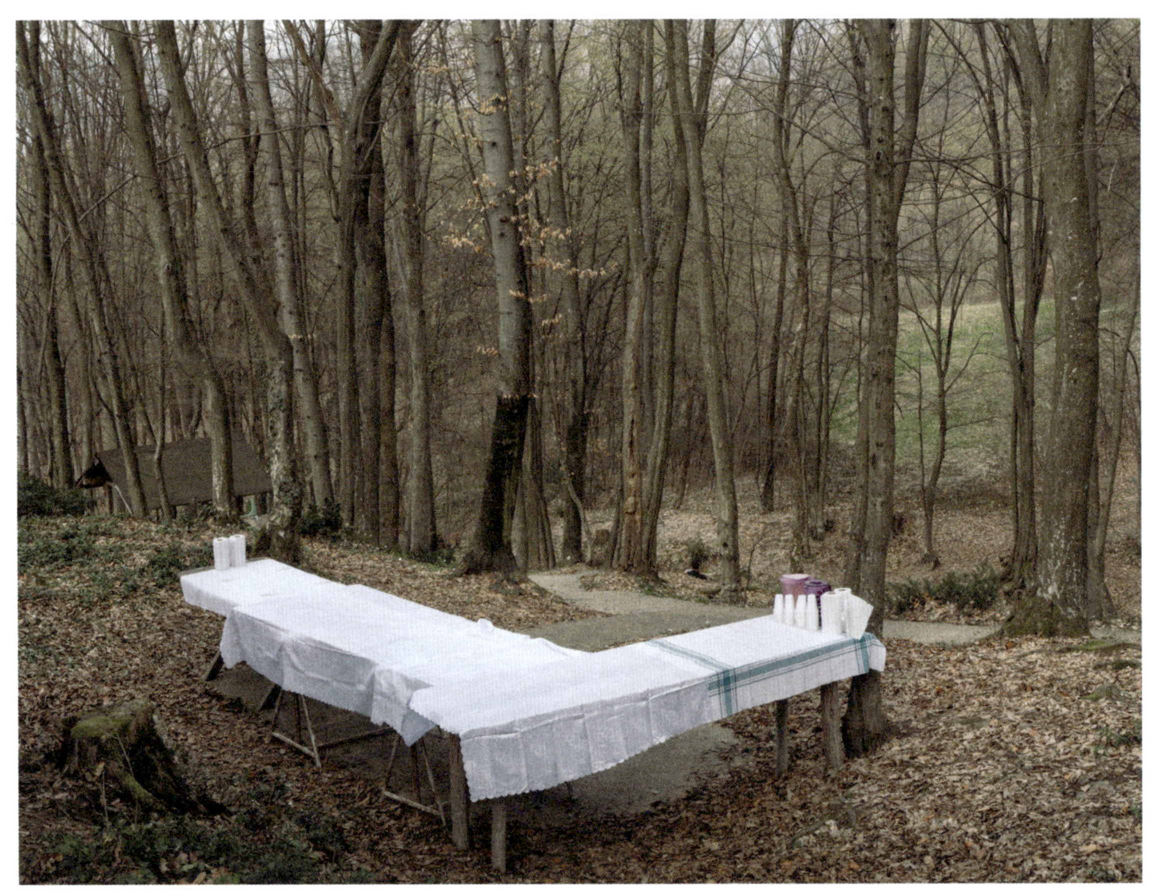

Plate XXII

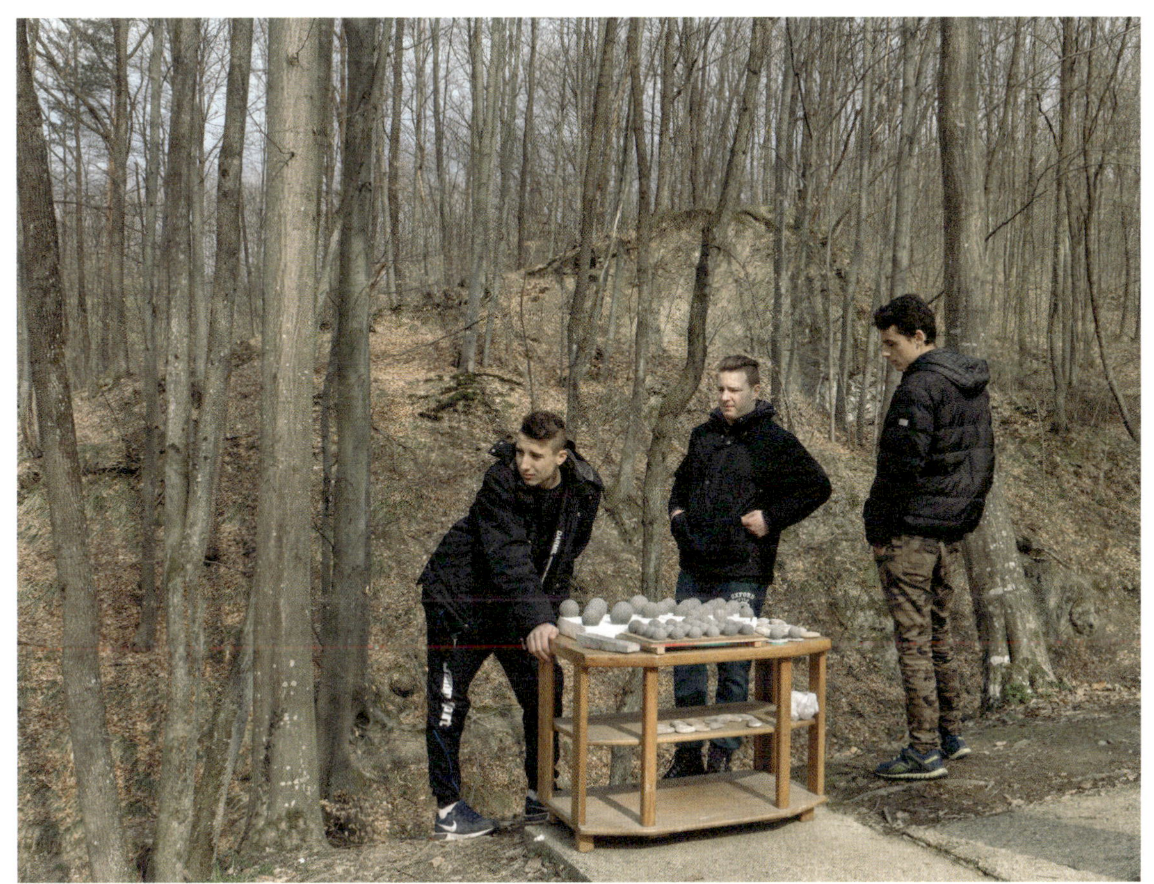

Plate XXIII

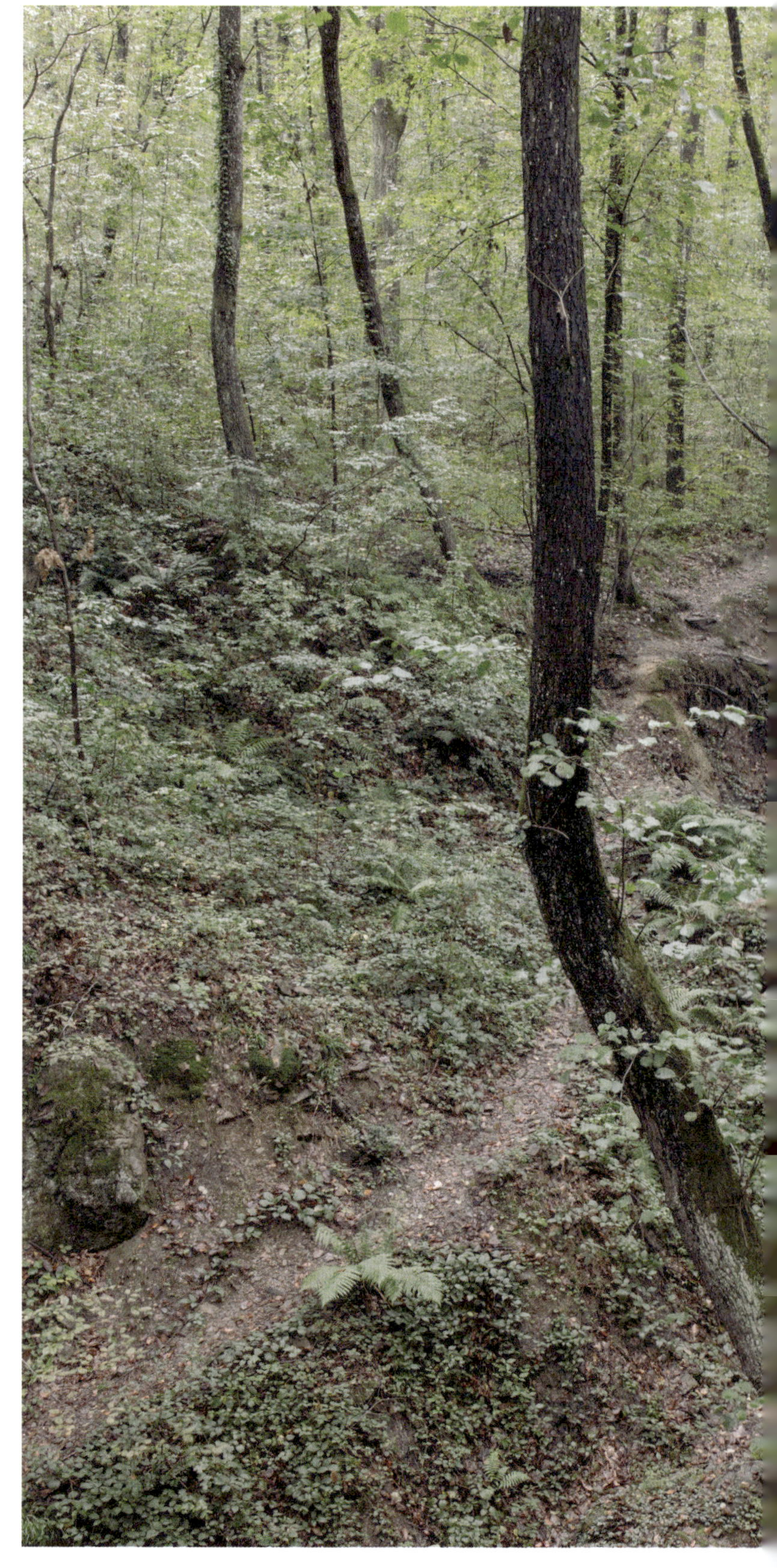

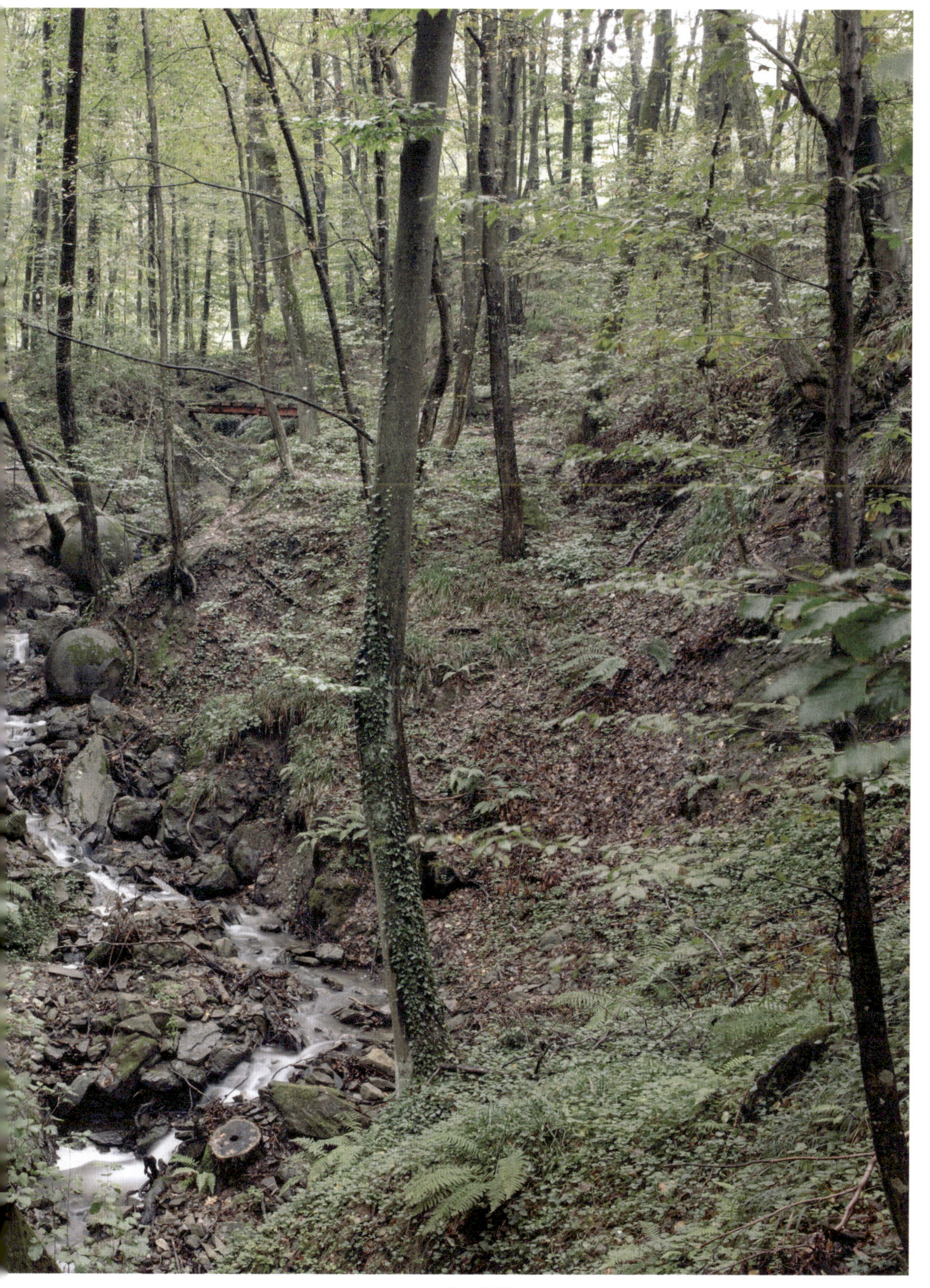

Plate XXIV

# BIGGEST STONE BALL IN EUROPE JUST DISCOVERED IN BOSNIA

Written by Dr. Sam Osmanagić, Ph.D. Friday, 25 March 2016 11:01

I've been researching prehistoric stone ball phenomenon for 15 years. I've visited several times shaped granite stone balls in southern Costa Rica, volcanic stone spheres in western Mexico, "cocina" stone balls in the small island in Pacific – Isla del Cano, volcanic stone balls on Easter Island, some of them in Tunisia, and Tenerife on Canary Islands. They are also present on Antarctica, New Zealand, Russia, Egypt, USA, Argentina … I wrote about stone balls found in Balkan region: northern Albania, province of Dalmatia in Croatia, western Serbia.

When I established non-profit "Archaeological Park: Bosnian Pyramid of the Sun" Foundation, our team has started investigation of this phenomenon in Bosnia. We have discovered them in twenty different locations, either shaped or, in some instances, made from different materials. We found granite stone balls in the Teocak village in northeastern Bosnia, volcanic stone ball near town of Konjic in middle Bosnia and sandstone stone spheres in many locations in western and middle Bosnia.

Most of the stone balls were located near small town of Zavidovići. It used to be 80 of them in 1930s. In the meantime, some were taken by the river further down to the river Bosna, most of them have been destroyed in 1970s after rumors of gold being hidden in the middle of them, some were taken by locals and moved to their backyards. Only eight stone balls remained in what we established as Archaeological Park: Bosnian Stone Balls". We've started promoting this location and it's been visited by thousands of tourists every year.

With the winter months over, again near the town of Zavidovići, excavation of the enormous stone ball has started. By the mid of March 2016, it became obvious that the most massive stone ball in Europe has been discovered. Name of the location is village Podubravlje.

So far, less than half of the ball has been uncovered. Preliminary results show the radius to be between 1.2 – 1.5 meters. Materials have not been analyzed yet. However, brown and red color of the ball point to very high content of the iron. So, the density has to be very high, close to the iron which is 7,8 kg/c.c. If we take value of only 5 kg/c.c. we have all the elements for the preliminary calculation of the mass. Mass comes to be over 30 tons !

It makes this Bosnian stone ball the most massive in Europe. However, if further lab testing shows higher content of iron, than this will be the biggest stone ball in the World surpassing those in Costa Rica (35 tons) and Mexico (40 tons). Over stone balls we see signs of natural sedimentation: layer of sandstone plates, then clay, soil and vegetation. It takes tens, even hundreds of thousands of years for this sediment to form.

What would be the significance of this discovery?

First, it would be another proof that Southern Europe, Balkan and Bosnia in particular, were home for advanced civilizations from distant past and we have no written records about them. Secondly, they had high technology, different than ours. Finally, they new the power of geometrical shapes, because the sphere is one of the most powerful shapes along with pyramidal and conical shapes. No wonder, that pyramids and tumulus phenomena can also be found in Bosnia.

While visiting the site group of dowsers were recorded that aura field improve and grow when exposed to the vicinity of stone ball. It seems that ancient did one more thing better than us. They new Planetary energies better, living in the harmony with our Mother Earth.

So, we're creating one more site in Bosnia which would be of global importance for researchers and visitors.

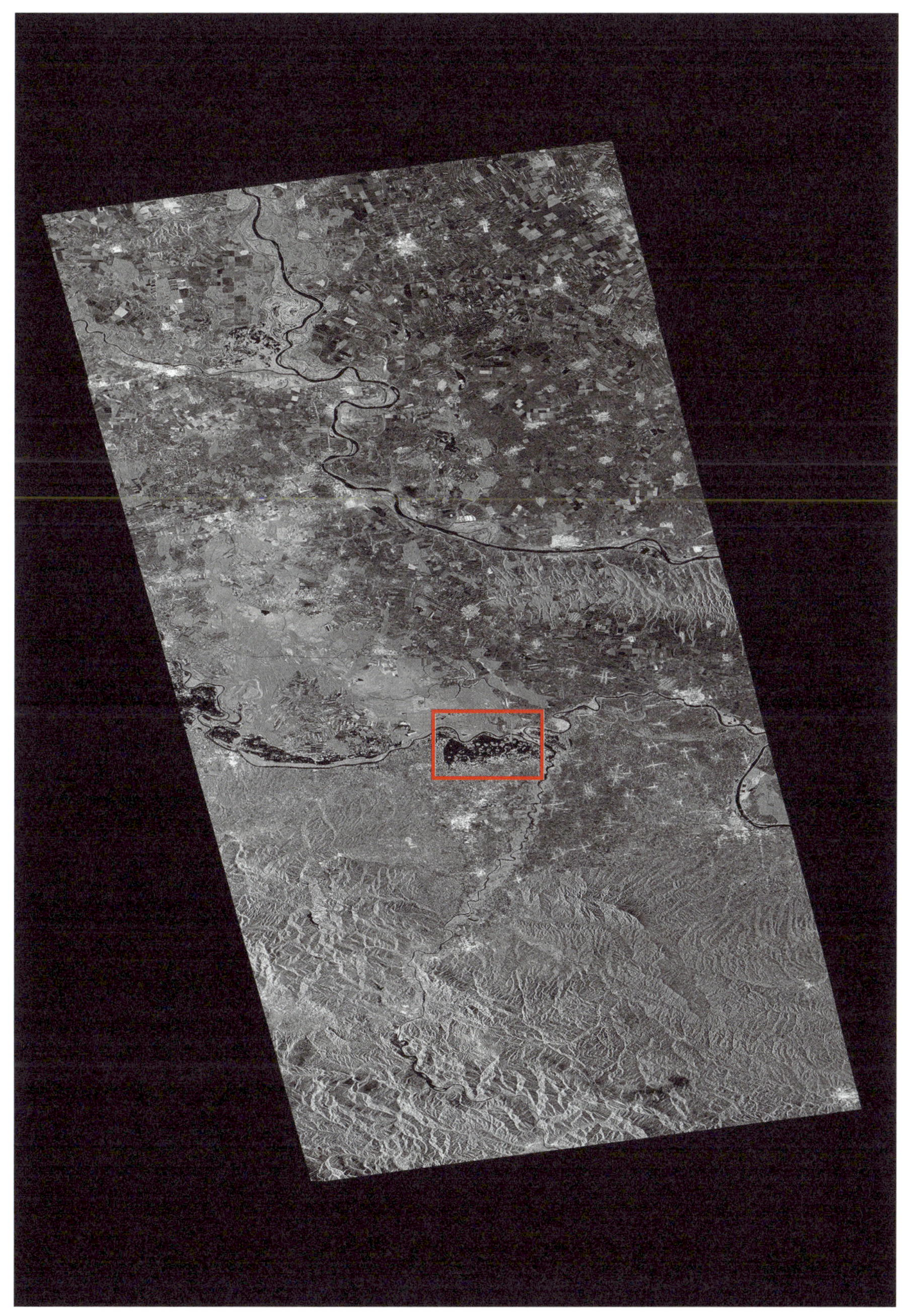

Plate XXV

# Misplaced Stones

This stone measures around two square meters and weighs about five tons. If one man can lift let's say fifty kilogram or two bags of cement. You would need one hundred people to lift one block. You cannot get hundred people around this block. In order to move and to lift it, they needed a technology.

— Semir Osmanagić at the megalithic city of Daorson, 2014

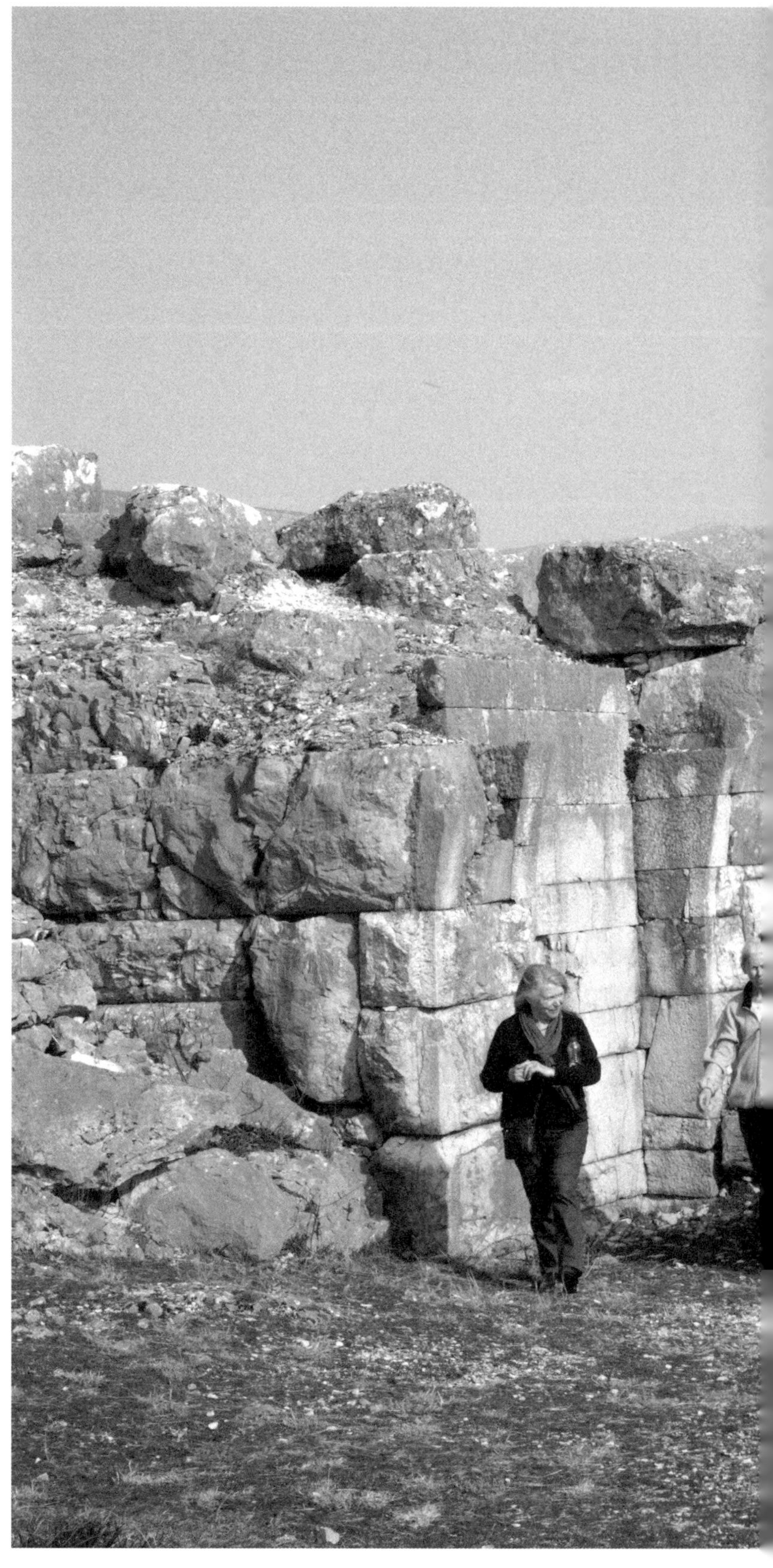

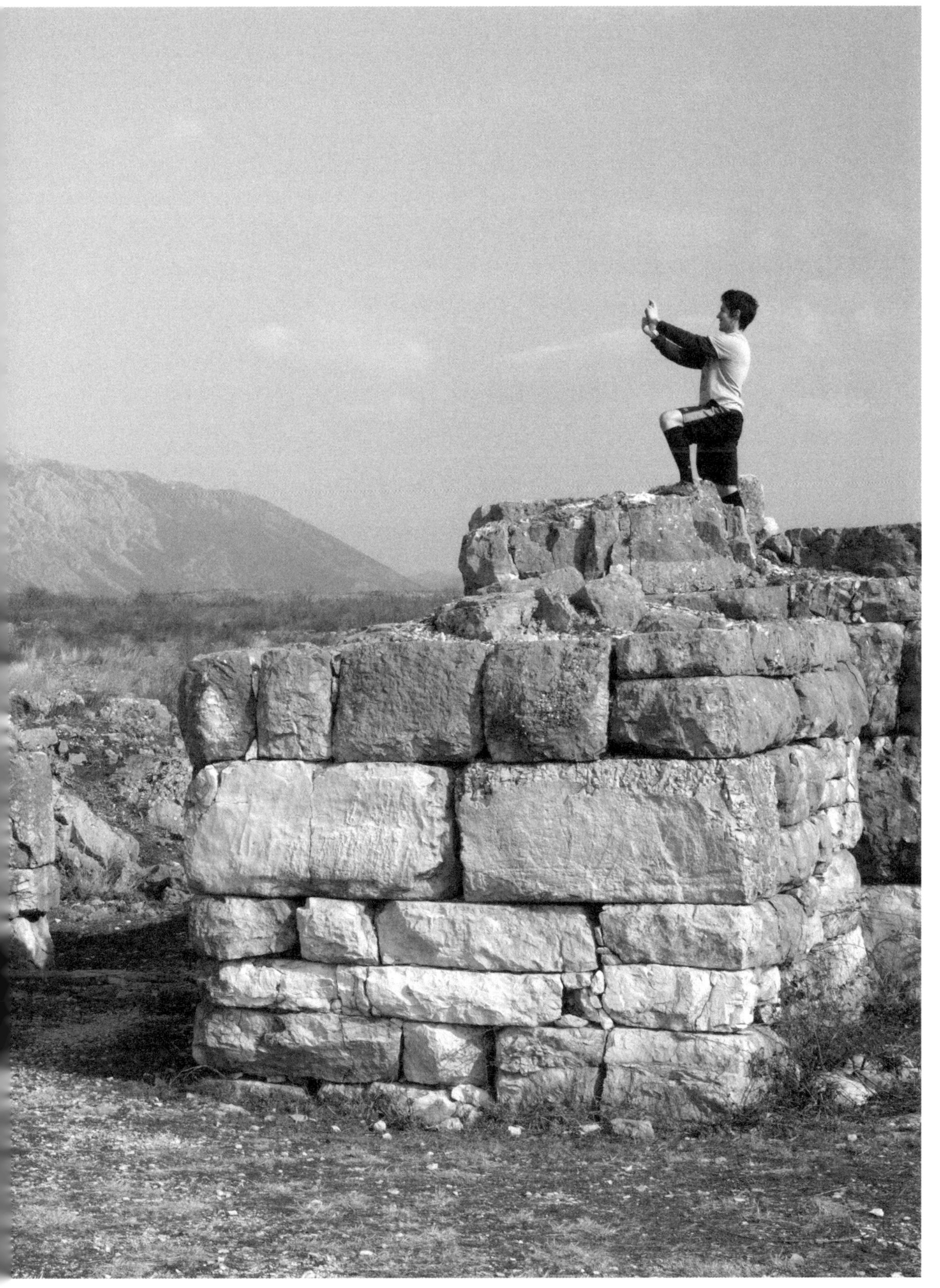

Plate XXVI

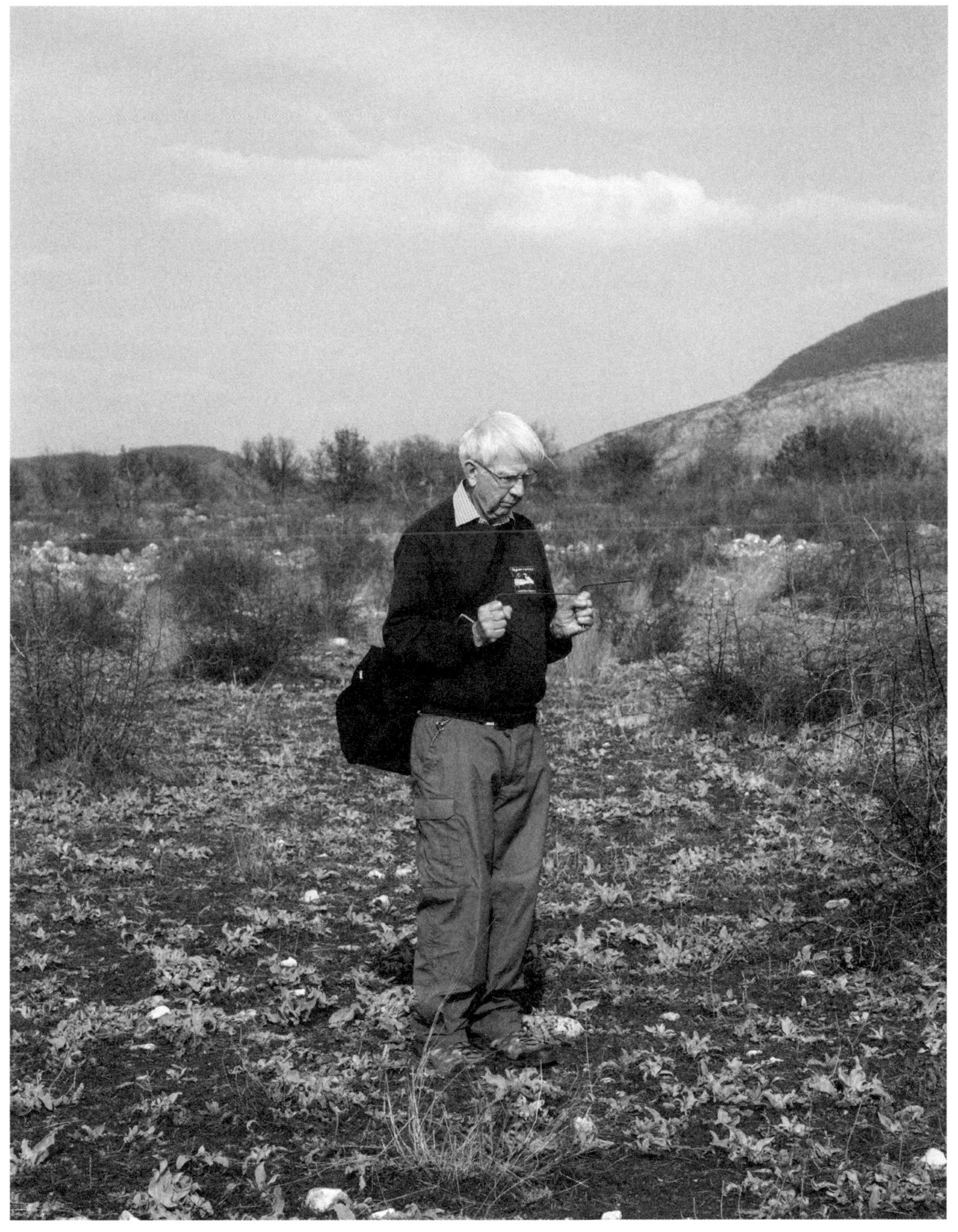

Plate XXVII

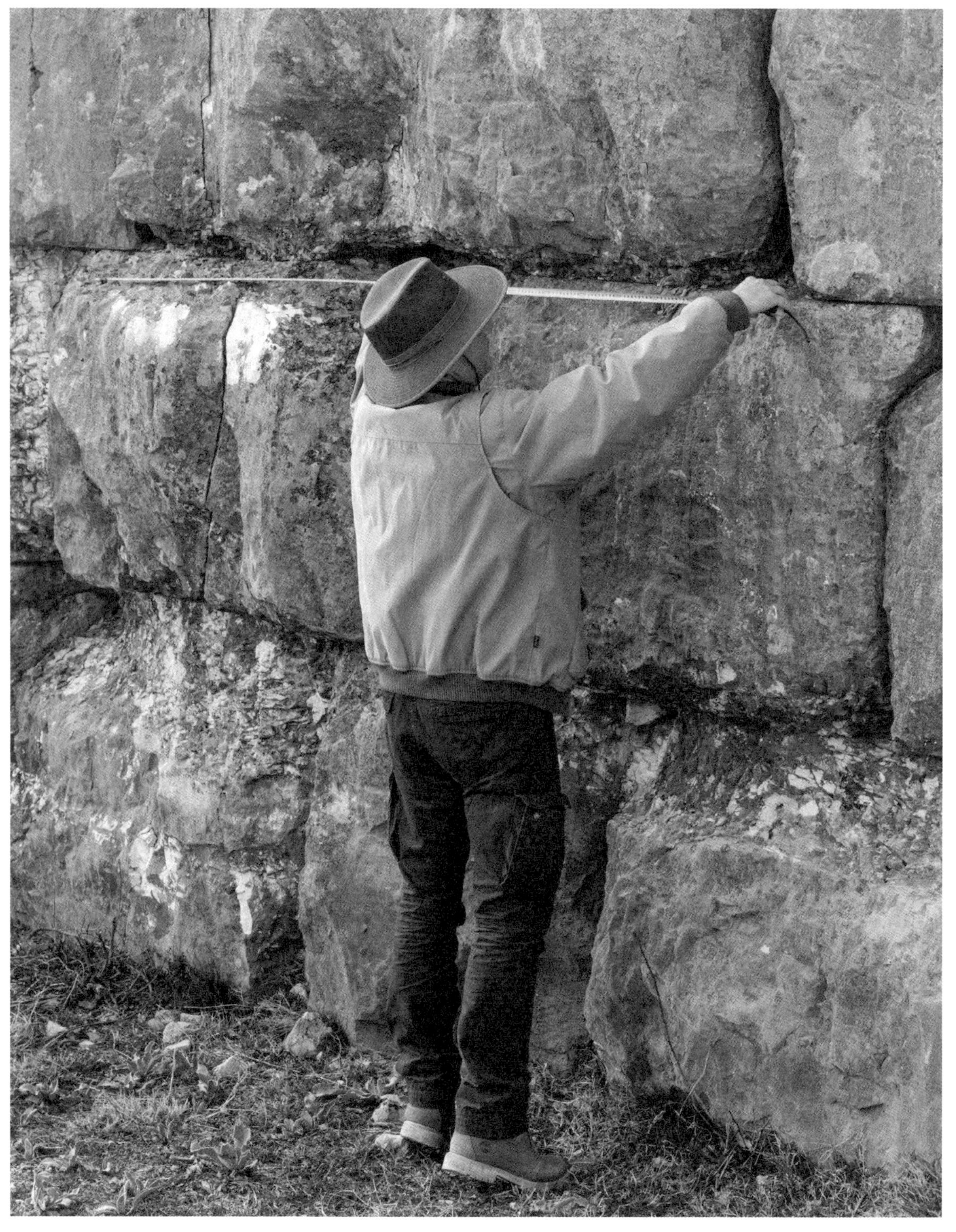

Plate XXVIII

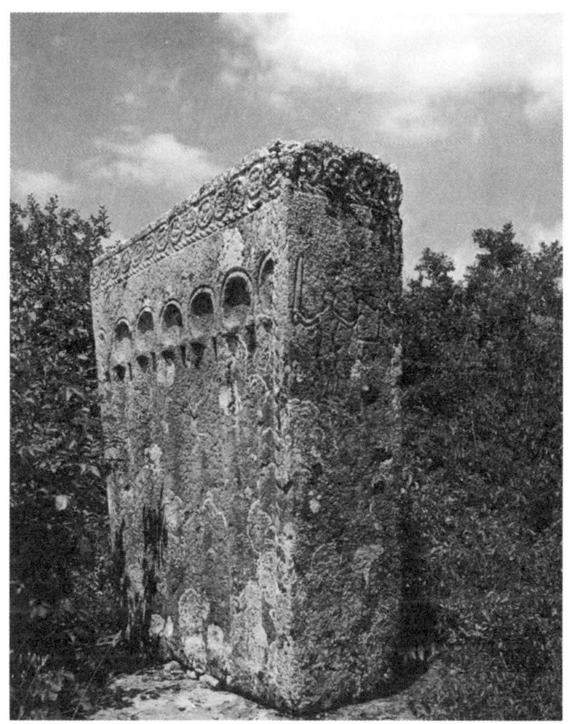

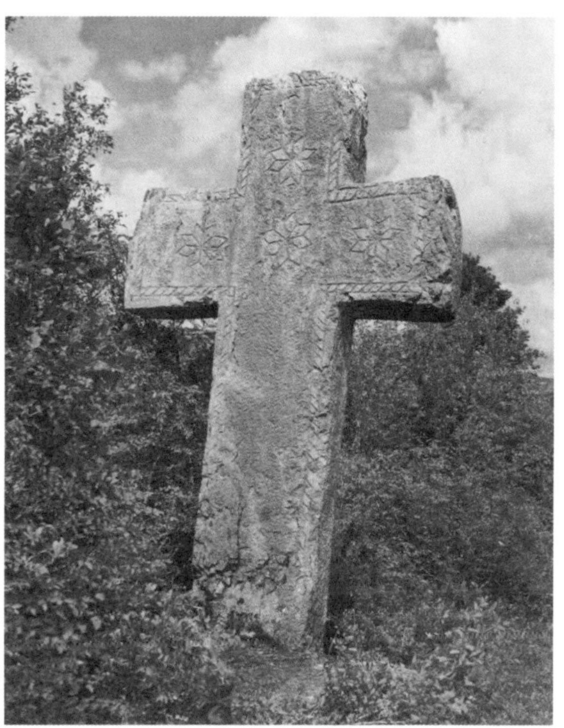

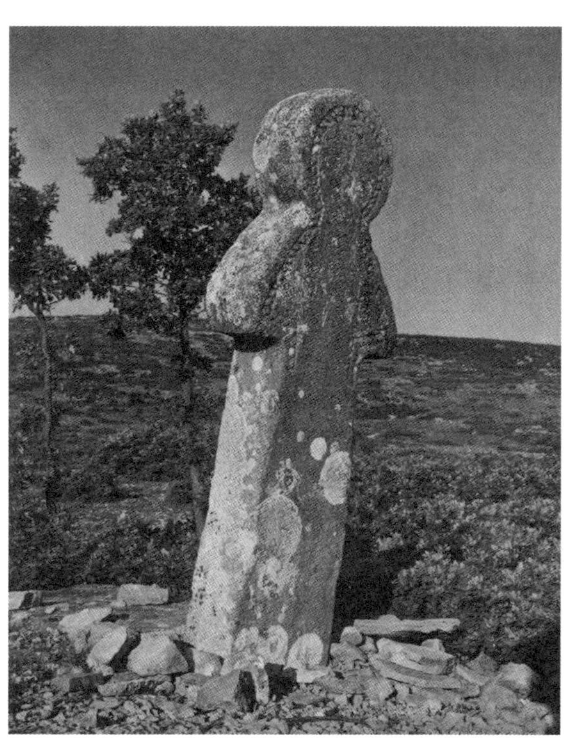

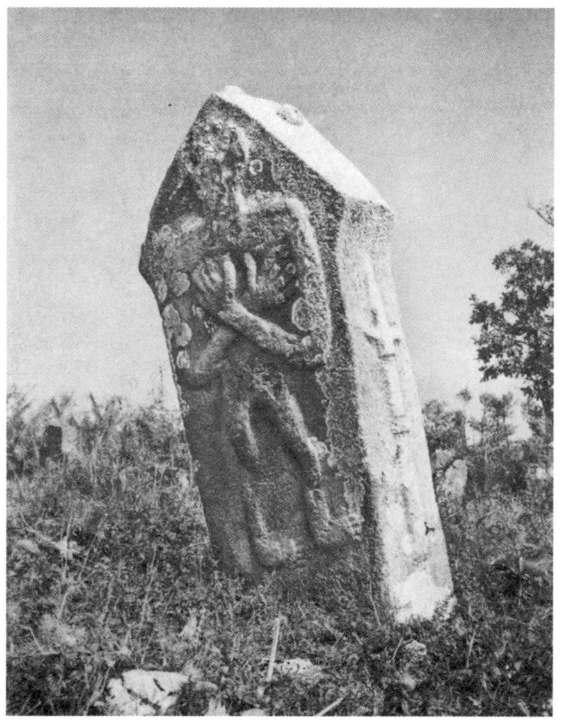

Plate XXIX

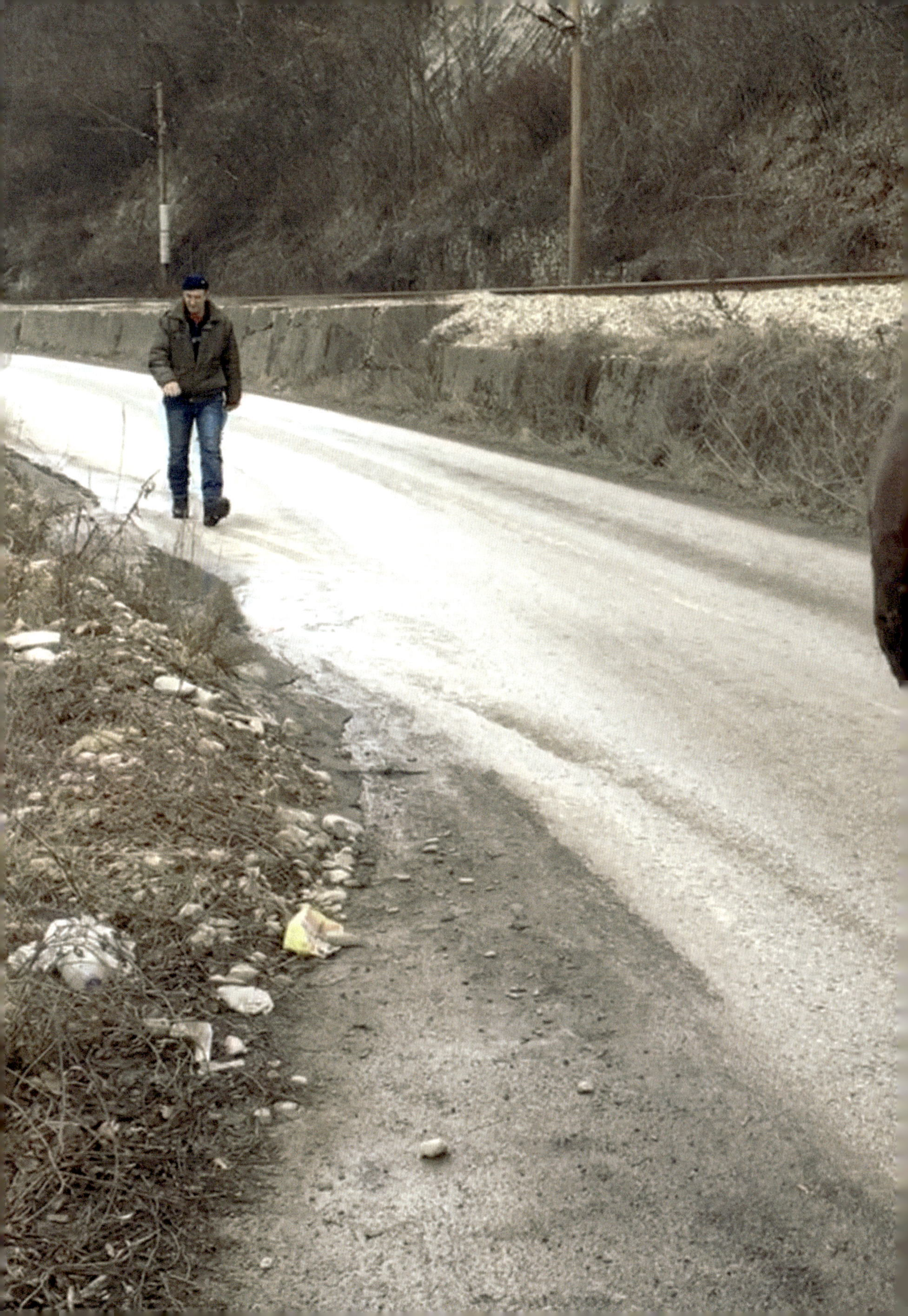

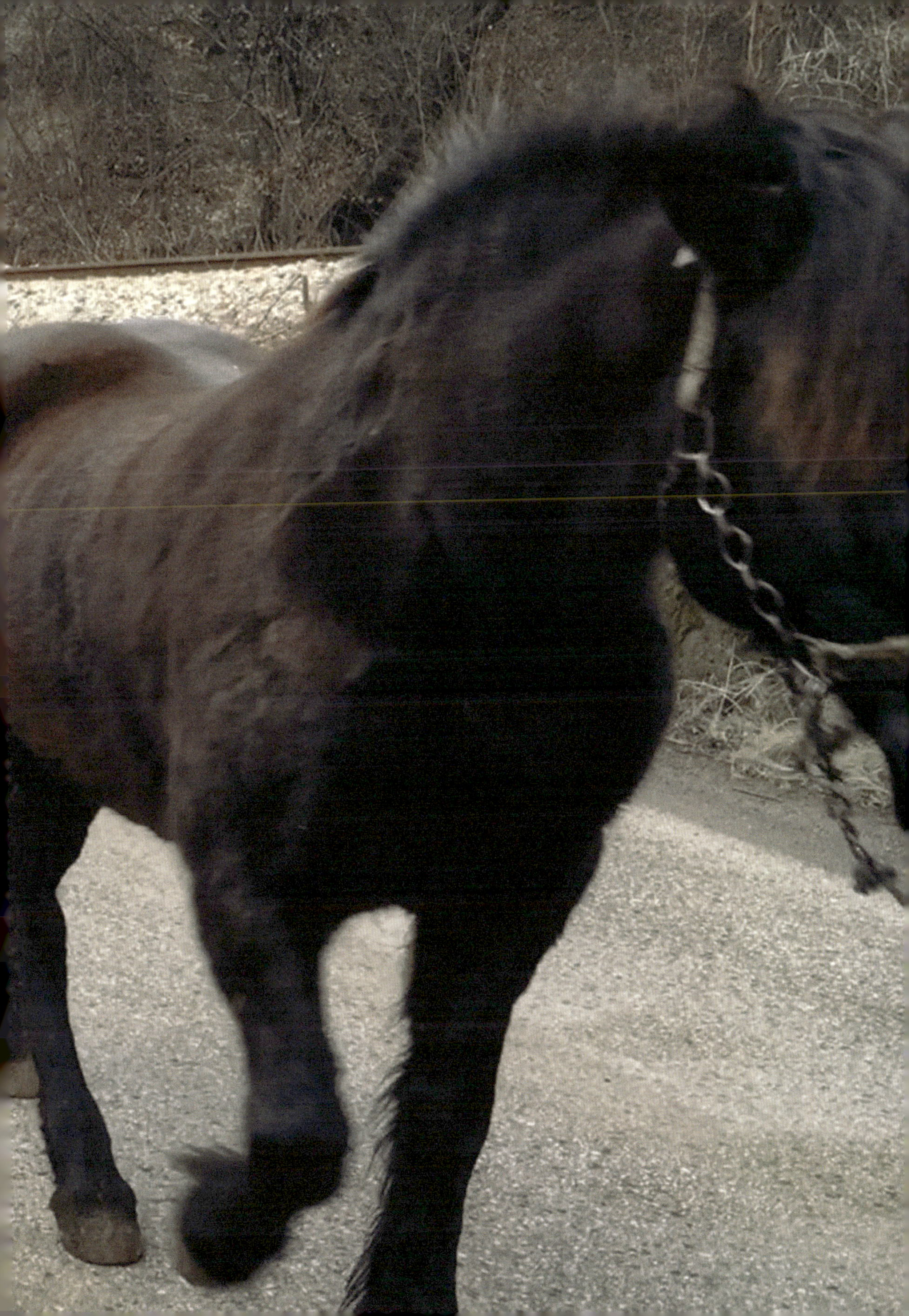

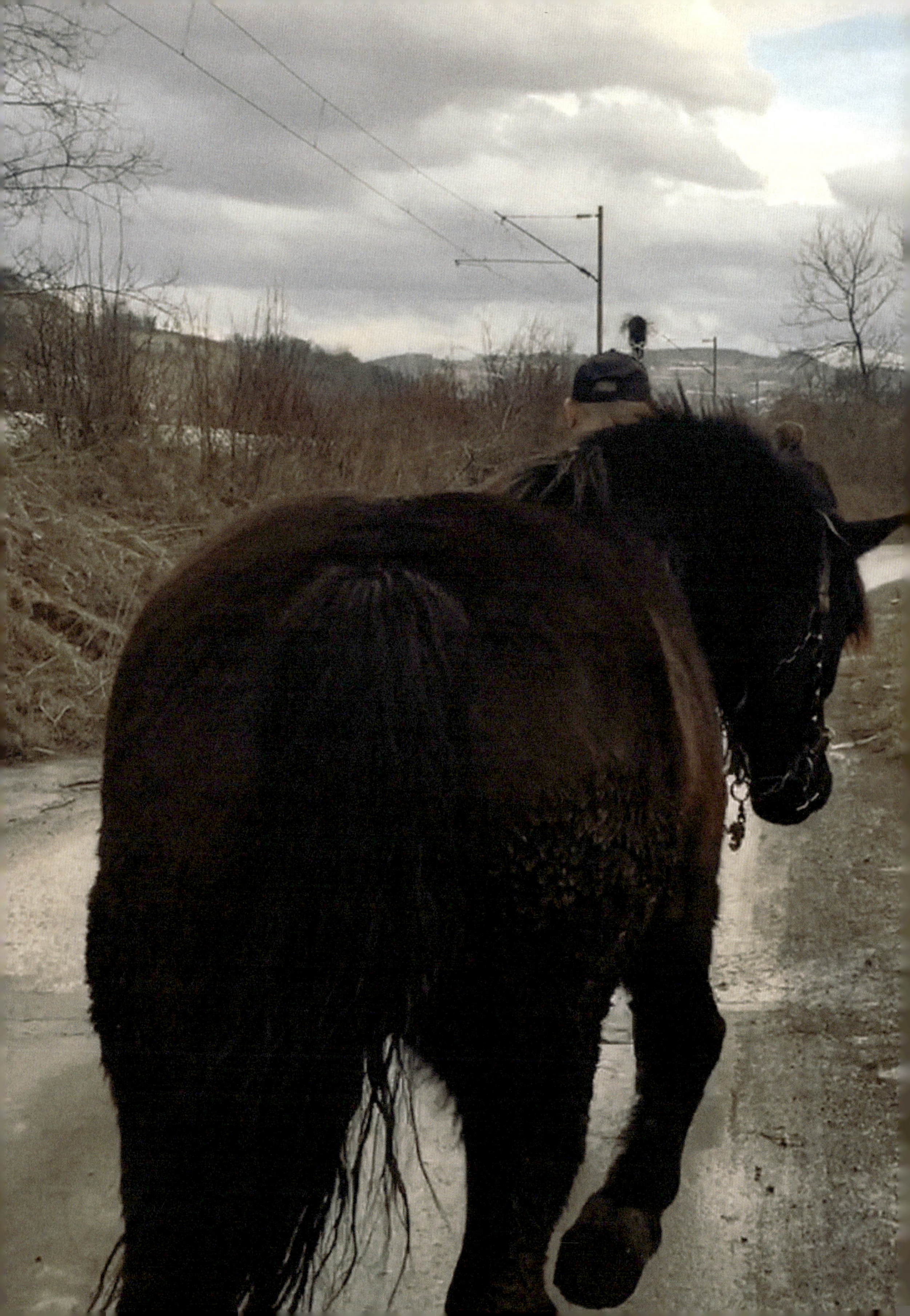

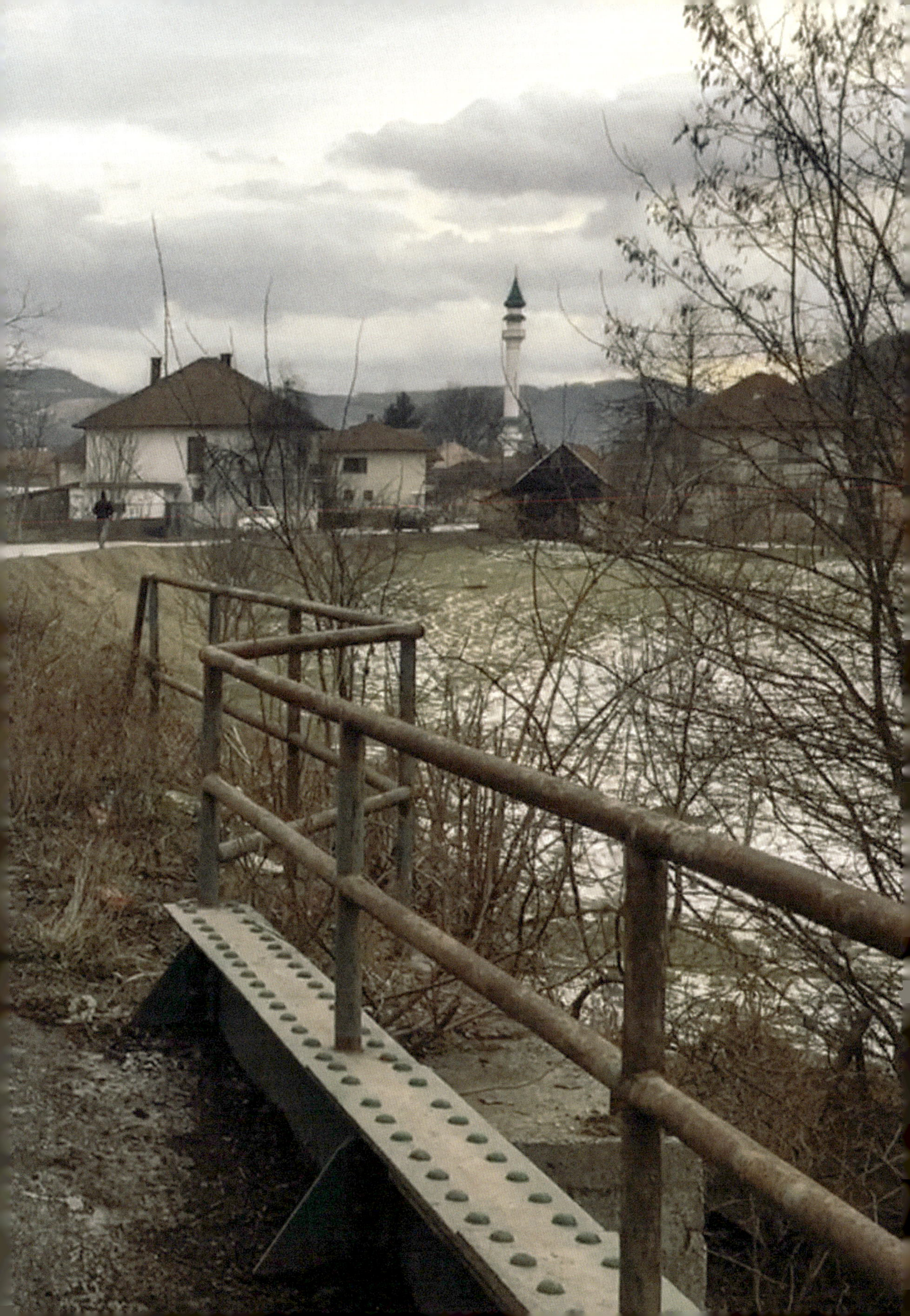

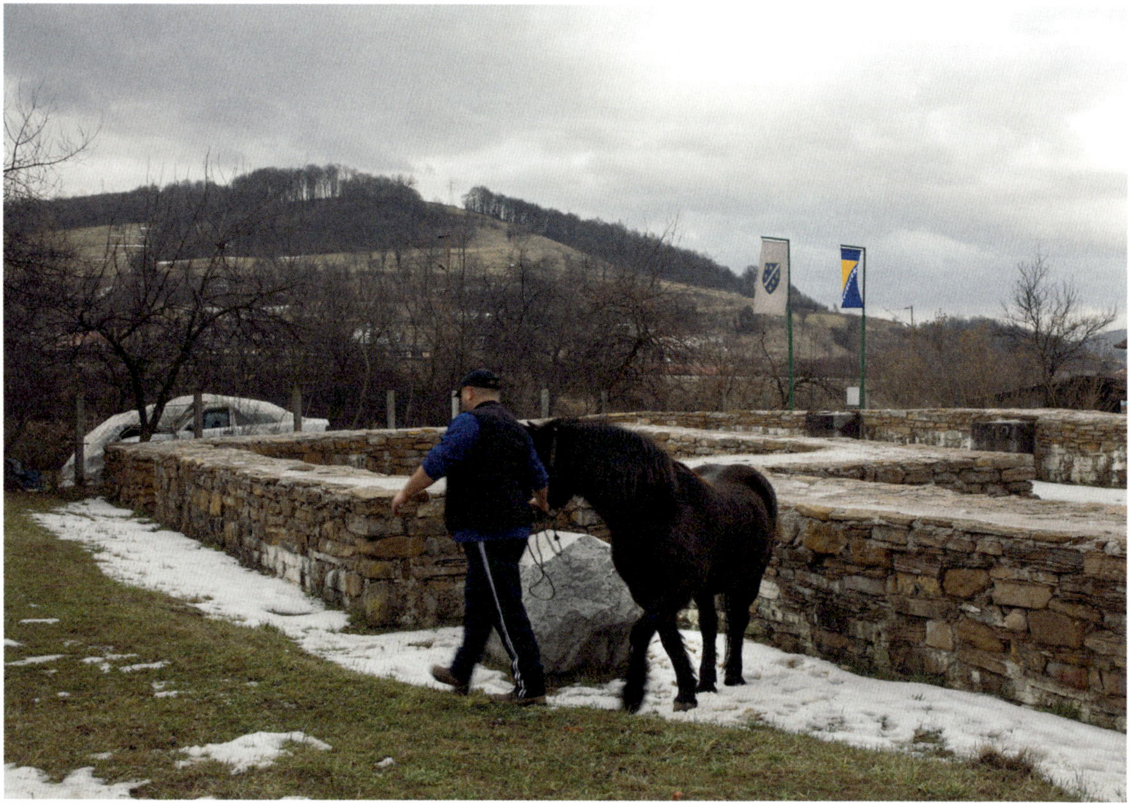

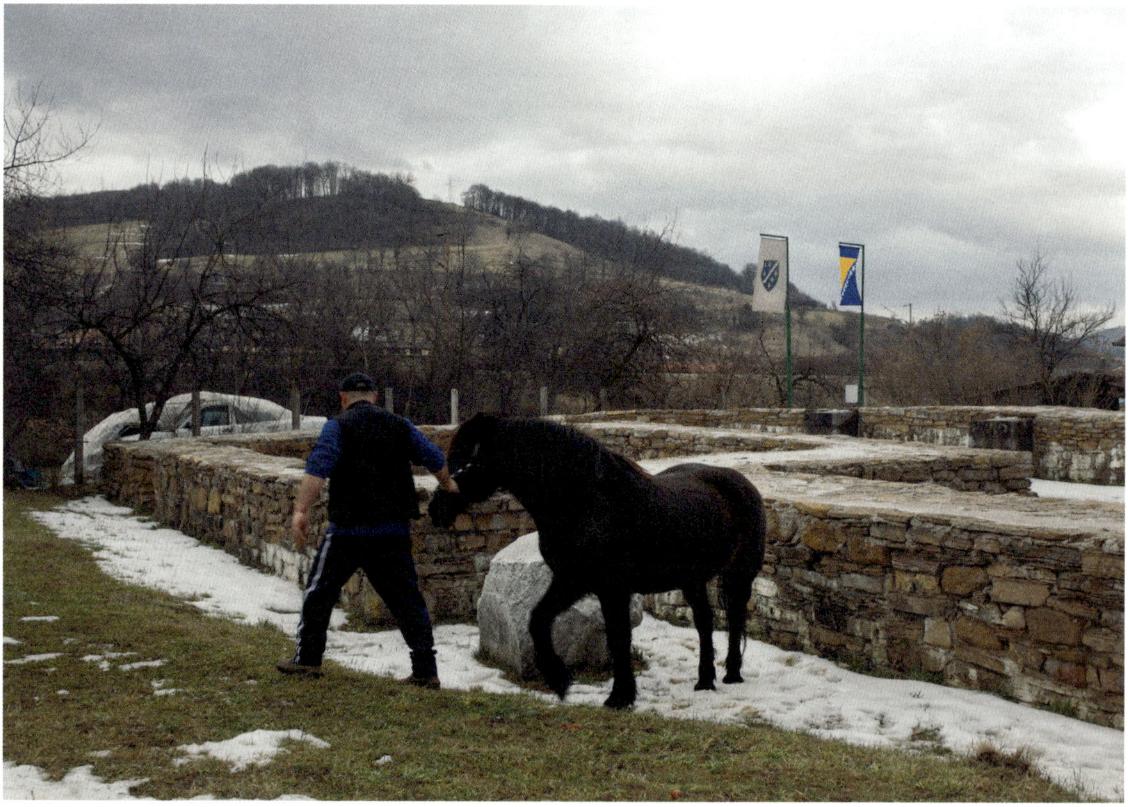

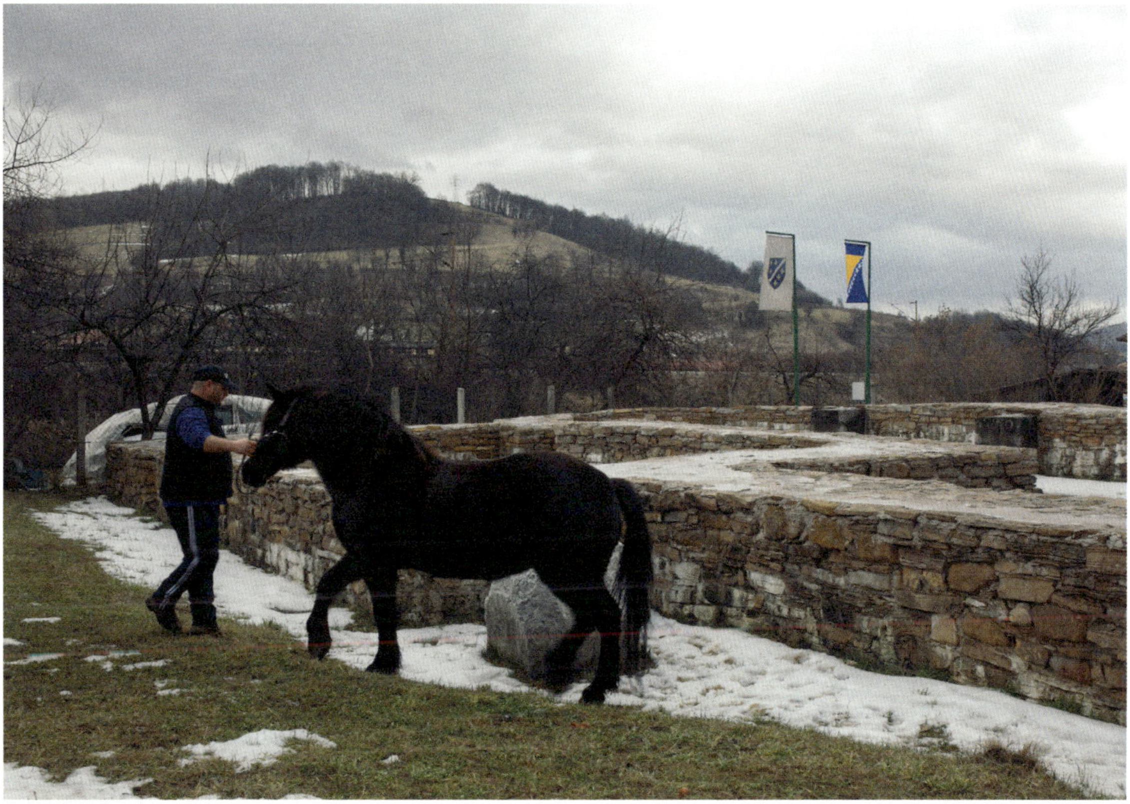

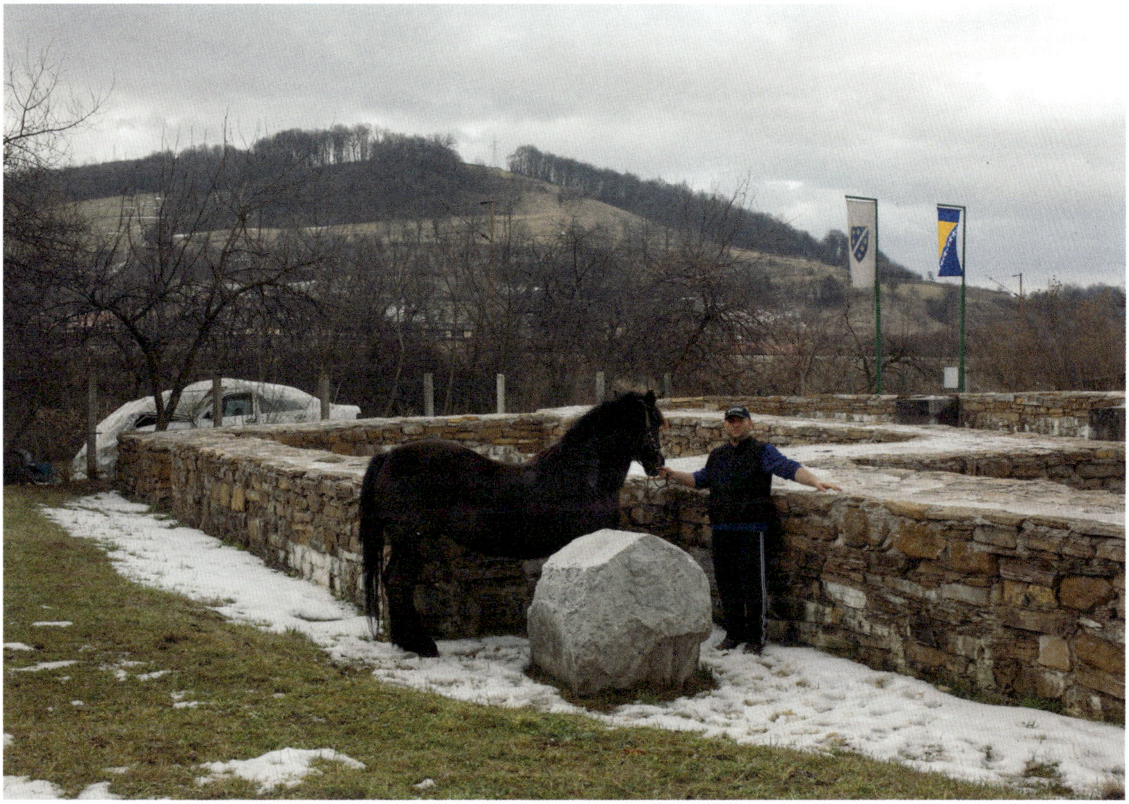

Plate XXX

# SEARCHING THE STEĆCI WITH A HORSE

The folk custom of walking with animals with urinary problems around a stećak (tombstone) is alive to this day. This, as part of a curing process, denotes the mysterious healing aspects of the stećak. It can be useful in unveiling the mysterious disappearance of a stećak in the Arnautovići church near Visoko.

When the Austrians in 1905, incidentally found a stećak inside an old catholic church they were terrified because it didn't fit their romantic Bogomil theory.

More, the discovery would uprise nationalistic feelings amongst inhabitants, so the Austrians destroyed the stećak, dragged it outside and later built a road straight through the church to give the site less importance.

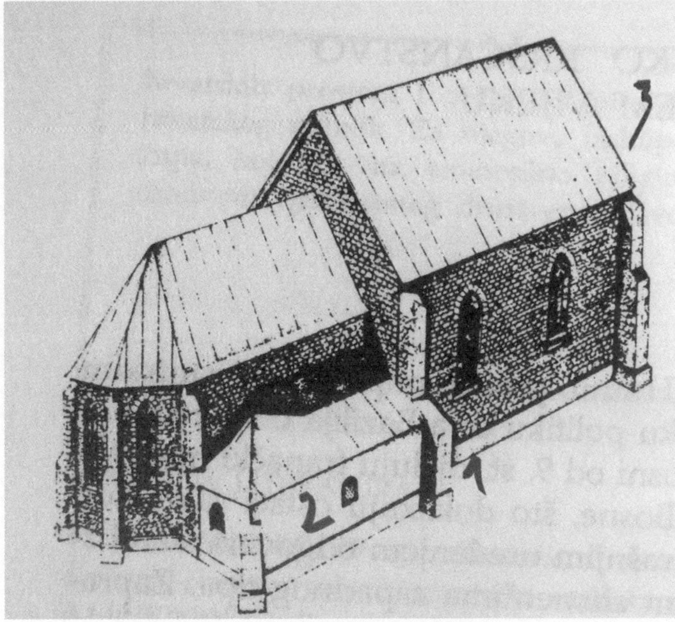


St-Nicolas Church

We found a horse at a farm in a village nearby, walked with him back to Arnautovići and tried different locations were remnants of a possible stećak could be discovered and waited until he urinated.

Locations:

1. Near the mausoleum: the horse was very stressed, probably because of the cars passing by or because of the snow. I asked the farmer to walk the horse around the remnant of a stone. Unfortunately the horse did not urinate.
2. Inside the mausoleum: the same and no reaction. The farmer although took his time and smoked a cigarette for 5 minutes, waiting until the horse would deliver.
3. On the other side of the road there was a larger stone. Unfortunately no reaction.

Conclusion: the stećak has not only been removed from the church, but from the entire site.

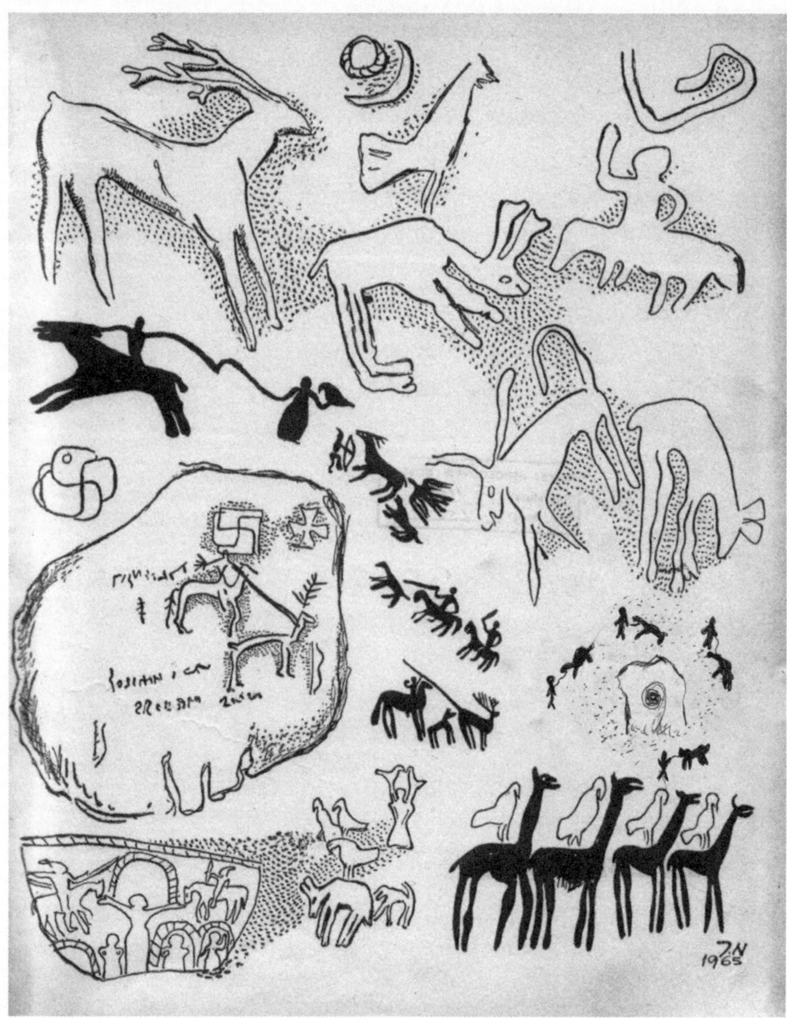


Different folk customs written on stećak

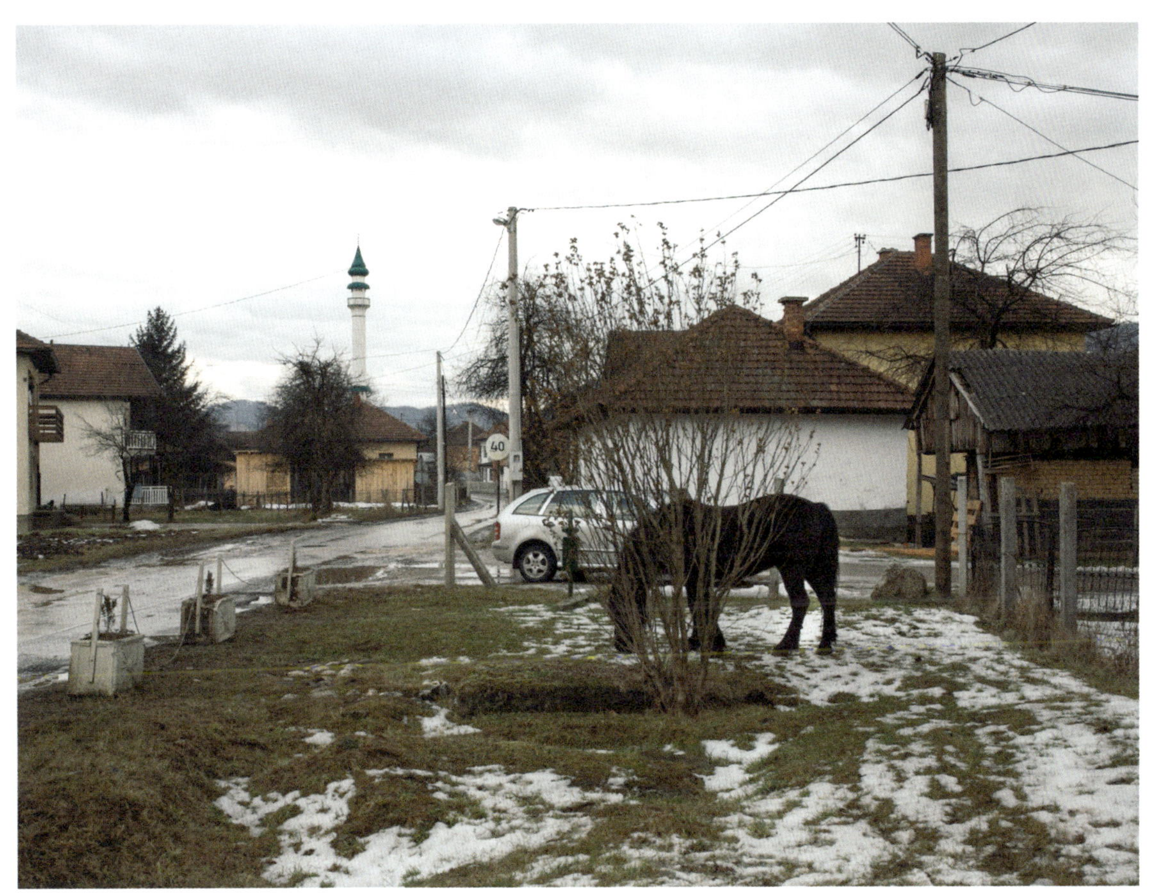


Plate XXXI

# Archaeology and the (De)Construction of Bosnian Identity

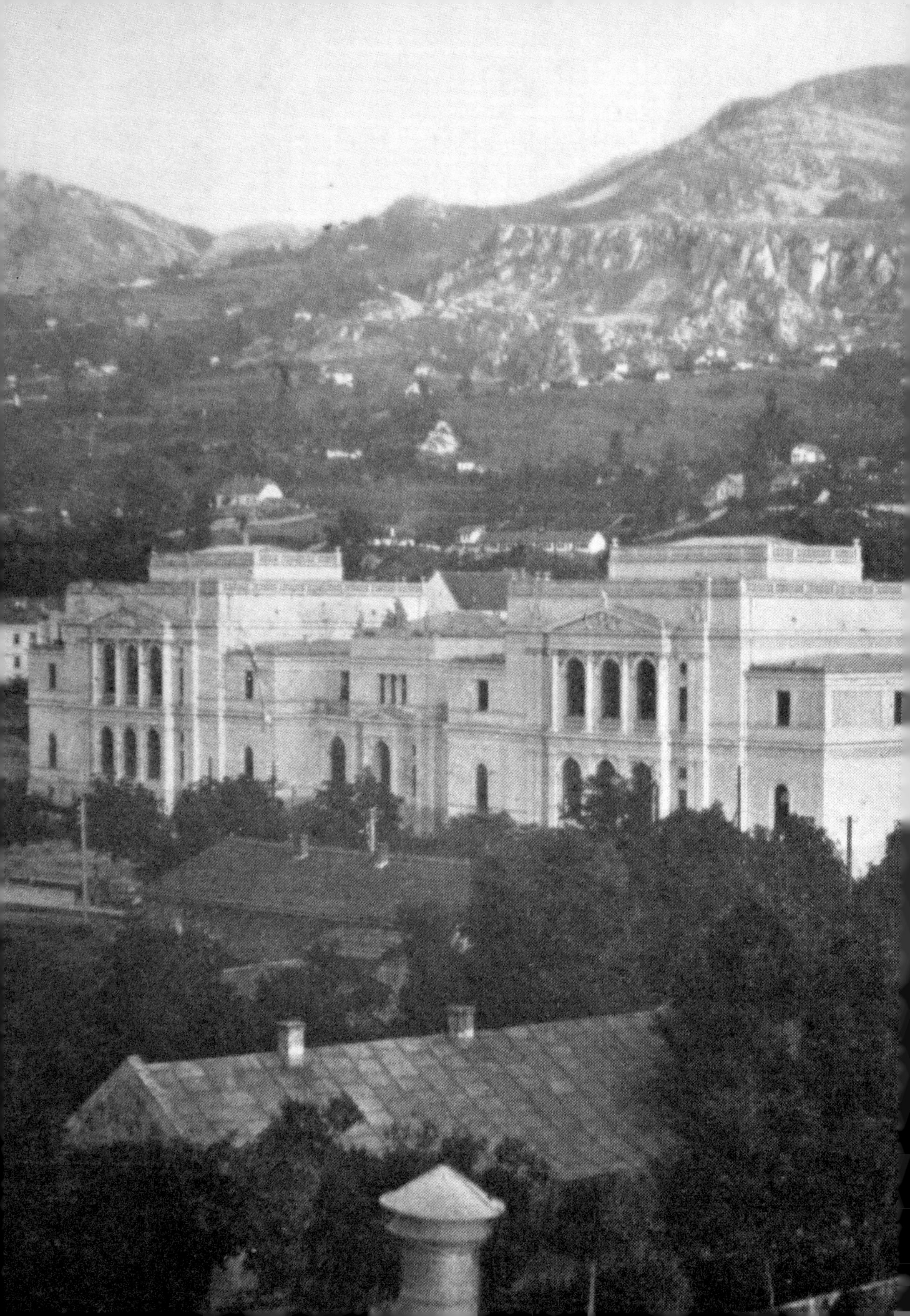

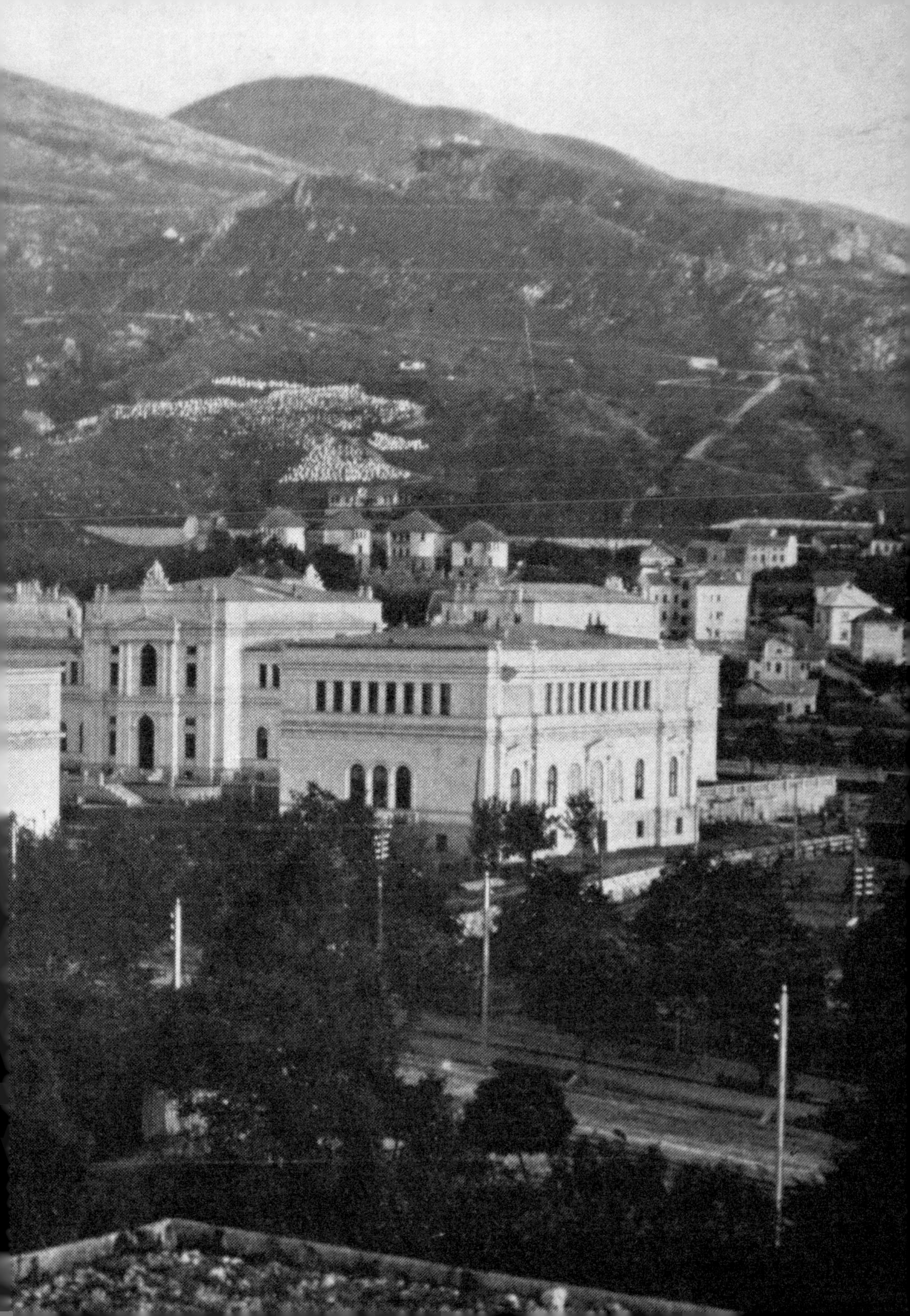

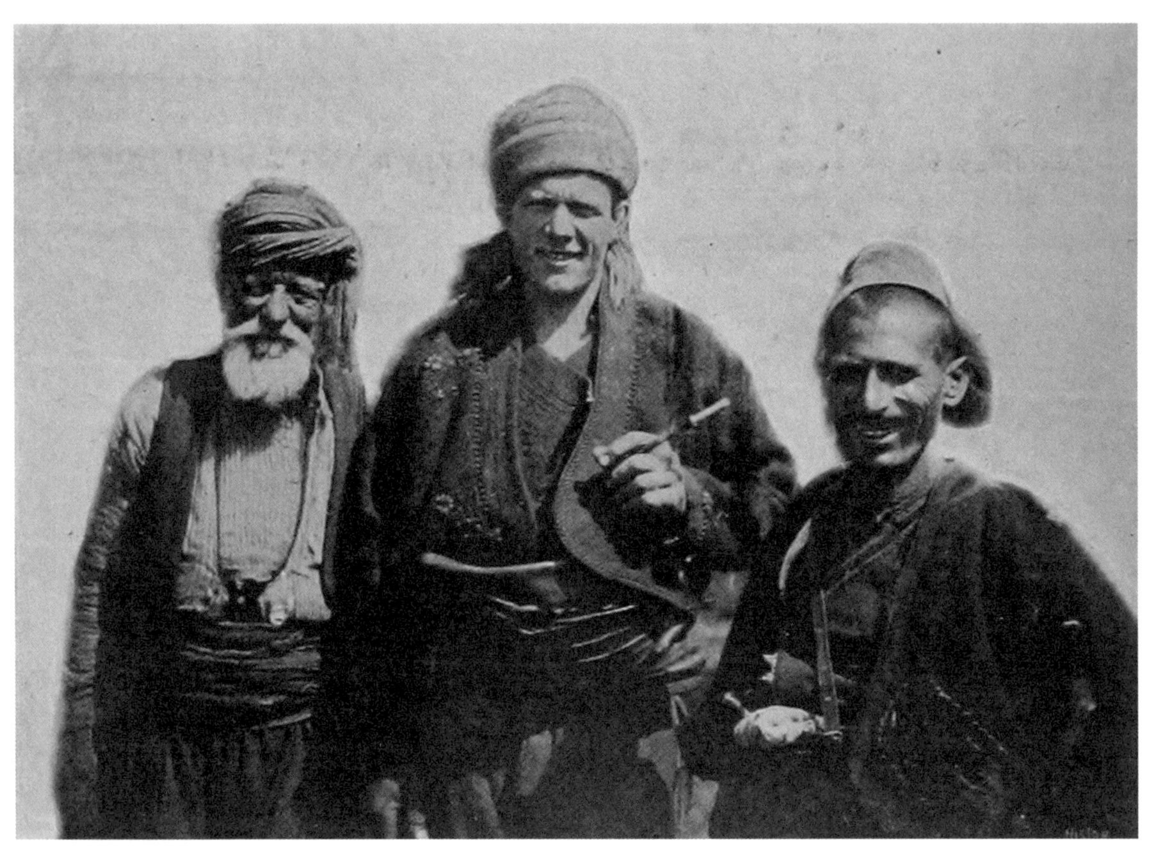

‘Western traveller with astonished natives’, Glasinac, August 20th, 1894.

# ARCHAEOLOGY AND THE (DE)CONSTRUCTION OF BOSNIAN IDENTITY

Dr. Danijel Dzino

The assessment of the relationship between the past and interpretation of the past has gained increased interest and popularity amongst archaeologists. The influence of ideology, colonialism and nationalism on archaeological research and interpretation of material evidence is perhaps its most attractive and most popular aspect (Díaz-Andreu 2007, Díaz-Andreu and Champion 1996, Fawcett and Kohl 1995; Galaty 2004). There is a strong connection between archaeology and the projects of construction of nations. They both developed at the same time – the late eighteenth and nineteenth centuries. Nationalism was a creative project of Western intellectual elites which were creating 'imaginary communities' connected by perceptions of common origins, history, traditions and destiny (Anderson 1991). These projects were initially internal developments, ultimately resulting in the creation of Western nation-states. However, the experience with nation-making projects proved to be very useful during European colonial expansion in the nineteenth century, as one tool for imperial domination over colonized peoples, such as colonial constructions of African nations (Young 1994).

Nationalism needed history to provide 'biographies' for those imaginary communities, to describe their 'birth' and tell the story of their development. Archaeology, which also developed as an academic discipline in the nineteenth century, was initially used as an auxiliary discipline illustrating with artifacts the historical narratives of written sources. Historical artifacts, but also monuments, landscapes and sites separated from their original historical contexts transform into images and symbols helping the wider audience to visualize the past. These images and symbols produce experiences of the past, which can be perceived as authentic and true, bringing the public into direct contact with 'their ancestors' and 'their past' (Russell 2006). The construction of national 'biographies' was effectively provided in museums, where images of the past were selectively placed in a particular, well-defined order, with the purpose of illustrating historical narratives, stories of nations – their birth and development (Kaplan 1994). Apart from museums, the ideas of nations as communities were also transmitted through historical sites, landscapes and monuments, new places of pilgrimage, which create shared experiences of the past for members of the imagined community.

Examples of the relationship between projects of nation-making and archaeology are very diverse, not only in their historical and regional contexts, but also whether national identity was constructed by 'outsiders' or 'insiders'. To demonstrate this diversity in a brief sketch, I will touch upon the use of archaeology in the attempts to construct Bosnian identity in two different historical periods in order to illuminate several wider issues connected with the relationship of archaeology and the construction of nations.

The territory of modern-day Bosnia and Herzegovina was shaped in 1699 from the reduced Ottoman province (*ellayet*) of Bosnia, named (but not shaped) after the medieval Kingdom of Bosnia, which was conquered in 1463 by sultan Mehmed II. Under the Treaty of Berlin, Habsburg Austria-Hungary was permitted to occupy and administer Bosnia and Herzegovina in 1878, which remained under nominal rule of the sultan. In 1908 Bosnia and Herzegovina was annexed to the Habsburg Empire as a special administrative region, under the joint administration of Austria and Hungary. Bosnia and Herzegovina is inhabited by three different ethnic groups: Orthodox Serbs, Catholic Croats and Slavophone Bosnian Muslims (from 1993 known as the Bosniaks). Bosnian identity was claimed by different groups in different historical contexts before the nineteenth century, mostly Muslims, but did not exist as a well-defined and shared identity-discourse bridging all three groups at the same time, apart from the sense of regional identity (Džaja 1984).

Habsburg rule was significantly affected by the personality of Benjamin von Kállay (B.ni Kállay de Nagy-K.II.), the Hungarian-born minister of imperial finances who was appointed as the administrator of Bosnia and Herzegovina from 1882, remaining in this post until his death in 1903. His personal agency and influence shaped the Habsburg colonial enterprise as a 'civilizing mission', not unlike the contemporary 'civilizing missions' of European imperial powers in Africa. Certainly, Bosnia and Herzegovina was a special case as it was not an overseas territory but directly adjacent to the Empire. In the 1880s and 1890s Kállay pursued the idea of a three-confessional Bosnian identity for clear political reasons. The Habsburg administration feared the politicization of Serb and Croat identity in Bosnia and Herzegovina, which participated in the creation of imagined communities of the Serbs in neighbouring Serbia and Croatians in Austro-Hungarian Dalmatia and Croatia-Slavonia. Certainly this policy cannot be seen as a clearly defined repressive imposition of Bosnian identity, or simplified endorsement of the continuity of medieval Bosnian kingdom.

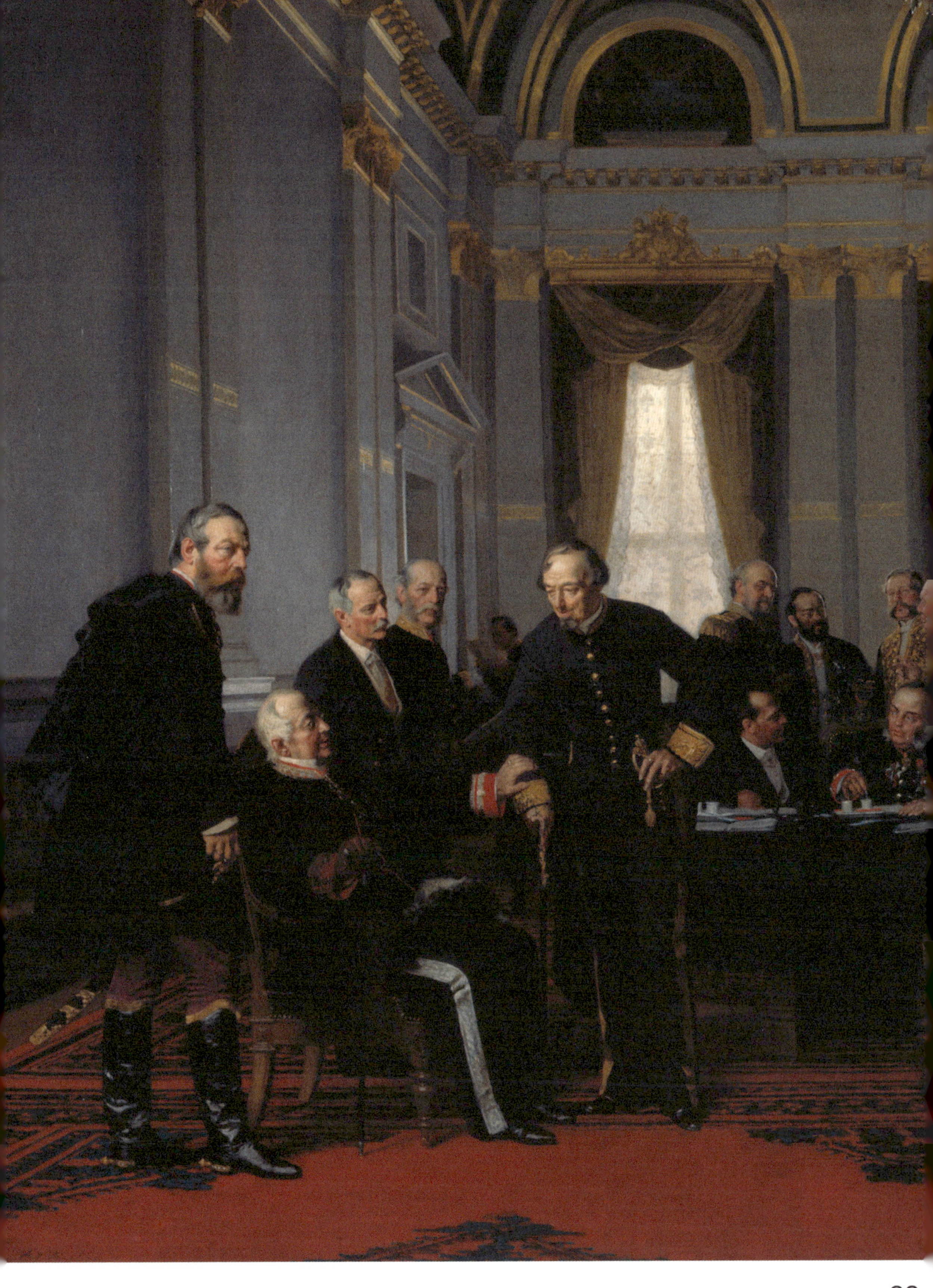

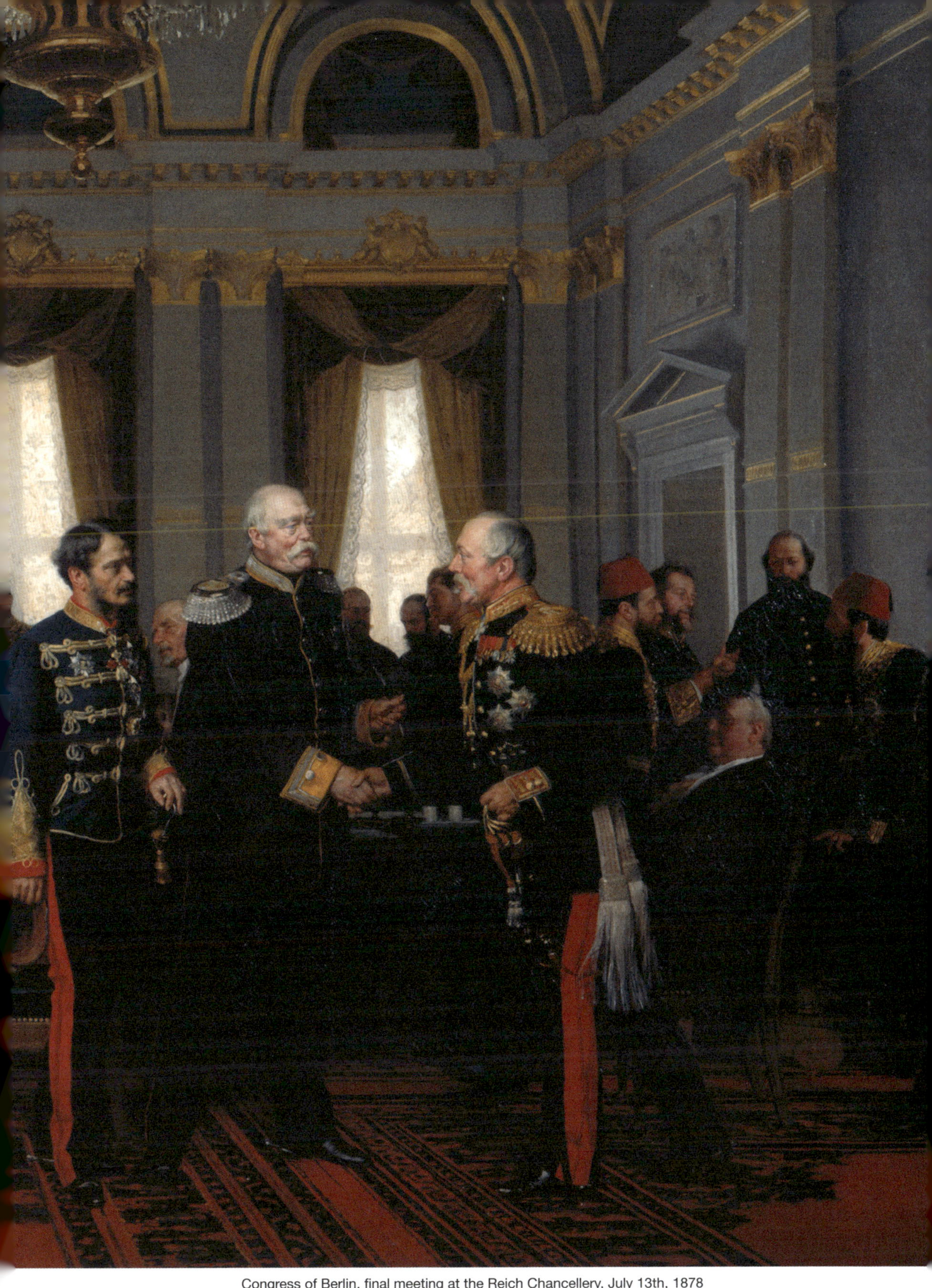

Congress of Berlin, final meeting at the Reich Chancellery, July 13th, 1878

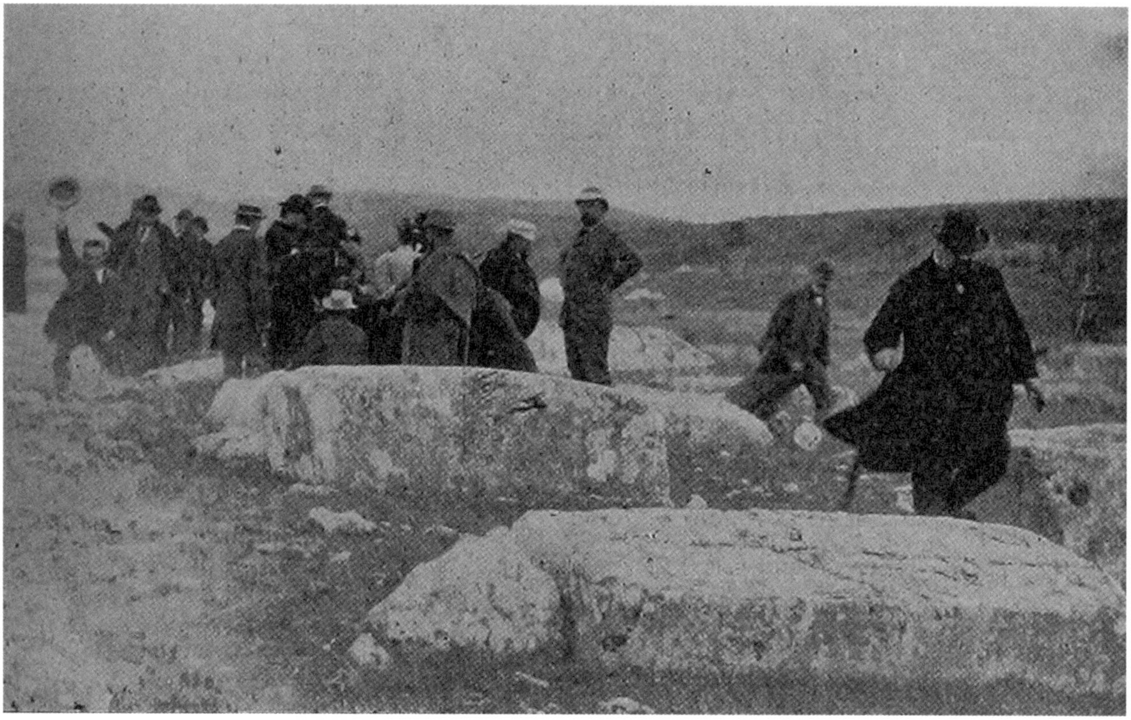

‘Archaeologists among the tombs’, August 19th, 1894

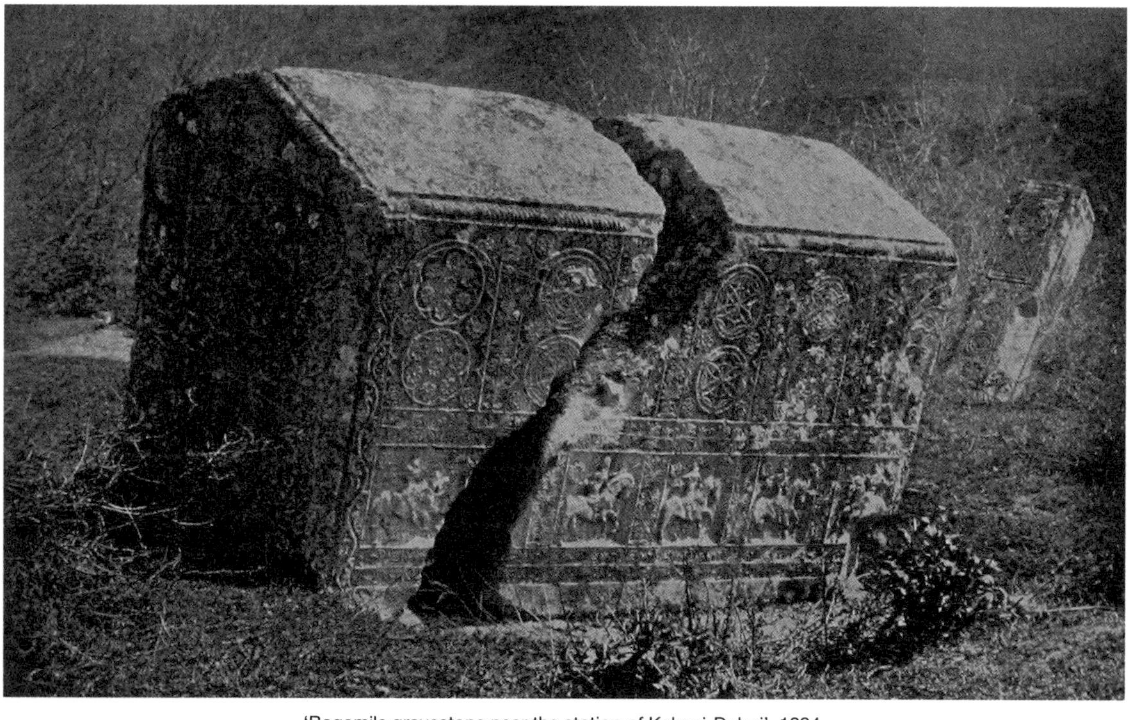

‘Bogomile gravestone near the station of Kakanj-Doboj’, 1894

It was rather focused to construct a new Bosnian identity as a multi-confessional and supranational identity, within an imperial ideological framework, loyal to the Empire, smoothing the transition of the region to Austro-Hungary (Kraljačić 1987; Okey 2007: 55–143, 253–255).

The development of archaeology in Bosnia and Herzegovina must be seen in this political and ideological context. While no organized archaeology existed under the Ottomans, the period of Austro-Hungarian rule resulted in significant investments and results in this field. Archaeology was developed as a colonial enterprise, part of the Habsburg 'civilizing mission', differing from the archaeological development in neighbouring regions. Its development, excavations and institutionalization, through the development of the Provincial (*Zemaljski*) museum, one of Kállay's ideas and pet projects, required significant material investment which was readily available through imperial structures (Novaković 2011: 402–404). The most significant archaeological work and discoveries were made in the Iron Age and Roman periods, as well as late antiquity. Medieval history had a special place in this colonial enterprise, and the Habsburg administration went to considerable length to shape a narrative from the Bosnian medieval past.[1] Stećci (sing. stećak), characteristic decorated medieval tombstones, were directly linked with the medieval heretic movement known as the Bogomils, who were chosen as useful 'ancestors' to the new Bosnian 'nation' because they could not be linked with either Catholic Croats or Orthodox Serbs. The archaeology of the medieval period was focused on *stećci*, rather than on any other medieval structures apart from fortresses, while the existence of Christian churches from the twelfth century onwards was usually denied (Truhelka 1914: 227–252). The positioning of the *lapidarium* with *stećci* within the newly built museum complex in Sarajevo (opened in 1913) emphasizes their importance as contemporary symbols (Truhelka 1914: 249-252). They were placed in the botanic gardens, between the archaeological and ethnological pavilions of the Museum, which displayed the past and present of Bosnia and Herzegovina. Thus, they directly connected the medieval kingdom of Bosnia and the duchy of Hum (Herzegovina) with the Austro-Hungarian present, skipping over four centuries of Ottoman rule, which was not present in any Museum exhibitions or structures (cf. Novaković 2012: 57). Furthermore, the discovery of an elite male burial under *stećak* in Arnautovići by Carl Patsch, ascribed to the medieval Bosnian king Tvrtko I, had not been published or even mentioned at this time (Wenzel 1999; Zadro 2004).[2] The problem with the discovery was that this grave was located next to the church – and the interpretative framework of the time insisted that the Bogomils were not supposed to be connected with churches. Thus, the discovery was not mentioned at all, and the church of St. Nicholas from the fourteenth century, was ascribed to the early Christian period, i.e. the fifth and sixth centuries, in a contemporary overview of provincial medieval history (Truhelka 1914: 226). Whether this discovery was hidden for ideological reasons, as Wenzel (1999: 175–180) convincingly argued, cannot be ascertained beyond reasonable doubt, but it would nicely fit into the contemporary colonial context.

A hundred years later a unique Bosnian identity was claimed once again through archaeology, but in different historical circumstances. In 1992 Bosnia and Herzegovina became an independent country but was immediately plunged into armed conflict. While the reasons for the conflict are numerous, one of the most important is disagreement about the political organization of the country between three ethnic groups. The Serb and Croat political options in Bosnia and Herzegovina supported a high level of political decentralization and/or dissolution of the country, while the most numerous group, the Bosniaks, supported the centralization of the country.
In 2006 Semir Osmanagić, a Bosniak-born amateur-archaeologist living in the US, claimed that the hill of Visočica and a few neighbouring hills, near the township of Visoko, were nothing less than 27,000-year-old pyramids. The discovery brought about brief interest in the world media but its validity was quickly and unanimously rejected by experts, local and foreign, who recognized it with good reason as a case of pseudo-archaeology (Harding 2007). However, work on the excavation of the 'pyramids' continued. It was coordinated outside of academic institutions by the Bosnian Pyramid of the Sun Foundation founded by Osmanagić, which continued to receive some degree of public, financial and moral support (Foundation 2012).

Pruitt (2009) enlightened the complex meanings and significance of this 'discovery' in different local economic and political contexts, although failed to clearly position this venture within current political and identity-narratives in post-war Bosnia and Herzegovina.[3] On one side, its discoverer and the Foundation claimed the site for a new supra-ethnic discourse on Bosnian identity, which is mostly accepted in Bosniak majority regions by the Bosniaks and some minority non-Bosniaks, as a secular and inclusive identity. It is best seen, on a symbolic level, in the logo of the Foundation which contains the new state flag of Bosnia and Herzegovina. The triangle from the flag has been incorporated as symbolic representation of the pyramid.[4] The site was immediately claimed by the Bosniaks, on a number of different levels.

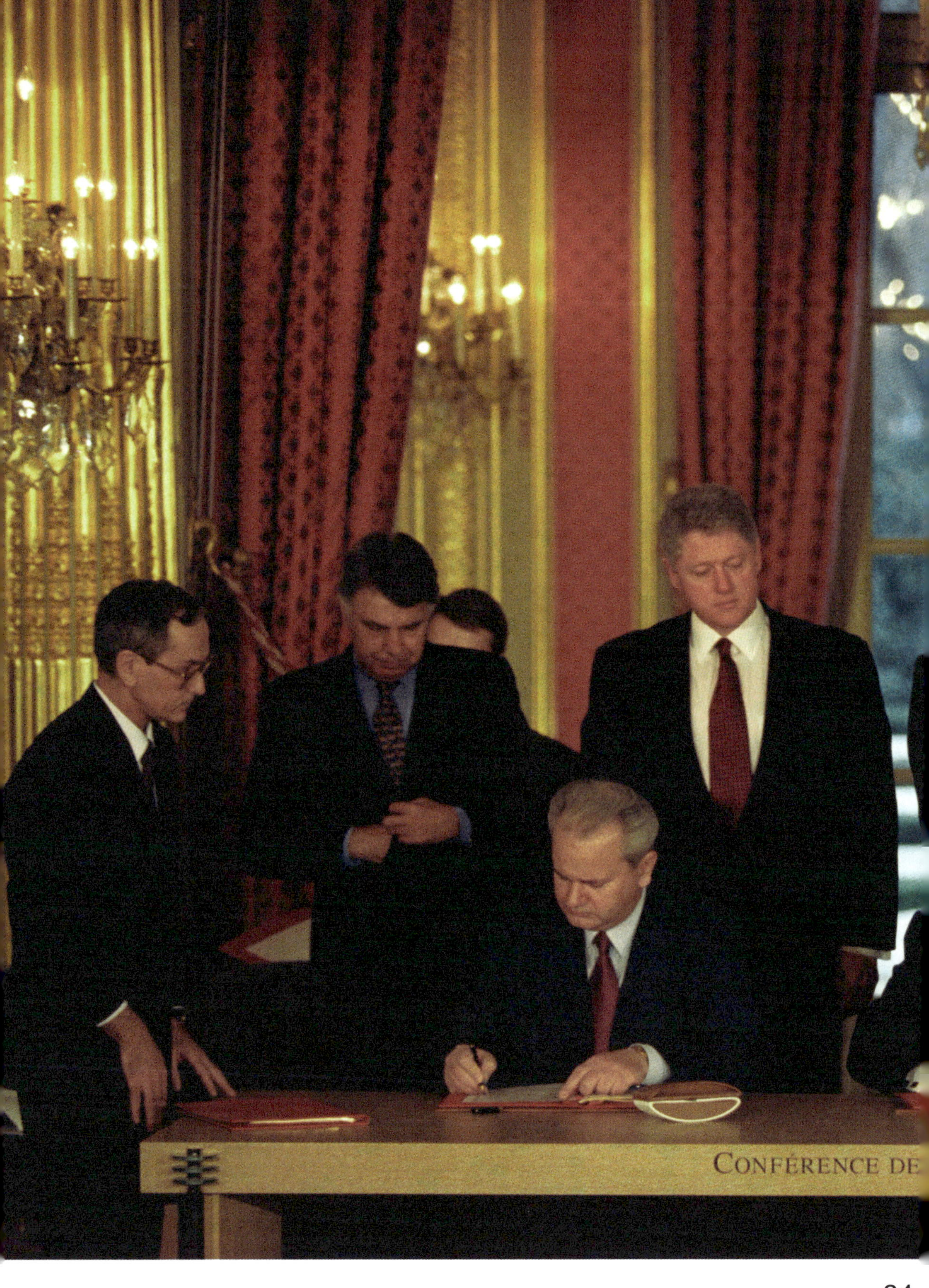
CONFÉRENCE DE

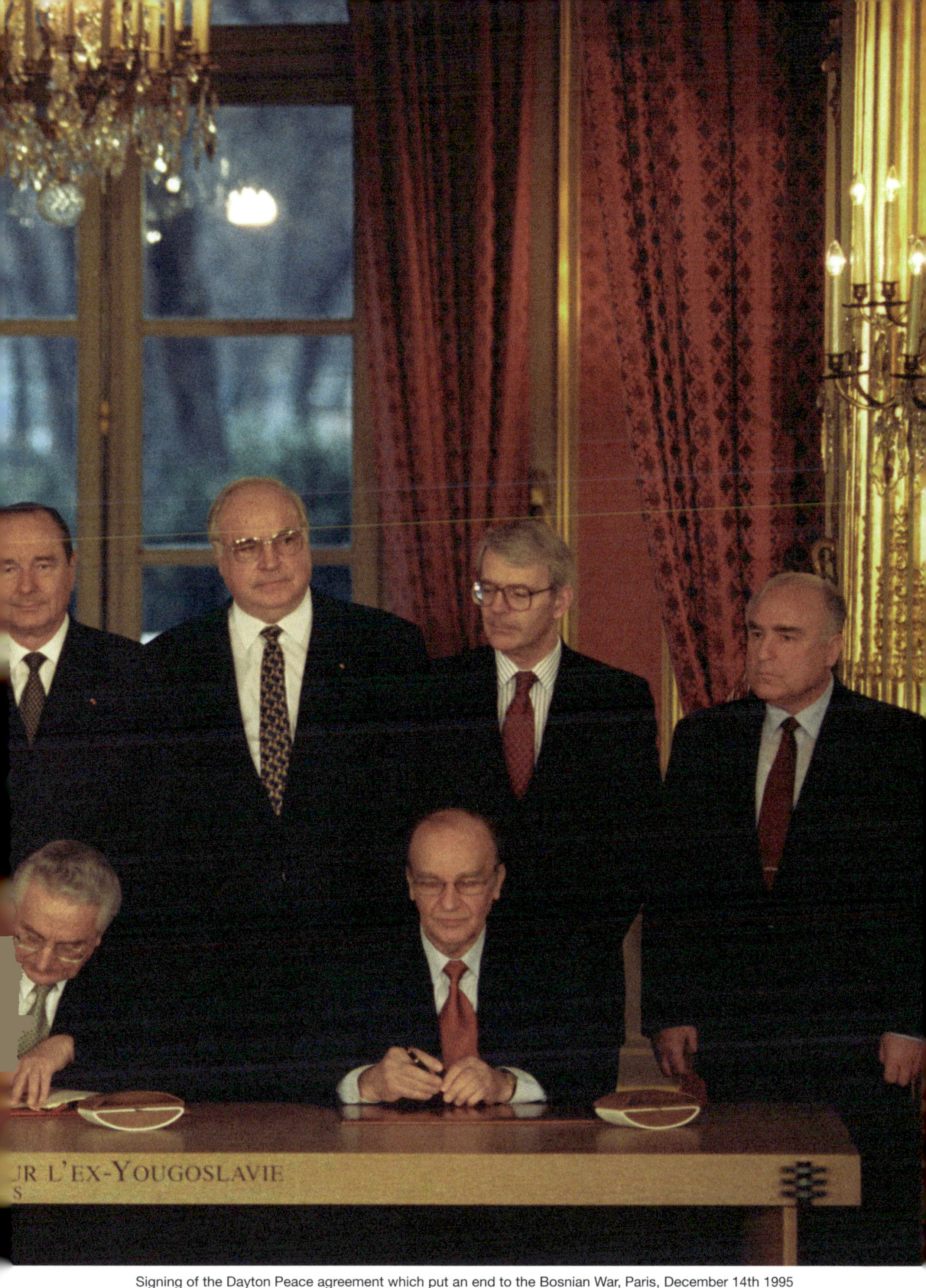

Signing of the Dayton Peace agreement which put an end to the Bosnian War, Paris, December 14th 1995

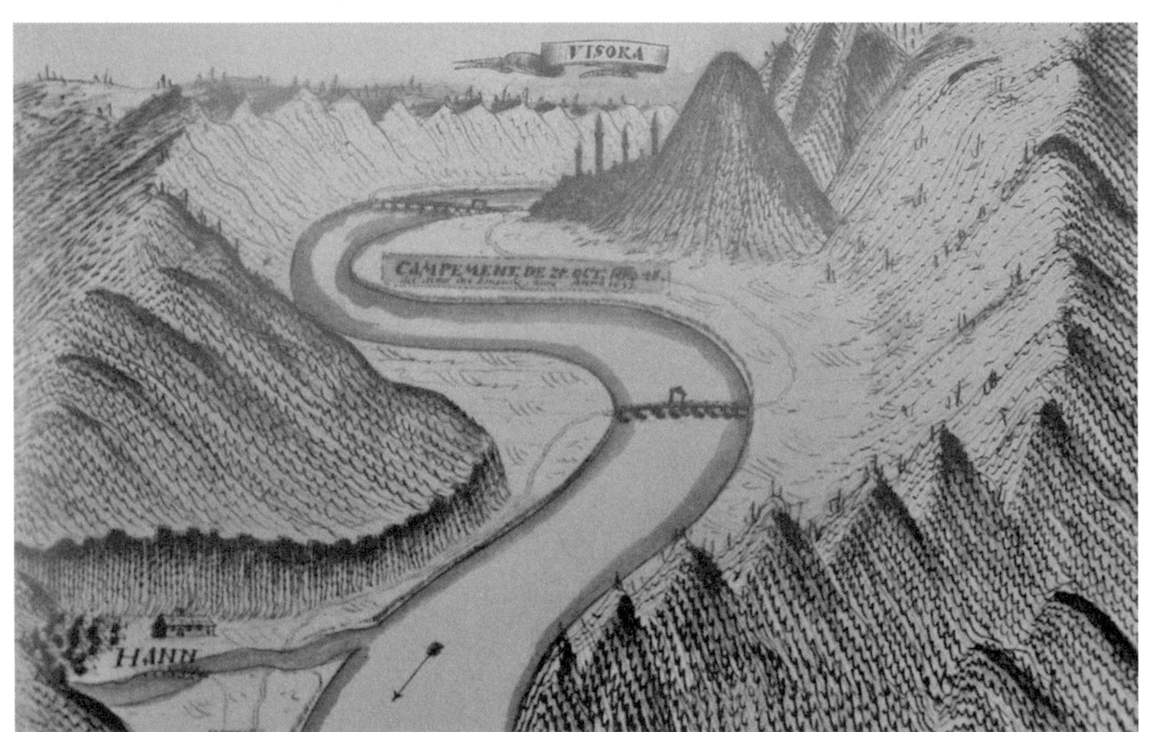


Visoko, 1697

On the level of public discourse, it offered a site of pilgrimage, a sacred space for marking and experiencing identity. For locals, Bosniaks by an overwhelming majority, it offered limited economic opportunities. Finally, it became a useful tool used by the Bosniak political and religious leaders for their own promotion. The 'discovery' of Osmanagić did not attract the Serbs and Croats in Bosnia and Herzegovina – both of these groups showed visible indifference towards the 'pyramids'. No political or religious leader representing the Serbs or Croats from Bosnia and Herzegovina has visited the site, and the pyramids have not attracted much enthusiasm, apart from amused interest, in public and media discourses in Serb and Croat majority-regions.

The two instances of the use of archaeology for constructing Bosnian identity discussed here are representative of wider issues related to the reconstruction and deconstruction of nations in archaeology. They show how the same identity can be used by both outsiders and insiders to assert political aims in very different historical circumstances. The Austro-Hungarian imperial bureaucracy attempted to construct a supra-national and multi-confessional Bosnian identity as an instrument of imperial control and colonial domination of Bosnia and Herzegovina. In order to do that, the imperial power felt the need to establish control of newly produced historical narratives of the Middle Ages. Archaeology played an important role in this project, focusing institutionalized research on medieval tomb-stones, which became recognizable symbols of historical 'foundations' for this identity. One century later, the 'discovery' of ancient 'pyramids' by an amateur archaeologist was used in an attempt to once again construct a supra-national Bosnian identity in independent postwar Bosnia and Herzegovina. This time, archaeology was used by internal forces. Pseudo-archaeology circumvented institutionalized archaeology and created an instant pilgrimage site and symbol, one which was connected with newly established state-symbols and identity-narratives of Bosnianness, fully accepted only in Bosniak-majority regions.

Both attempts ultimately failed. The Habsburg Empire gave up on the wider project of constructing Bosnian identity even before its own disintegration, as the three ethnic groups were not interested in developing a joint imaginary community.[5] A century later, the 'pyramids' were, on a popular level, accepted by the Bosniaks but failed to attract the acceptance of the other two groups as a shared symbol. The role of archaeology in both examples was to produce recognizable images and symbols related to two different projects aiming to form the same imaginary community. This brings us to the very essence of the relationship between archaeology and nation-making projects. Archaeology produces artifacts which, through their public display and exposition, easily transform into recognizable images, ready to be claimed as symbols in different contexts. Symbols are necessary in order to bring together imaginary communities like a national anthem, or a flag, and in the case of archaeological artifacts and sites, to relate to a 'joint' past by sharing experience of that past. Archaeology is a crucially important discipline, which provides a window into the past, providing a type of 'family album' illustrating biographies of imaginary communities, ultimately providing proof that the past really happened. On some level, it 'proves' that fluid and unstable social constructs, such as nations, can be regarded as fixed and immutable realities.

1 The Habsburgs did not have monopoly on these narratives, see for example Evans (1877: xxiii–civ).

2 As Zadro (2004: 68) first points out, the discovery was mentioned in the annual report of the museum activities for 1909, and publication of the finds was announced for the foloowing year (Anonymous 1909: 605–606) but not published for unexplained reasons.

3 Surprisingly for someone quite familiar with 'local knowledge', Pruitt does not show awareness that 'Bosnian public' and 'Bosnian identity', frequently mentioned in the paper, are identity-narratives limited only to the Bosniak-majority regions.

4 The flag of Bosnia and Herzegovina is not historical. It is a new design adopted in 1998 on the decision of a foreigner, Carlos Vestendorp y Cabeza, High Representative of the UN in Bosnia and Herzegovina (1997–1999), who, through his office had powers to implement laws and dismiss elected local officials. The flag is today mostly accepted by the Bosniaks, but it is very rare to see it publicly displayed in the Serb and Croat majority areas.

5 To be precise, 'Bogomil romance' resonated positively amongst some Muslim intelligentsia at the time, who started to claim the Bogomils as their ancestors (Okey 2007: 242, 246).

# Valley of the Bosnian Pyramids

According to local legend, when the Turkish empire started to invade Bosnia in the 14th century, the Turks heard a story from an old woman who was living at the bottom of the Visočica hill. She said: "Nobody is allowed to live in the ancient town located at top of the hill unless they are prepared to guard its secret, hidden under the town, with their life." The old town was once the base of a Bosnian king, Tvrtko of Kotromanic (1338-1391). She said that the town hid a secret 'that wears two layers'. She said : "One layer has been brought there and is getting worn off by the rain (the earth layer). The second layer is an 'eggshell' layer which is thin and fragile. If the eggshell gets damaged and its contents are taken away by water (flood), this will cause bad luck for the people of the Valley."

Legend says that Turks were so scared at this story that they never invaded the town on top of the Pyramid of Sun, even though it was the capital of the Bosnian state at that time. They moved on with their invasion, taking the towns of Travnik and Jajce. As a result, Bosnia became part of the Turkish Empire as its most western point in Europe at that time.

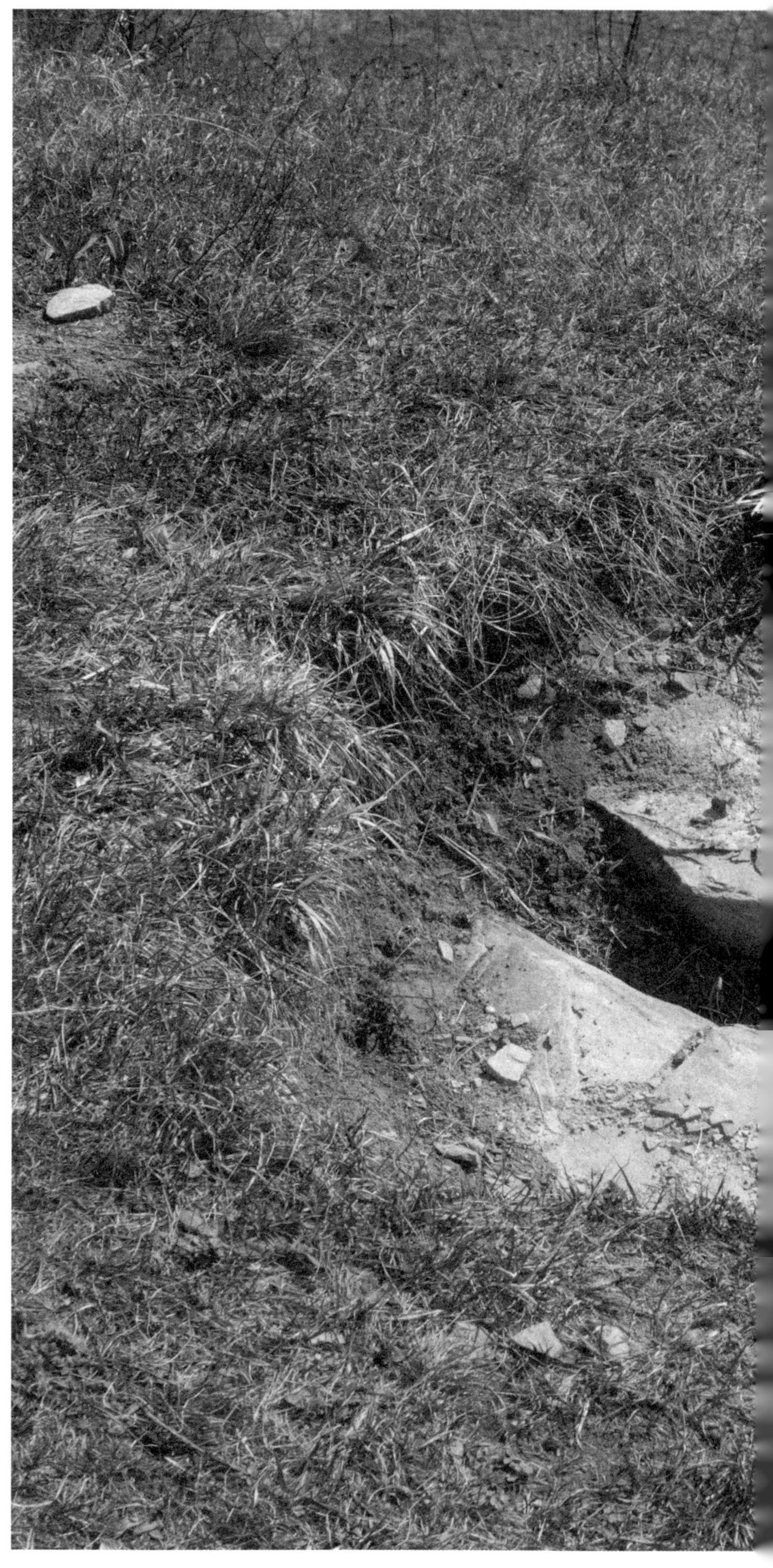

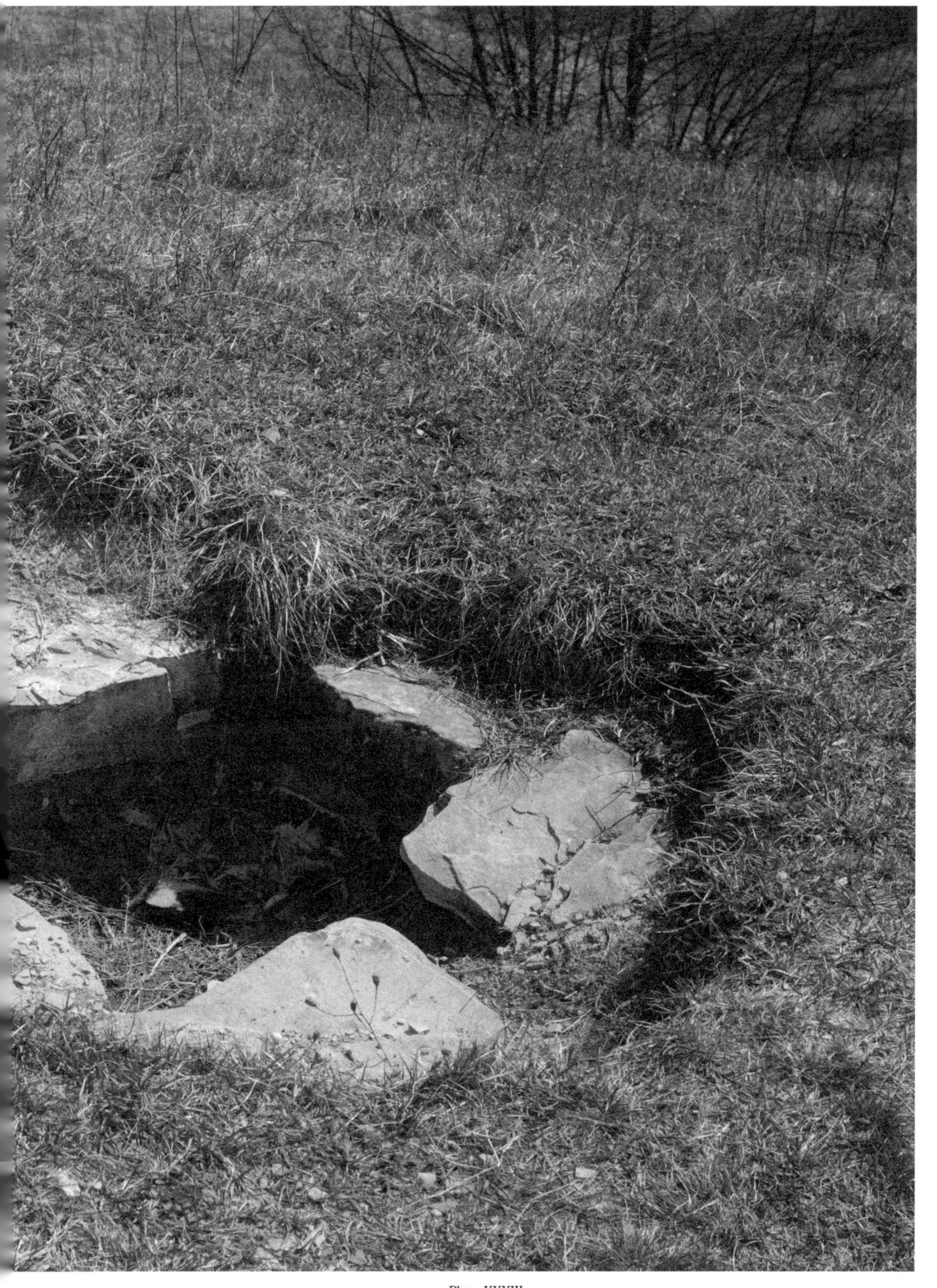

Plate XXXIII

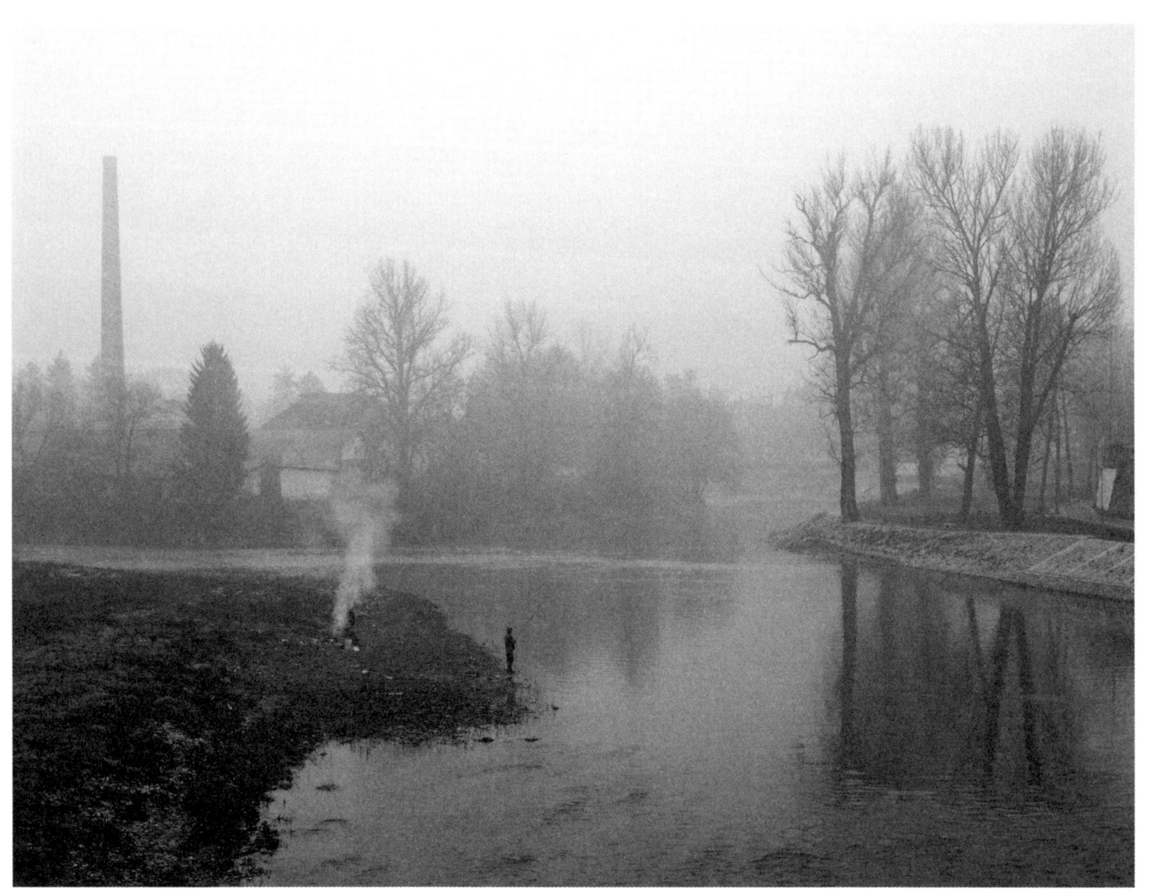

Plate XXXIV

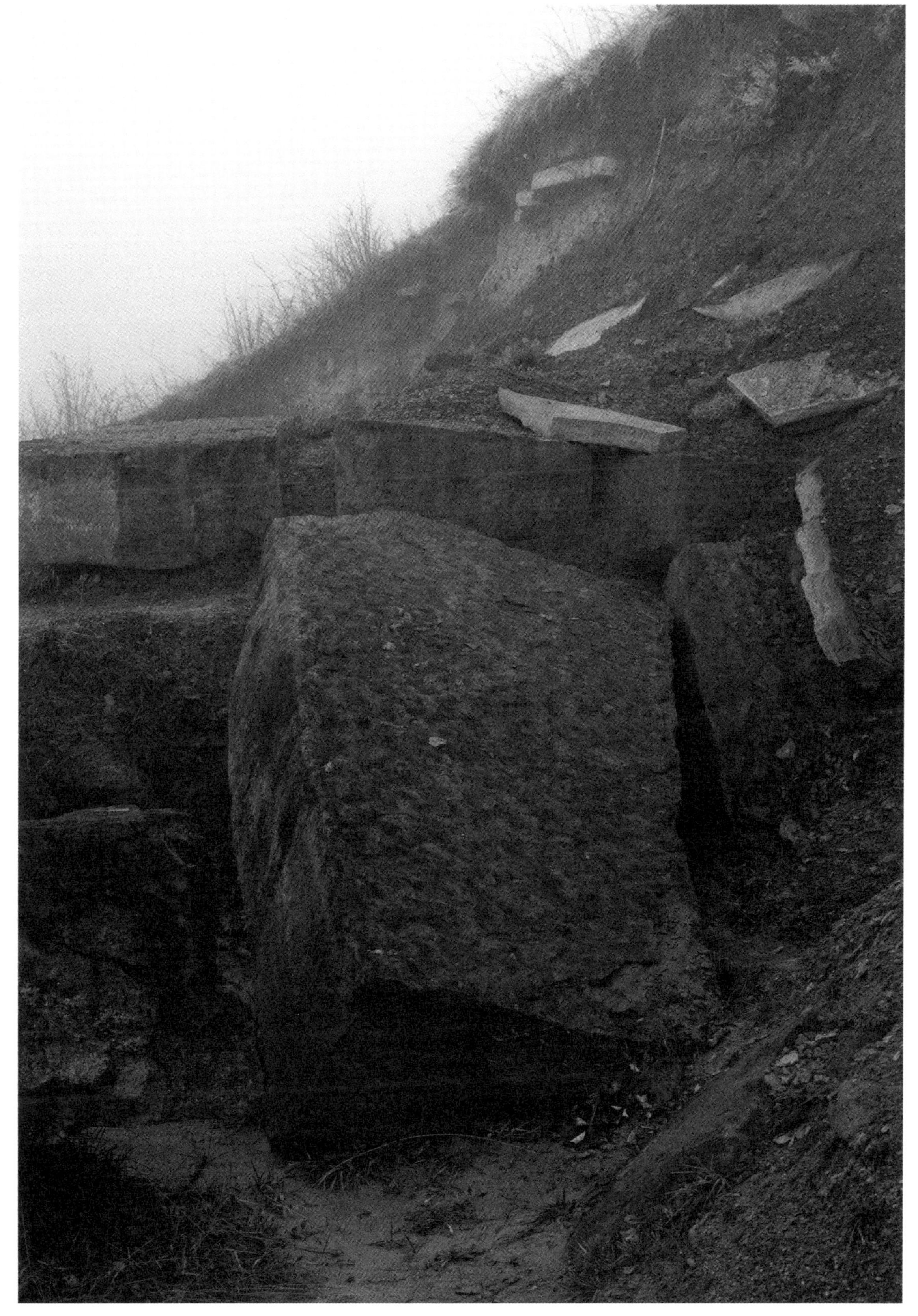

Plate XXXV

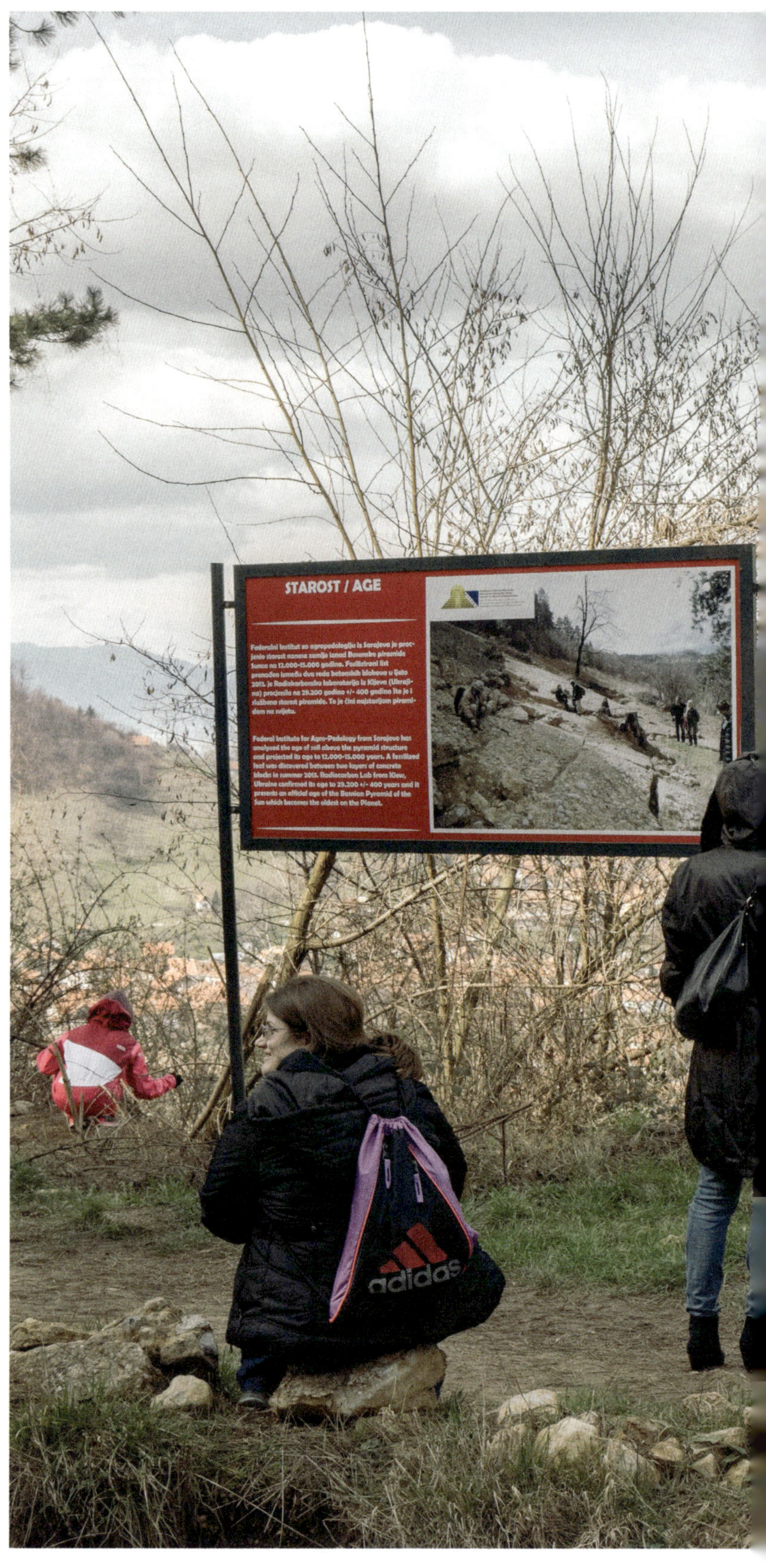
STAROST / AGE
Federalni Institut za agropedologiju iz Sarajeva je procjenio starost nanosa zemlje iznad Bosanske piramide Sunca na 12.000-15.000 godina. Fosilizirani list pronađen između dva reda betonskih blokova u ljeto 2013. je Radiokarbonska laboratorija iz Kijeva (Ukrajina) procjenila na 29.200 godina +/- 400 godina što je i službena starost piramide. To je čini najstarijom piramidom na svijetu.
Federal Institute for Agro-Pedology from Sarajevo has analysed the age of soil above the pyramid structure and projected its age to 12.000-15.000 years. A fossilized leaf was discovered between two layers of concrete blocks in summer 2013. Radiocarbon Lab from Kiev, Ukraine confirmed its age to 29.200 +/- 400 years and it presents an official age of the Bosnian Pyramid of the Sun which becomes the oldest on the Planet.
adidas

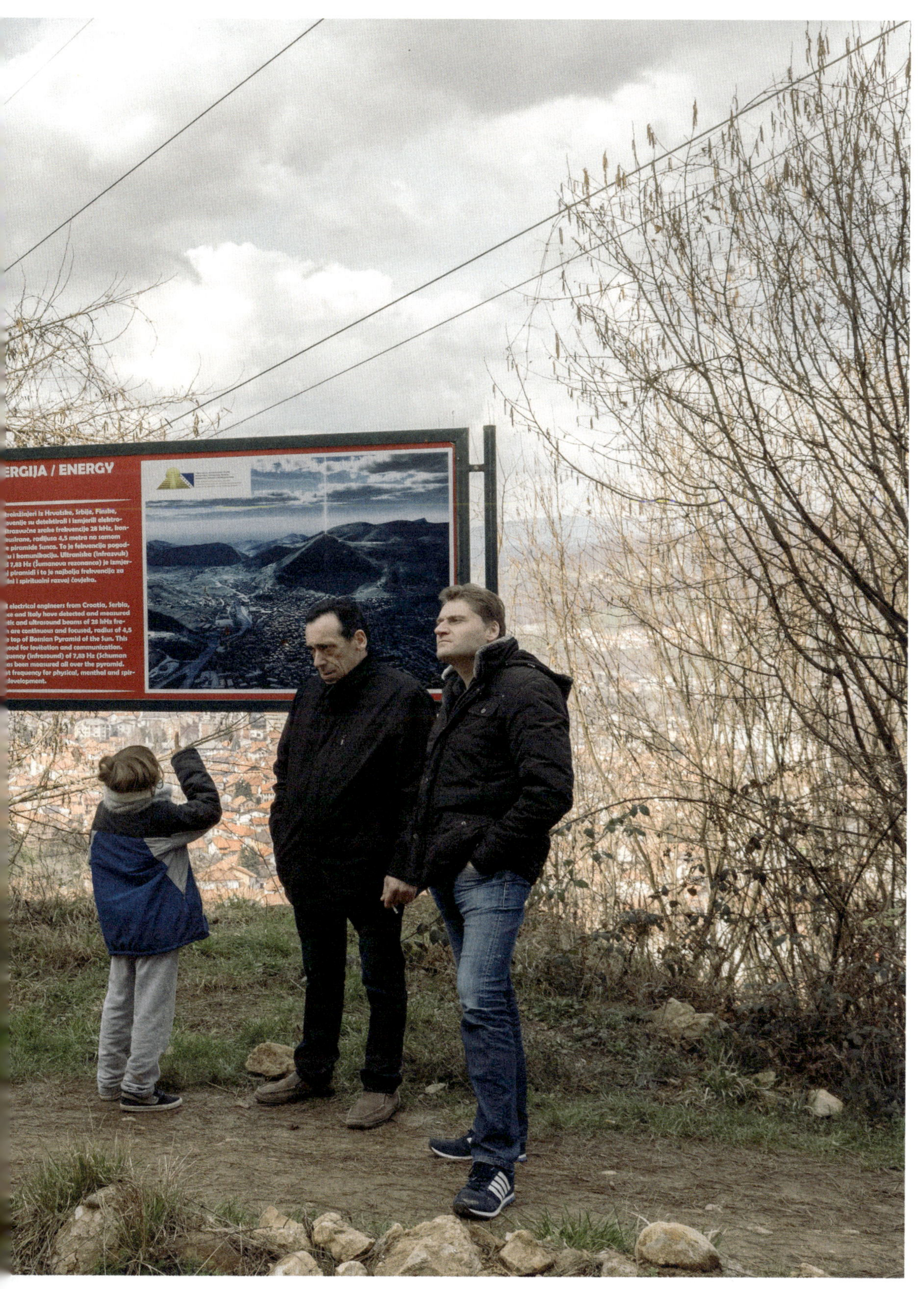
ERGIJA / ENERGY
troinžinjeri iz Hrvatske, Srbije, Finske,
ovenije su detektirali i izmjerili elektro-
trazvučne zrake frekvencije 28 kHz, kon-
kusirane, radijusa 4,5 metra na samom
e piramide Sunca. To je fekvencija pogod-
u i komunikaciju. Ultraniska (infrazvuk)
d 7,83 Hz (Šumanova rezonanca) je izmjer-
j piramidi i to je najbolja frekvencija za
lni i spirituaini razvoj čovjeka.
electrical engineers from Croatia, Serbia,
ce and Italy have detected and measured
tic and ultrasound beams of 28 kHz fre-
are continuous and focused, radius of 4,5
top of Bosnian Pyramid of the Sun. This
ood for levitation and communication.
quency (infrasound) of 7,83 Hz (Schuman
as been measured all over the pyramid.
t frequency for physical, menthal and spir-
development.

Plate XXXVI

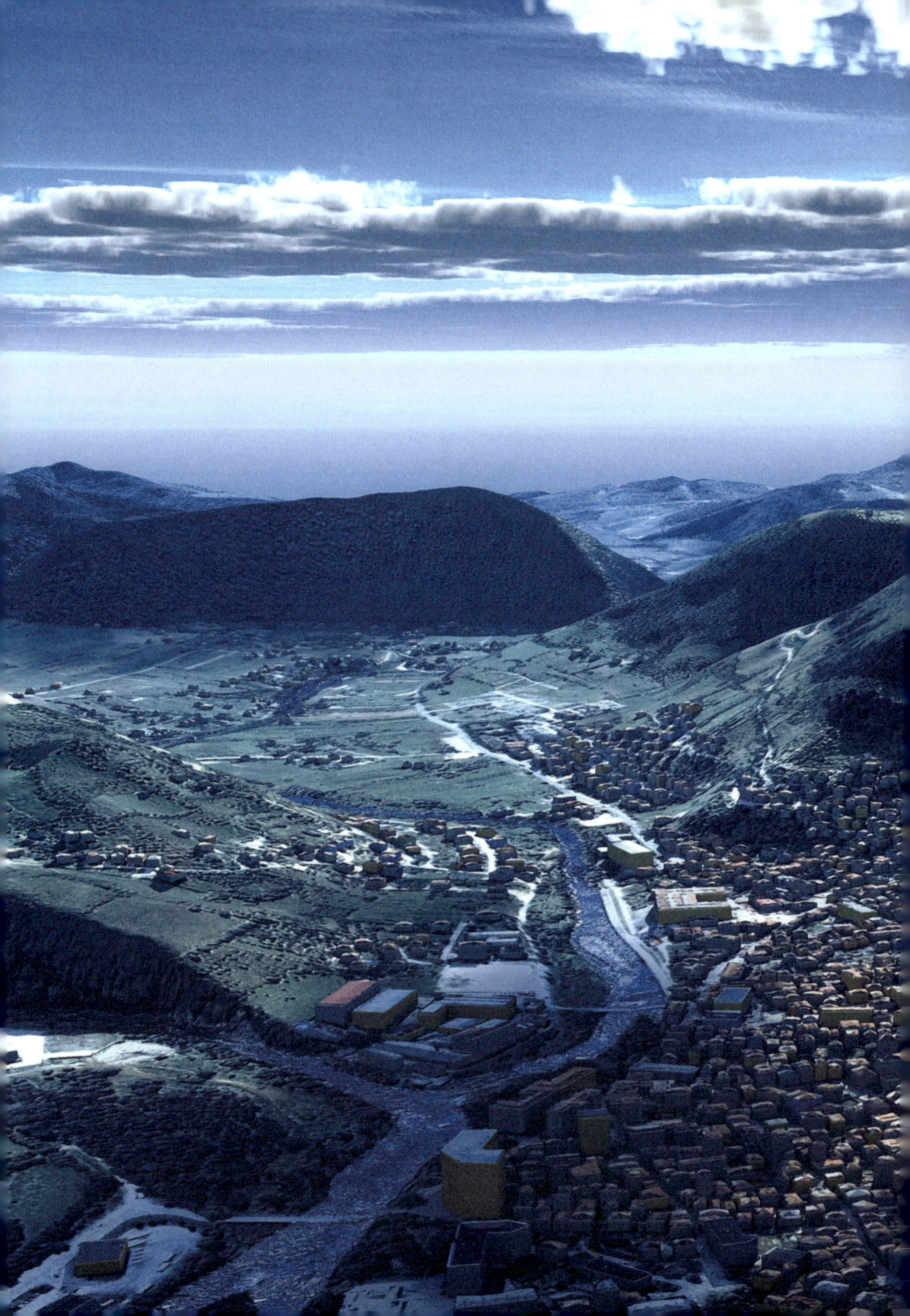

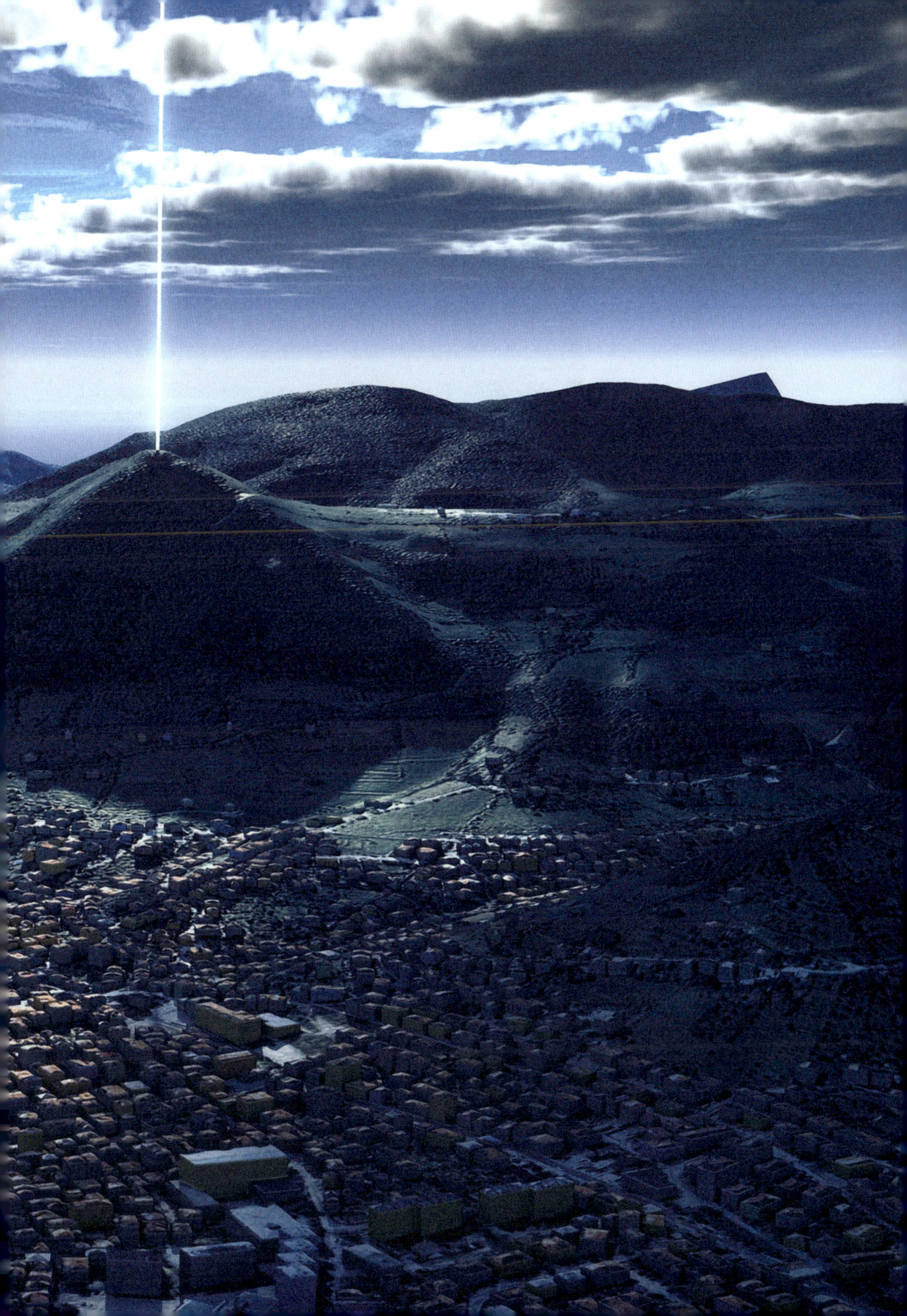

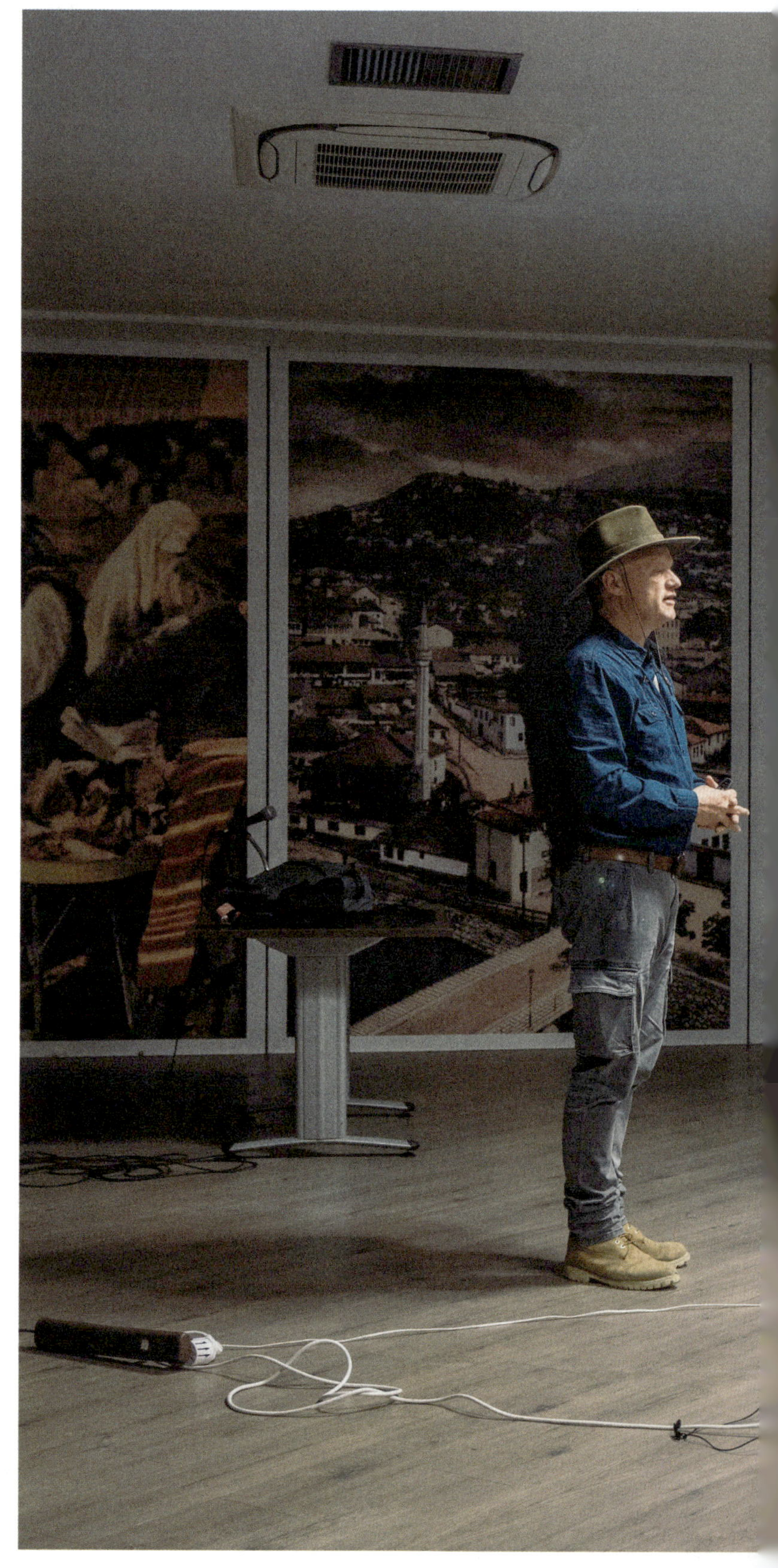

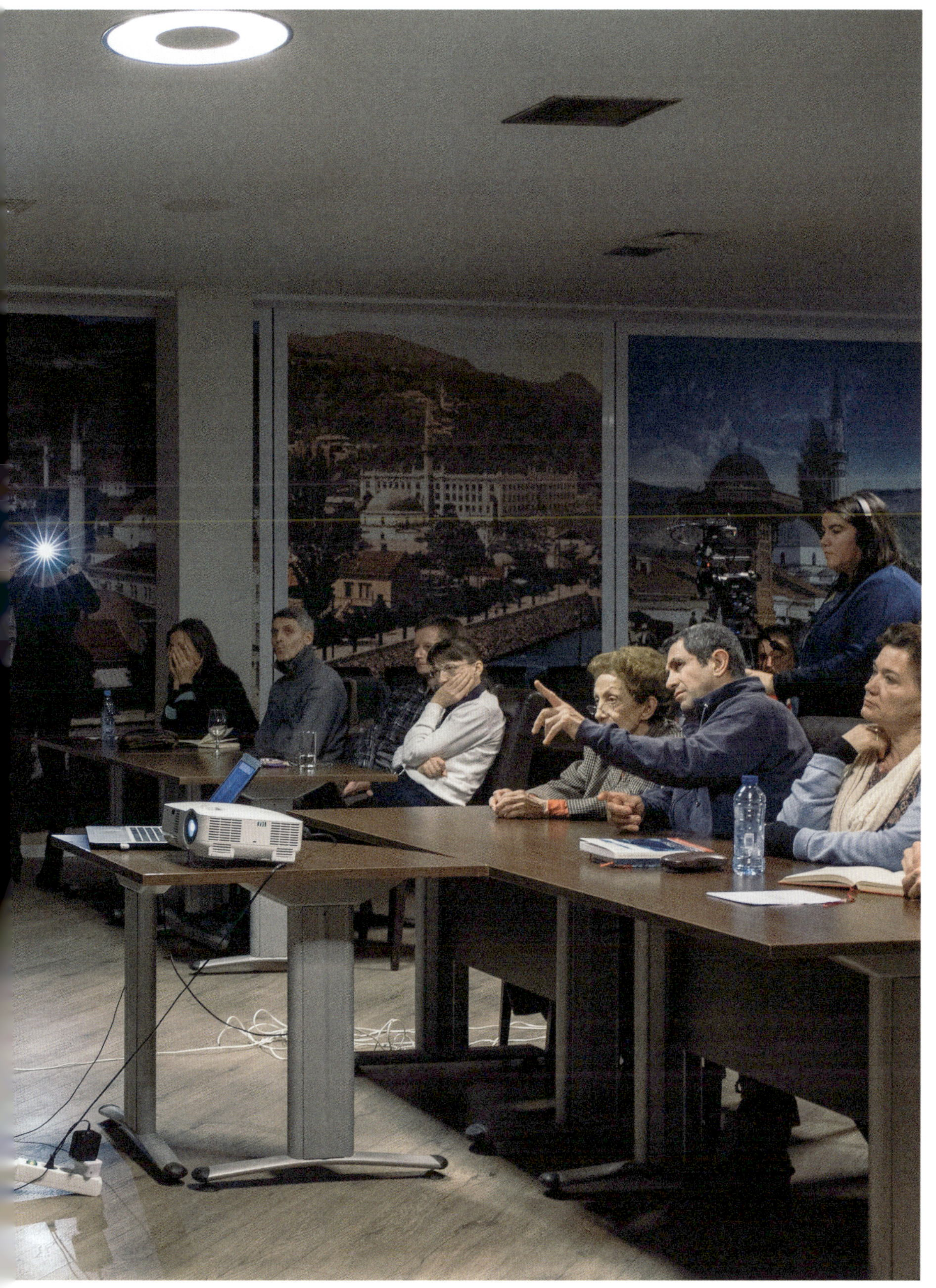

Plate XXXVIII

March 21th, 2014, Hotel Saraj, Sarajevo, conversation with a tourism officer

Do you have an office here in Sarajevo?
Yes, we've made a small gallery in the centre. Just some photos to get the idea what we're doing … We also want to open a museum with the artifacts. We used to exhibit in the local museum but they kicked us out.

In Visoko?
Yes … They are changing their minds all the time … I used to make the exhibition there … It was so stressful to put these pictures together and then suddenly being told to take them all away … So they accept you and then they suddenly they …

They don't know what to do with the pyramids?
Yes, they are in the position between the officials and us …

Officials, you mean the government?
Yes, you know … This country has lost 20 years … moved backwards 20 years in every sense … It's an awful condition, I mean … the state of mind of the politicians and the people who stayed here to work is really … the situation is not bright at all. So we are … But Semir is a wonderful person and he is …

Are there any volunteers at the moment?
Yes, we have now 7 employed people that are cleaning the tunnels, and honestly they do much better then the volunteers.

So you have volunteers?
Yes, but we also have official archaeologists and geologists. Most of the time we have anthropologists and people who are not obsessed with general, official knowledge(laughing).

Like pseudo-archaeologists?
Yes, pioneers, the whole new concept of … Have you ever been to the pyramids?

No but I would like to …
When you drive next to them you will see a hill on which they planted some trees in the sixties. If you see photos from the beginning of the 20th century you see more clearly that it looks like a pyramid. Like normal pyramids.

This project is completely different from any other archaeological site in the world. We are open for any kind of investigation. Anyone who wants to come to do measurements and help us find the real purpose and function of the pyramid is welcome. For instance, we discovered that this pyramid is an potential energy place, just like other pyramids. To have this, you need to have certain conditions like underground waters, which Bosnia has. And not only that, Georadar shows us that 2.5 km under these pyramids there is a huge natural iron block with a strong magnetic field around it. So can you imagine this piece of iron, the water streams and then the sacred geometry of the pyramid which is all amplifying this energy in the space? So at this very moment the pyramid is creating energy. The light beam that we have photoshopped on the image is not imagination, it's what measurements have told us through three years of constant research. The pyramid can be seen as a machine.

Have you been there ?
Of course … I was a bit sceptic about this idea back in 2005 when we were all invited by Dr. Osmanagić. I thought he just wanted to be popular but three years ago he invited me again, because I was working in tourism and he wanted me to help him because he wasn't getting donations from the government. So the only way was to bring tourists. But I was really ashamed, honestly, I didn't know what it was and I was sceptic … until I entered the tunnels. For me the tunnels are … I don't know, you feel it, even me who is not crazy about energy and such. You can't deny you become peaceful, that this environment doesn't scare you … Since that moment I regularly visit my tunnels, I'm in love with them.

Why are you digging tunnels 2,5 km away from the pyramid ?
It's really simple, this is a corrupted country and they wanted to give us some money but only with a proportional revenue. Semir refused to that and now we are on the blacklist. The State pursued a law that allows them to buy the area of the hill. They say they want to protect the medieval castle which is located on the top of the hill. The worst part is that they didn't only buy the property of the castle … but the whole mountain …

So you can't dig anymore?
No … Now we are discovering tunnels that will lead us under the soil to the pyramid. So our only hope is to reach the pyramids through tunnels. To shut everybody up.

But are the tunnels completely safe?
Yes they are safe, they are beautiful, and we have the K2-megalith. This block is very popular for tourists.

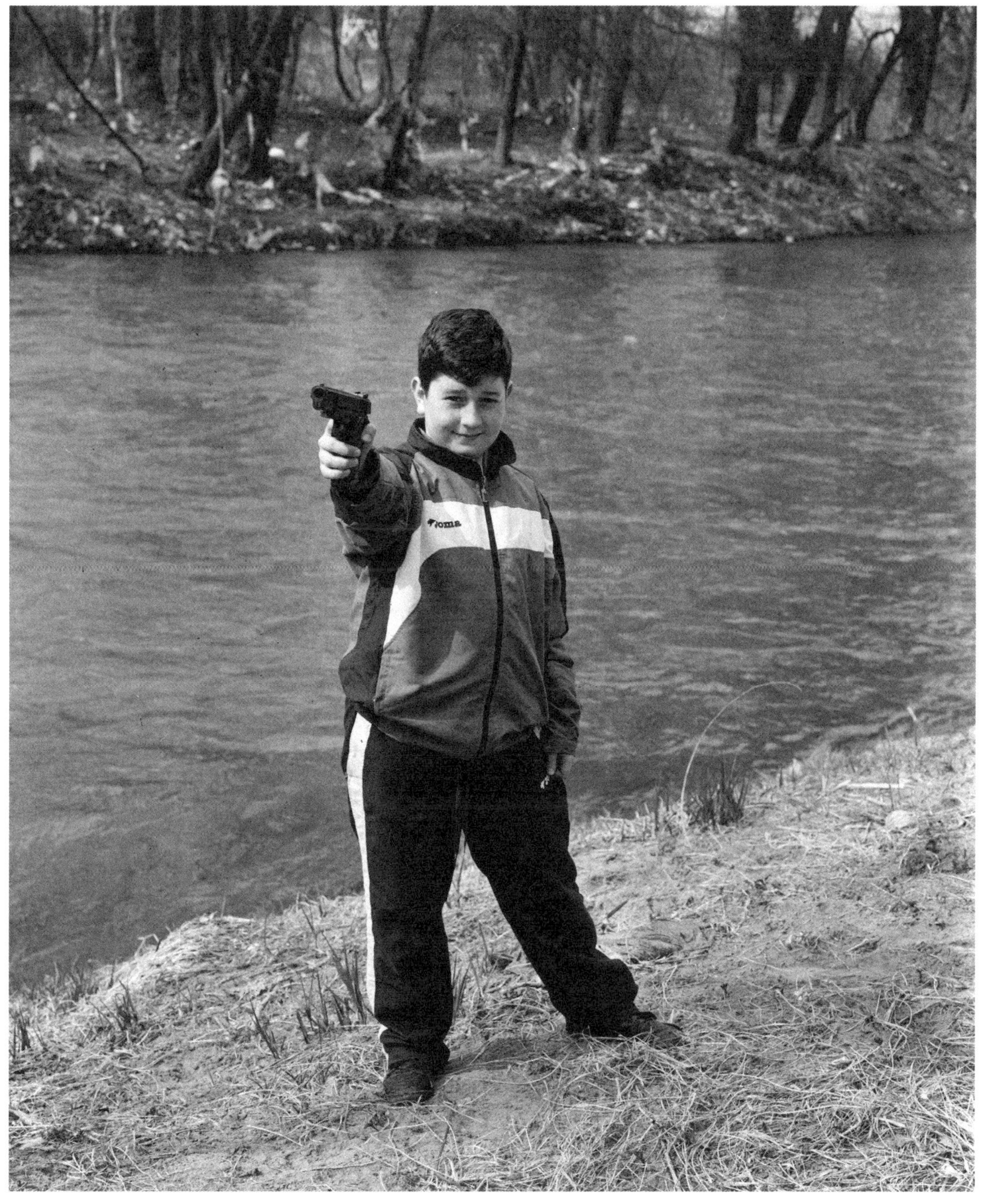


Plate XXXIX

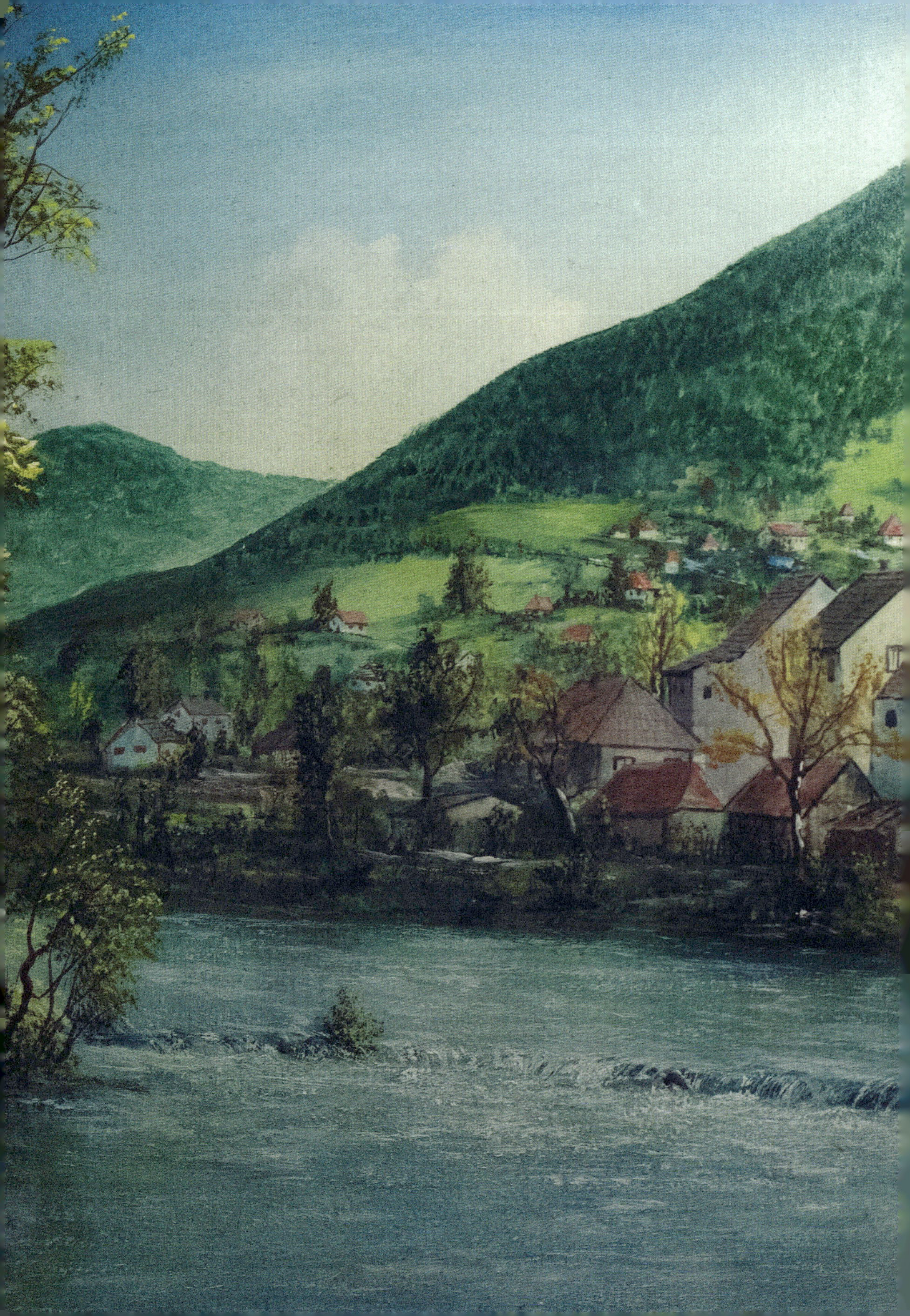

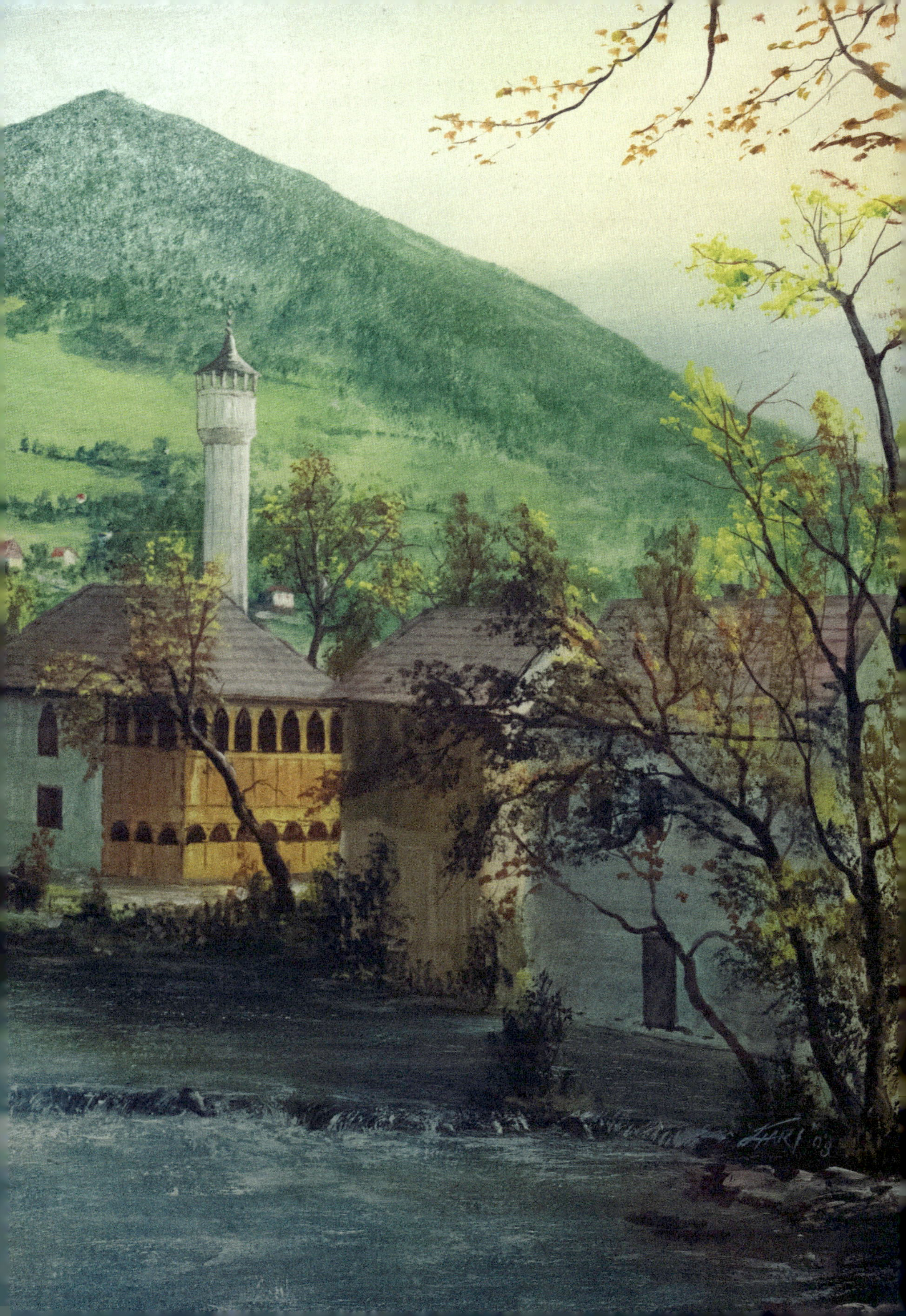

THE SOUTH SIDE
is separated from a hill to the south by a valley. It is incomparable with the N and E sides

THE EAST SIDE
demonstrates a little less perfection.

THE WEST SIDE
is regular for a distance of 40–50m long along the NW corner line, but the plateau merges with it beyond that.

THE NORTH SIDE
comes closest to perfection; its plane is roughly an equal sided triangle of: 250–230m length and 60°. When one looks from ground level southwards along the NS axis, it appears as if it had two 45° and 90°apex.

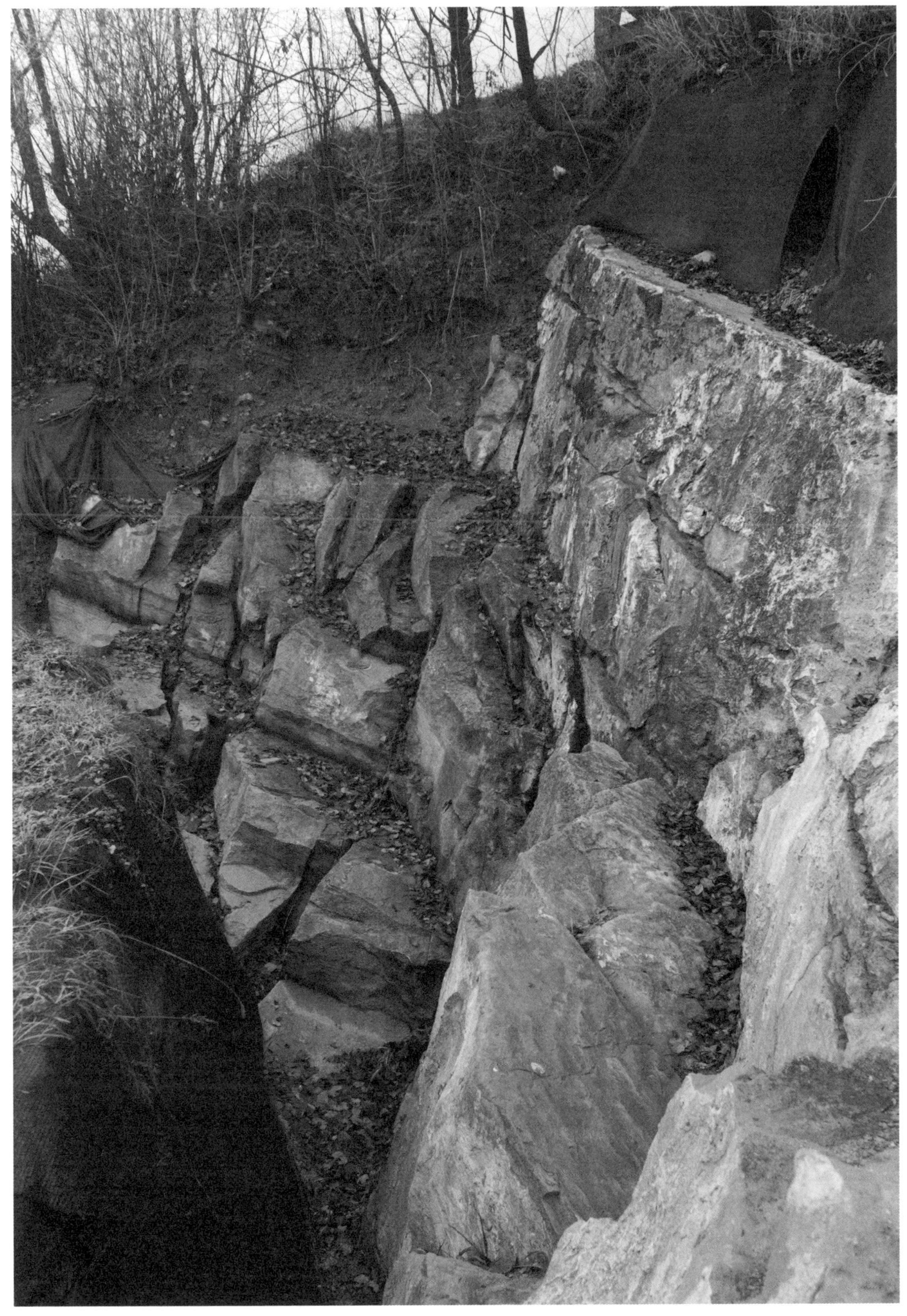

Plate XLI

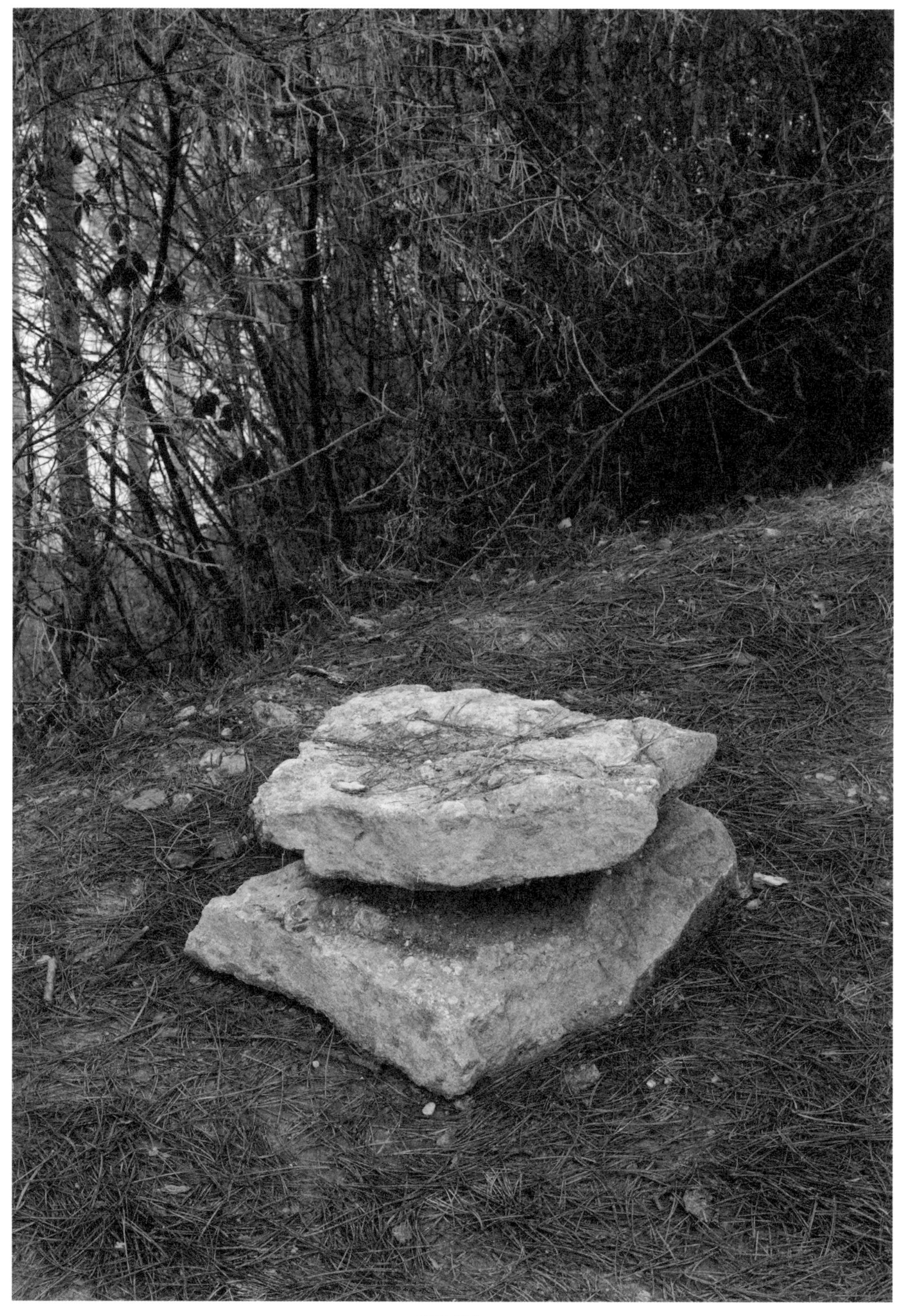

Plate XLII

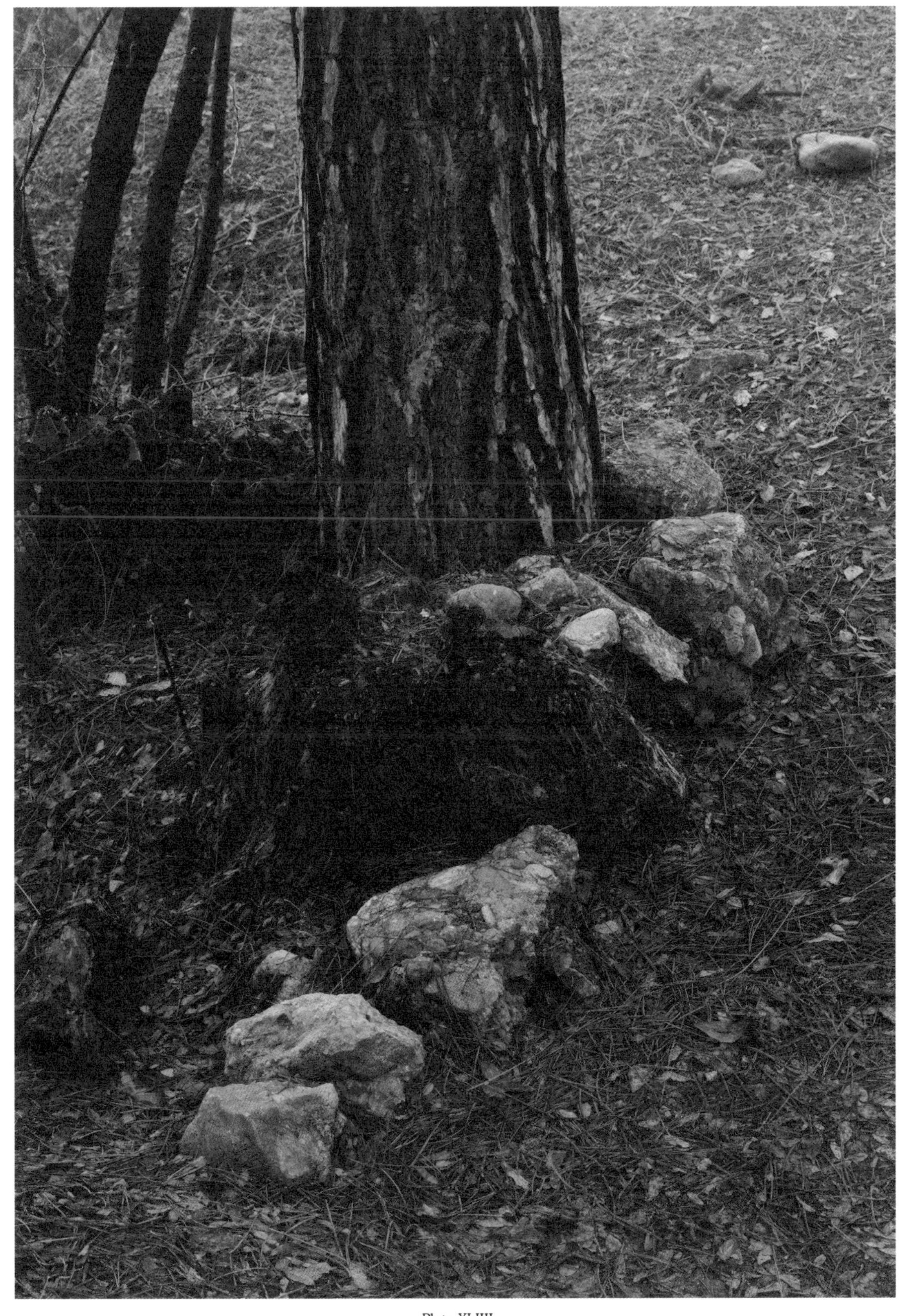

Plate XLIIII

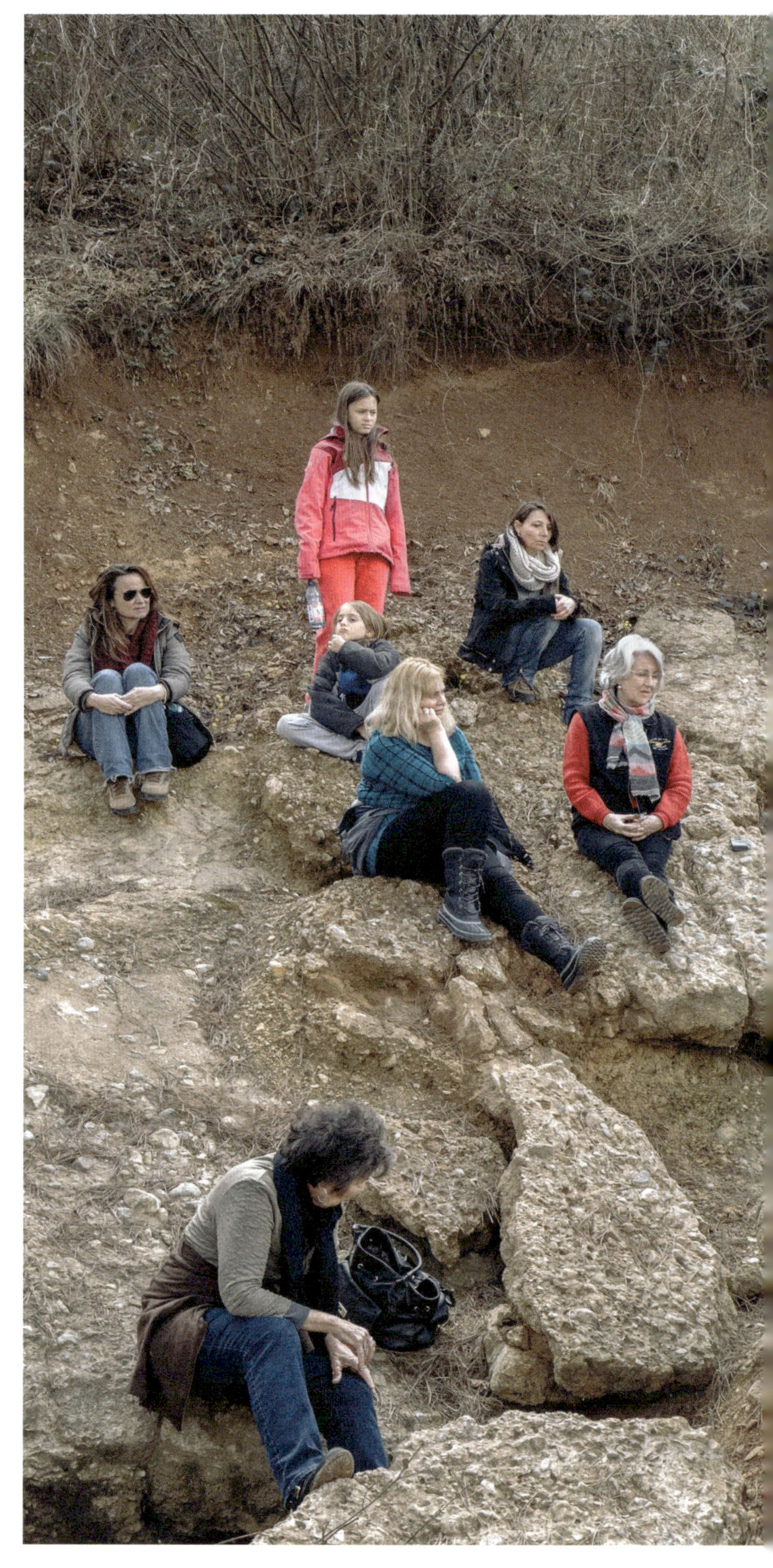

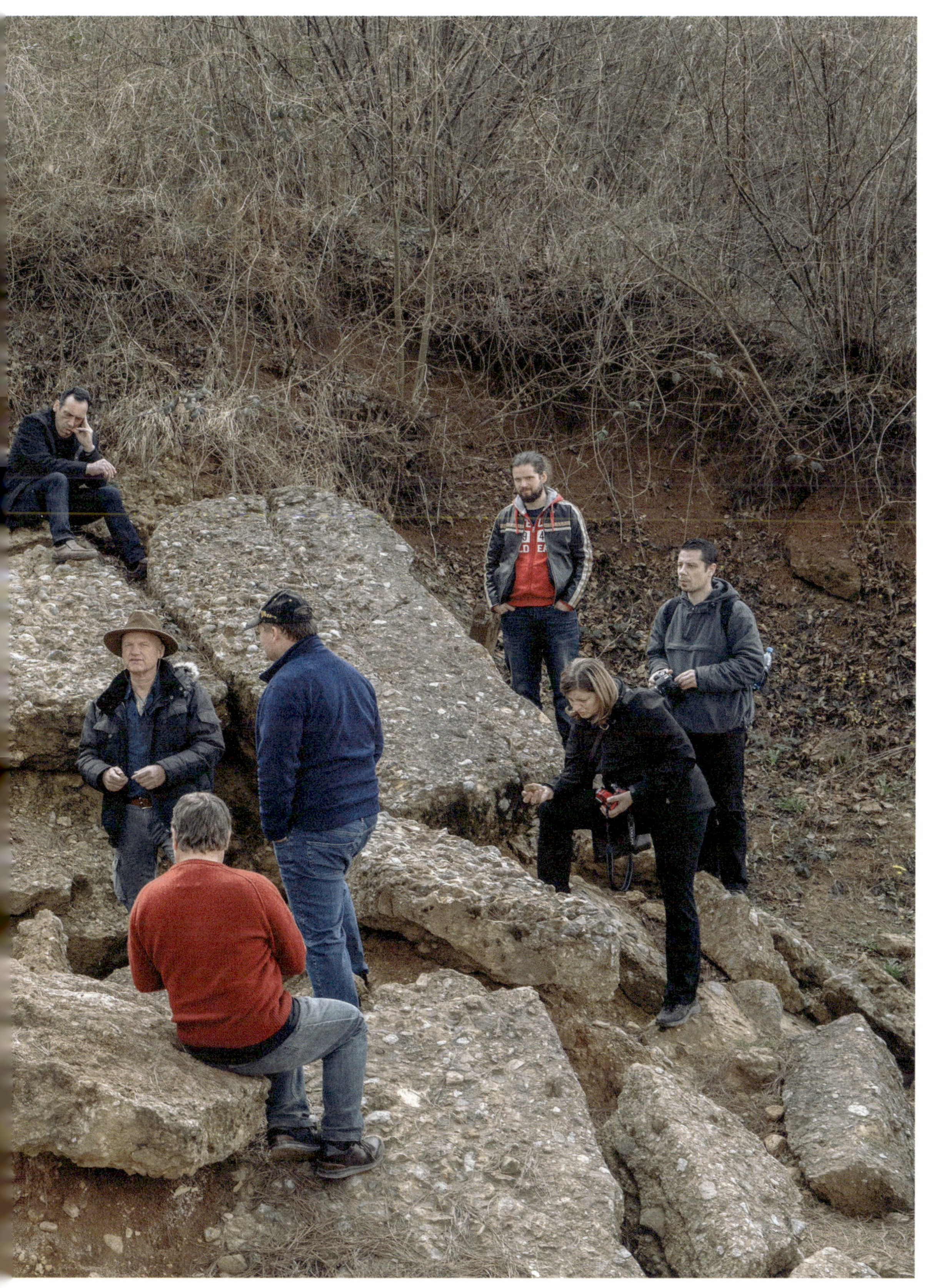

Plate XLIV

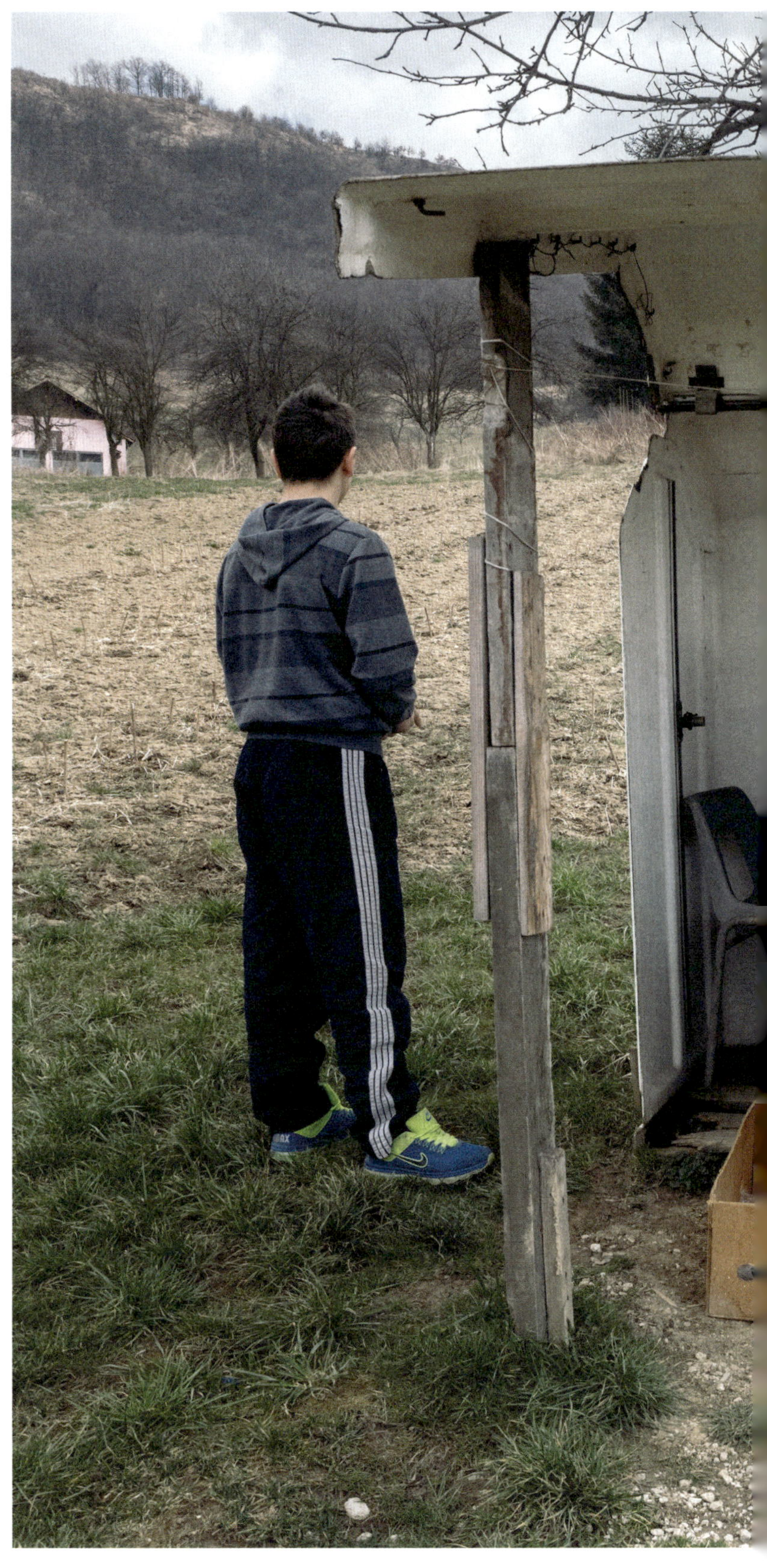

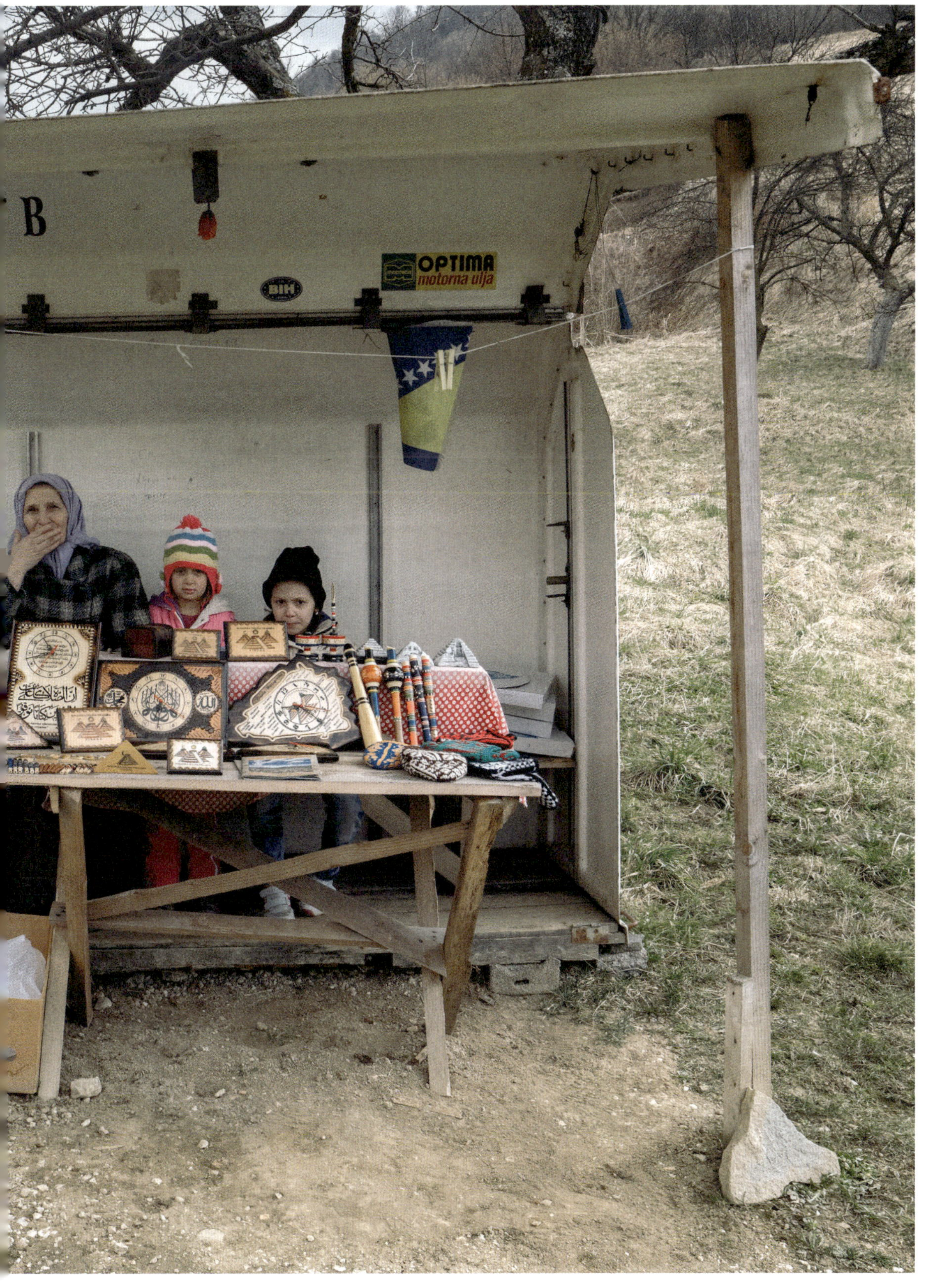


Plate XLV

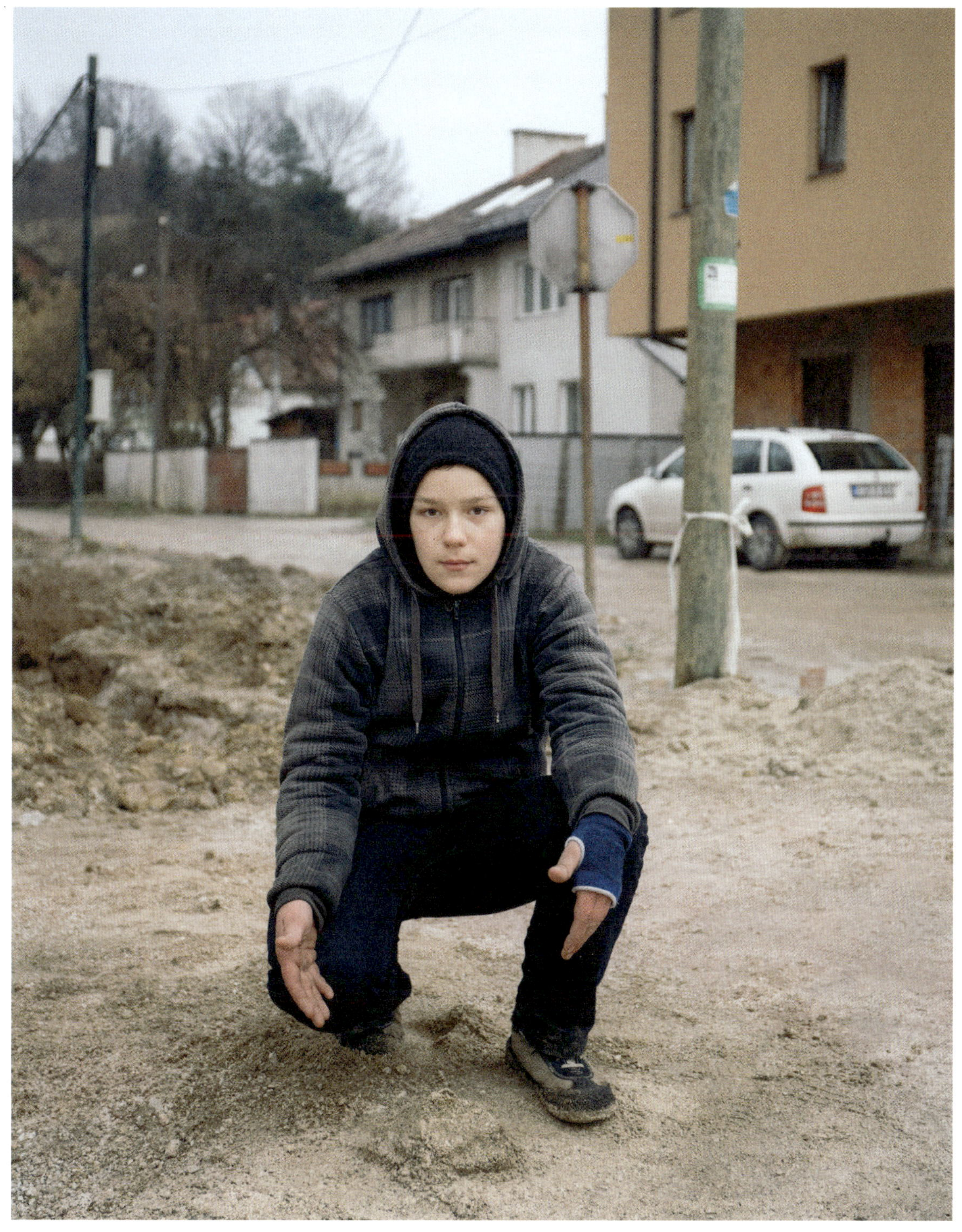

Plate XLVI

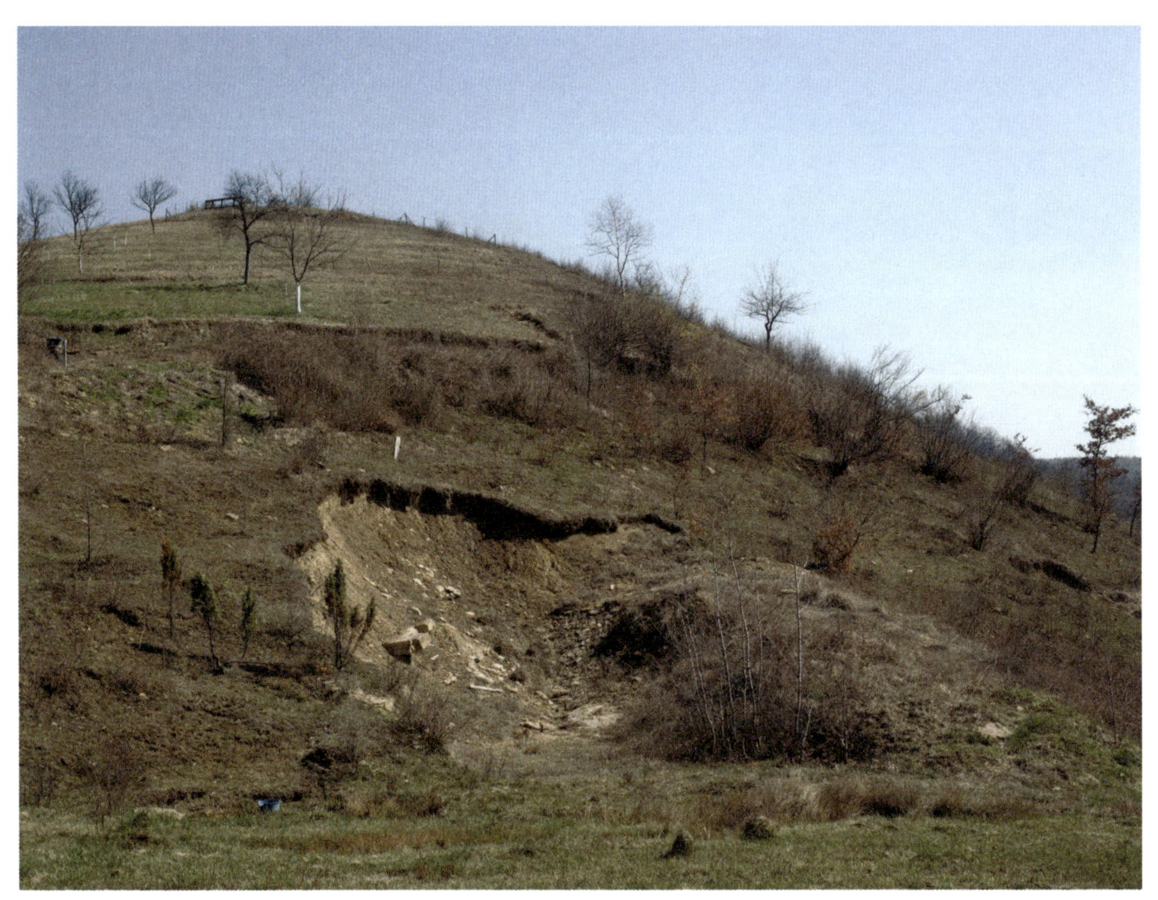

Plate XLVII

# HOW DID "PHARAOH" DR ZAHI HAWASS TRY TO STOP BOSNIAN PYRAMIDS PROJECT

Written by Dr. Sam Osmanagić, Friday, 14 March 2011 20:25

With fall of Hosny Mubarak's regime in Egypt, numerous affairs of corrupted state officials came out. During decades of reign some ministers have managed to sling billions of dollars on their accounts. Undoubtedly, among the wealthiest is Dr. Zahi Hawass, who ruled for decades in Supreme Council of Antiquities. Though legally he had to retire three years ago, he succeeded, thanks to friendship with the wife of Hosny Mubarak Suzanne, to preserve his stay at the most powerful position in the domain of archaeology. Finally, last year he succeeded in getting assignment as the State minister for antiquities and lifelong position. At least, that's what he hoped to be.

With revolution in Egypt it wasn't possible to hide 1.600 documents that demonstrate that Dr. Zahi Hawass stole precious artifacts, falsified historical findings (making them appear younger than they really are, because they didn't fit into official history), and fired archeologists, Egyptologists, guides and state officials, who spoke loudly about corruption of his office.

Dr. Hawass is recognized face from leading world scientific programs: National Geographic, History Channel, Discovery, BBC and others. He seats on their Boards, serves as their scientific advisor. More than decades, Zahi Hawass is the only one who announces all discoveries in Egypt, as if the real authors weren't the teams of researchers from Poland, Hungary, Germany, Great Britain, Italy, USA, Japan or Egypt. For decades, none of documentaries about Egyptian pyramids or temples have been recorded without the permission of Hawass, his presence in the movies and financial benefits that are given to him.

In order to retain his position as incontrovertible ruler in the domain of Egyptology, Pyramid Science and archeology, he even tried to patent the name "pyramid" as unique Egyptian product. He labeled all of those who had different ideas concerning the age, constructors and purpose of the pyramids (Hancock, Davidovits, Bouval, Dunn and many other experts). He would insult them, calling them names and didn't allow them to freely explore and to analyze samples. If by any chance researches with modern instruments (of Japanese, Germans and Americans) showed that pyramids have unique electromagnetic properties and energetic anomalies, which would reject the idea of most superior pyramids being tombs, it was the end for those researchers and free and unobstructed scientific investigation in Egypt.

And when he thought he had everything under control, series of pyramid discoveries appear across the world: 250 pyramids in China, hundreds of pyramids in Peru, hundreds of new Mayan pyramids in Central America, tens of pyramids in the Canary

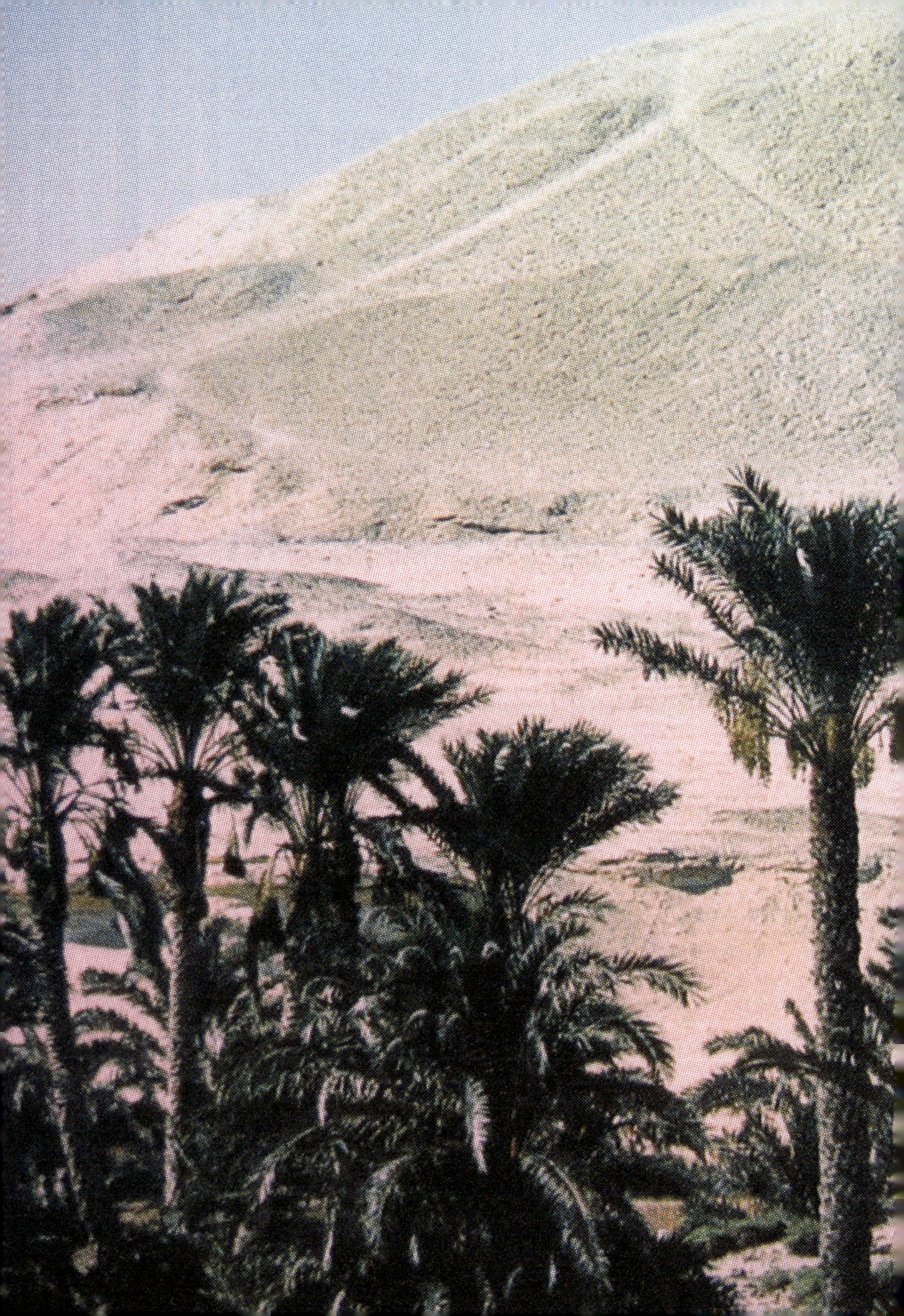

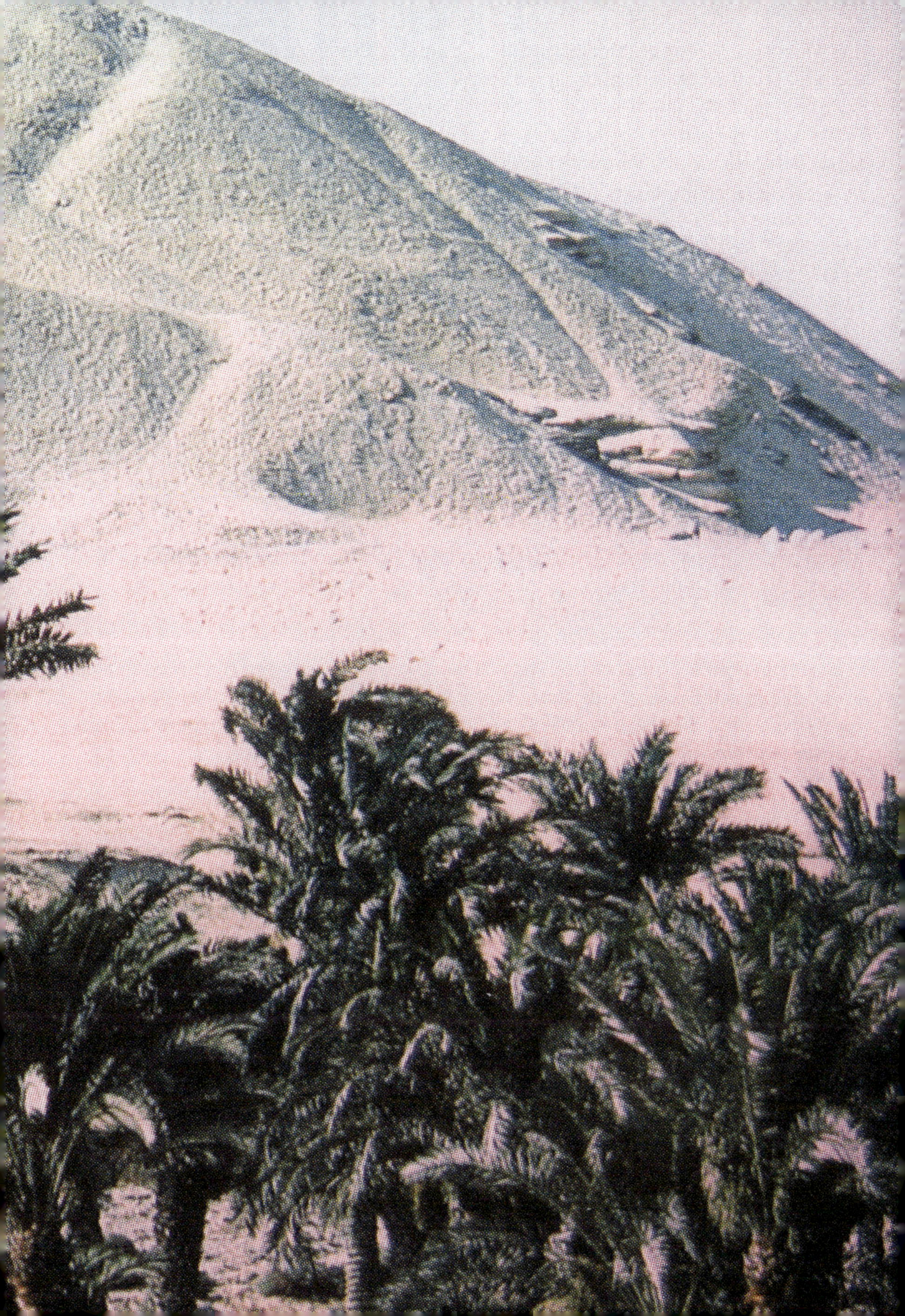

and Mauritius. Wrong considerations that pyramids were created as the product of local scenario crush down. Pyramids were the worldwide concept. The greatest shock came from the small Bosnia: discovery of the first European pyramids, the biggest in the world and at the same time the oldest in the world! Carefully nurtured idea of ancient Egypt being the most important cradle of civilization and the only home of the pyramids disappears forever.

**Year 2005**
In October 2005 I announced to the world that I've discovered pyramids in Visoko, Bosnia-Herzegovina. In interview with BBC I spoke about the possibility that they were older than all known pyramids. That was later confirmed by the State Institute for the pedology. Right after me, Dr. Zahi Hawass in program spoke with wobbly voice that it "is possible to discover new pyramids, but he doubted they were older than Egyptian ones".

**Year 2006**
In April of 2006 archeological excavations at Bosnian pyramid of the Sun began, after our non-profit Foundation "Archaeological Park: Bosnian Pyramid of the Sun" received all necessary permits, hired experts, acquired equipment and tools, carried out proer satellite, thermal, radar and topographic recordings. Group of Bosnian historians, archeologist and geologist were against research and wrote petition to stop the project. The Federal Government rejected petition after prime minster Mr. Hadzipasic and the member of his Cabinet visited archeological locations and were convinced in their artificial character. Afterwards, upset Bosnian archaeologists and historians asked for the help from European Archaeological Association from London requested their assistance in stopping research in Visoko. The president of Association Dr. Anthony Harding launched new petition full of untruths in which he tried to stop the project.

At the same time, they asked that every national archaeological organization in Europe boycott project and openly threat that all archeologists engaged in Visoko research will no longer work in their vocation-profession once they return to their countries. Under pressure of European boycott, Foundation turned to the Government of Egypt asking that it sends three experts. Upon recommendation of Dr Zahi Hawass, experienced geologist Dr Ali Barakat arrived in Visoko, in May of 2006. After 42 days of research, at the press conference in Sarajevo, on June 23rd he stated in his written report that Bosnian pyramid of the Sun was "man-made pyramid". (More: www.piramidasunca.ba/en/en/index.php/Unearthing-Europes-Oldest-Pyramid-Complex.html)

Dr. Ali Barakat investigating concrete blocksof the Bosnian pyramid of the Sun
The same day, custodian of National Museum in Sarajevo and opponent of the project who never came to see the pyramids herself, Zilka Vejzagic-Kujundzic, writes a letter to Dr. Zahi Hawass asking him to react and to confute Dr. Barakat. Two days later, Dr. Zahi Hawass convenes urgent meeting in Cairo: between Ministry

of Tourism of Egypt, Ministry of Culture and his Supreme Council of Antiquities. They have just one agenda: “Influence of Bosnian pyramids’ discovery on tourism in Egypt”. Considering that tourism and pyramids is the main Egyptian industry earning $ 15.5 billion of dollars per year, fear that they could loose, let’s say 20% (or more than 3 billion of dollars) because of discovery of Bosnian pyramids, disgusted them. After the meeting on June 25th, at noon time, Zahi Hawass hold press conference during which he says: “There aren’t pyramids in Bosnia, just a pile of stones. Blocks weighting 30 tons are natural. Barakat is no pyramid expert and Osmanagić is hallucinating”. Hawass writes a letter to Institute of Minerals of Egyptian Government, where Dr. Barakat works, and asked his boss to fire Dr. Barakat. Part of Sarajevo’s, Zagreb’s and Belgrade’s cultural establishment, who opposed the Bosnian pyramid project, is exulting. Several reporters, archeologists, historians, even writers thought this was the end of project. They weren’t aware that their complex of low self-esteem deceived them. Project was just getting started.

Foundation intensively continued with its works in which 90 full-time workers and hundreds of volunteers were involved. The Government of Egypt sends another requested expert, Egyptologist Lamia El Hadidi. She discovered that Bosnian pyramid of the Moon had rectangular structures, vertical walls and paved terraces. Excitingly, she calls Dr. Hawass in front of me and invites him to come to Bosnia. After the phone conversation, she asked me to send him official invitation to his personal fax number which I did. However, Hawass didn’t come, he ignored.

Discoveries in Bosnian Valley of the Pyramids continued. Hawass sent to Visoko his most loyal man and personal friend: Dr Mohamed Ibrahim Ali an Egyptologist from Ein Shams University in Cairo. During his visit that lasted eight days, Dr Ibrahim Ali couldn’t hide his enthusiasm with what he had seen and claims it is obvious that human hand built these structures, and it is yet to be determined whether it is a pyramid, a temple or something third. There again, no sign of Hawass, because the news he hears do not suit him.

**Year 2007**

During 2007 I was holding the lecture about Bosnian pyramids in Cairo which was organized by the Egyptian Ministry of Culture. At lecture were the leading figures of Egyptian science and archeology: vice minister, assistants to the minister, ambassadors, leading archaeologists and Egyptologists, deans and vice-deans. Dr. Zahi Hawass’ absence is flaring.

That same year more Egyptian experts come to Visoko: distinguished Egyptologist, PhD in archaeology and finder of four pyramids in Egyptian deserts Dr Nabil Swelim, vice-dean of Faculty of Archaeology at the Cairo University Mona Fawad Ali, an Egyptologist Dr Soliman Hammed and geologist Dr Ali Barakat. After seeing all locations many times this team sends messages to Bosnian and international public that the greatest

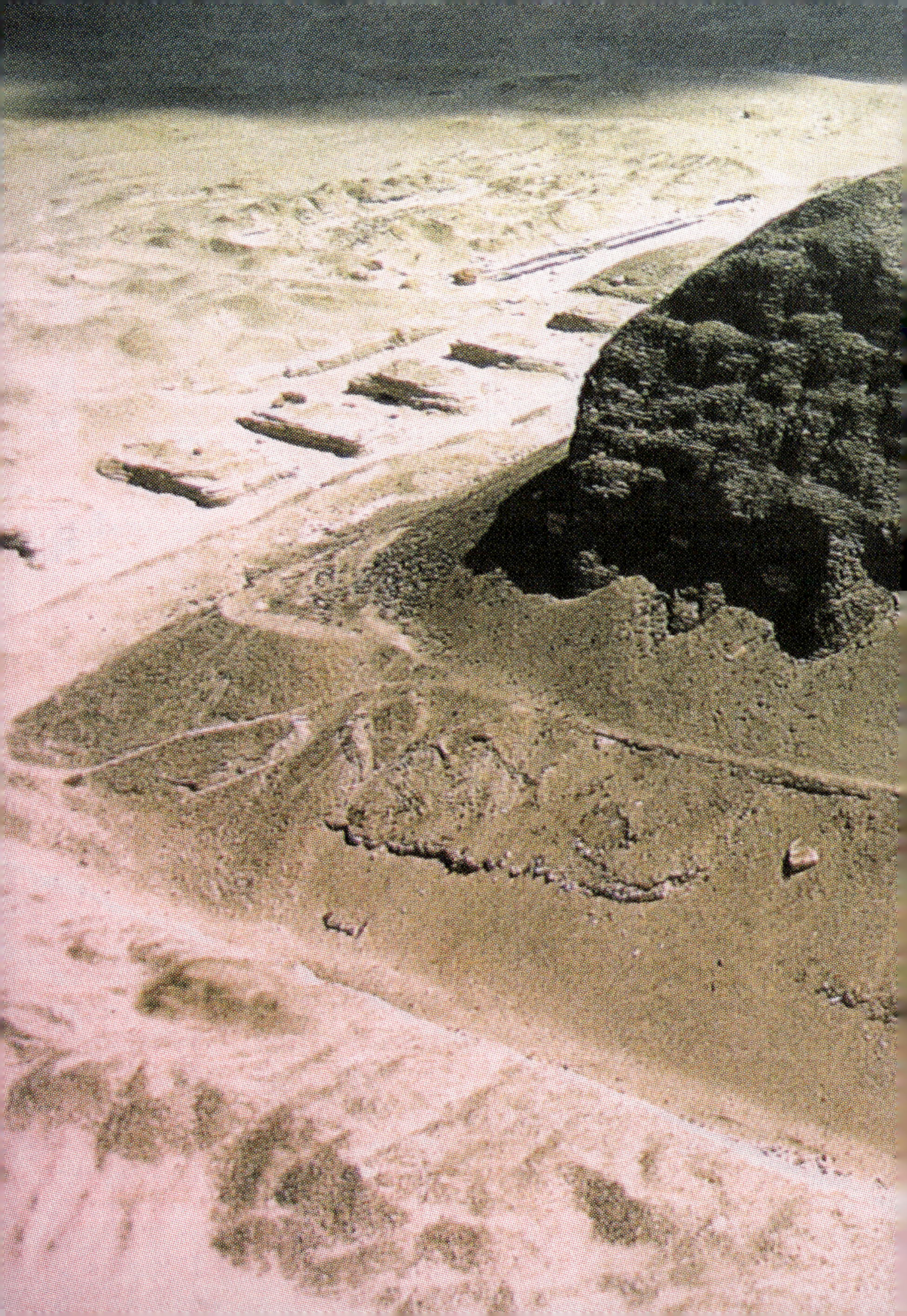

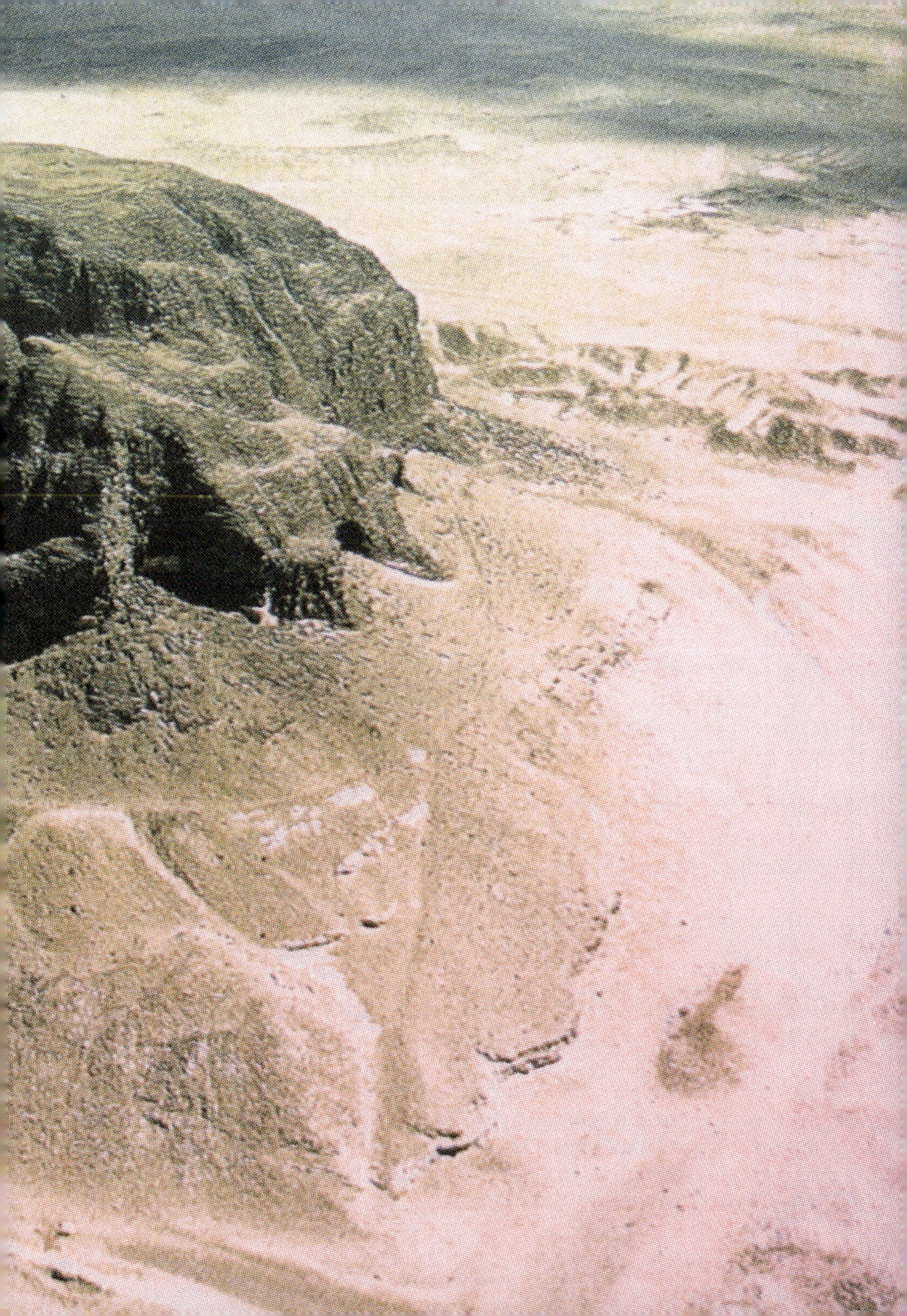

pyramids in the world are discovered here. Silence appeared in the region. Mouths were closed to opponents such as Govedarica, Imamovic, Vejzagic, Lovrenovic, Novakovic, Vrabac on local level or people like Harding, Schoch and others on international level. Even though these opponents were trying to continue with their game of labeling the discoverer, they were not bringing any scientific arguments on the table.

That same year, I visited Cairo again. In the most read Arabic daily "Al Ahram" we arranged our project to be regularly followed at their pages. However, after my visit to Cairo leading journalist of Al Ahram (Alaa Sabet) consulted with Zahi Hawass and changed arranged plan and hasn't published any of affirmative article.

**Year 2009**
In 2009 I signed an exclusive contract with Canadian producer for the project about the documentary and series for History Channel and Discovery. After director's visit to Visoko, that left her impressed, everything was ready for the big project. They have signed their preliminary contract with the world most watched scientific TV programs. However, they needed confirmation of scientific consultant on these TV productions. Suddenly, everything stopped. Instead of project's affirmation and affirmation of country of Bosnia and Herzegovina to the entire world, standstill came up. It wasn't surprise, because the name of scientific consultant was: Zahi Hawass.

**Year 2010**
After several lectures in Houston's branch of ARE center, organizers urged their home office in Virginia's Beach to invite me to their annual conference in the autumn of 2011. Polite refusal-rejection happened. The reason: Dr. Zahi Hawass will be this year among speakers and they didn't want to upset him with my appearance.

**Year 2011**
By summing up relation of Zahi Hawass, as one of world leading figures in archaeology, towards Bosnian pyramids project, I can notice the following:

- Dr. Zahi Hawass wasn't capable to raise above political role which he played and to behave as the real scientist who cares about scientific progress

- Careerism of most of the people around him overcame scientific dignity and citizen's courage

Precisely because of his enormous desire to impose and sometimes to falsify scientific achievements with strength of his political position, he will be soon forgotten. And this will happened the moment he has no political position. It's been happening so many times in history, it will happen now, as well. Despite everything, true values, like discoveries in the Bosnian Valley of the Pyramids, continue to live on.

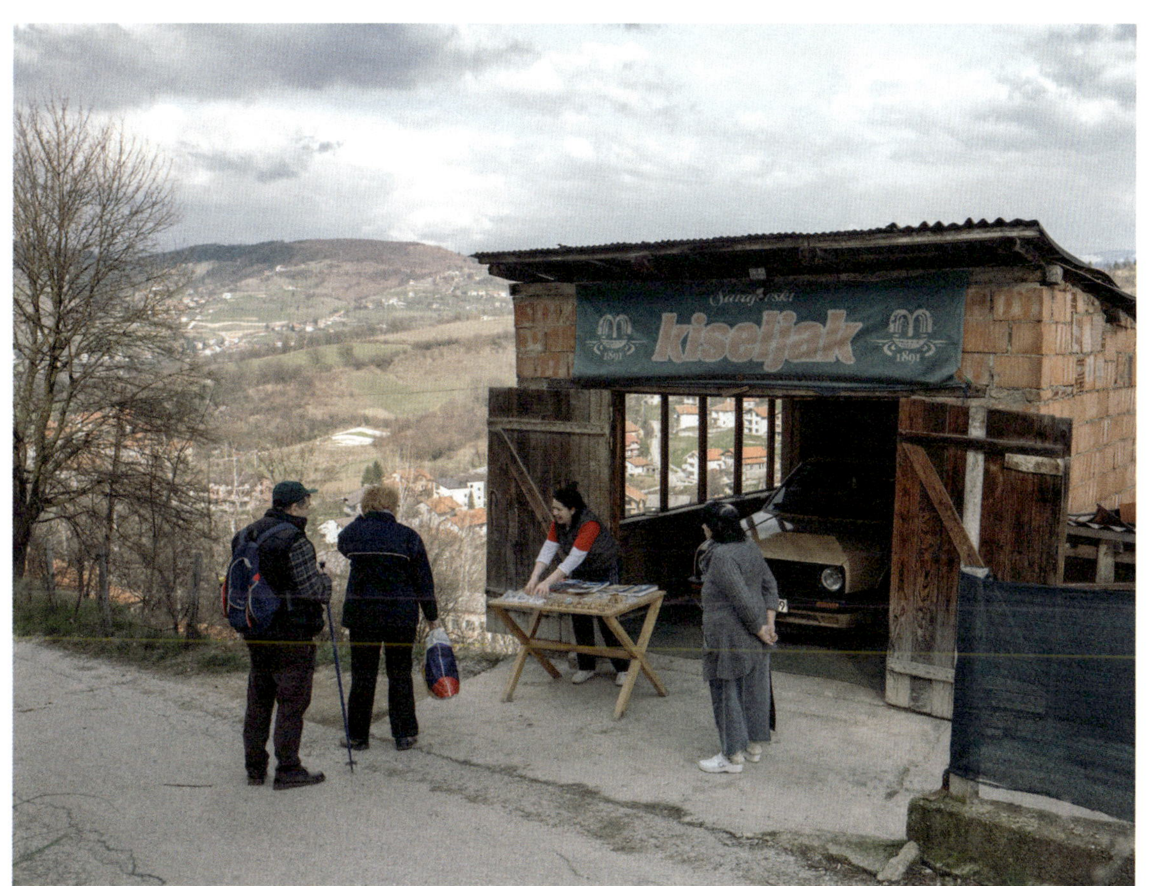


Plate L

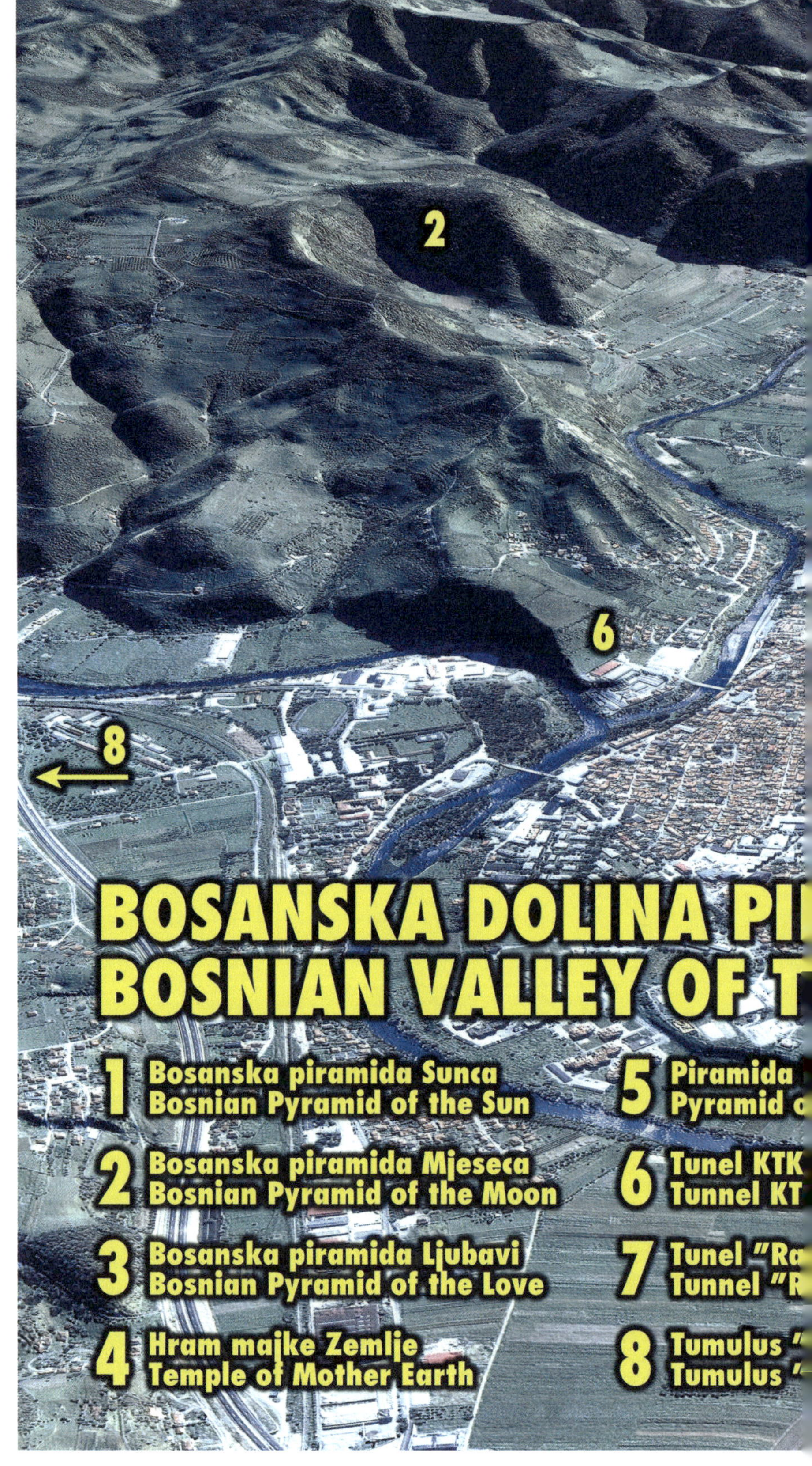
2
6
8
BOSANSKA DOLINA PI
BOSNIAN VALLEY OF T
1 Bosanska piramida Sunca
Bosnian Pyramid of the Sun
2 Bosanska piramida Mjeseca
Bosnian Pyramid of the Moon
3 Bosanska piramida Ljubavi
Bosnian Pyramid of the Love
4 Hram majke Zemlje
Temple of Mother Earth
5 Piramida
Pyramid
6 Tunel KTK
Tunnel KT
7 Tunel "Ra
Tunnel "R
8 Tumulus "
Tumulus "

Fondacija Arheološki park:
Bosanska piramida Sunca
Sarajevo, Bosna i Hercegovina
The Archaeological Park:
Bosnian Pyramid of the Sun Foundation
Sarajevo, Bosnia and Herzegovina
4
5
3
1
MIDA
PYRAMIDS
kog Zmaja
osnian Dragon
7
hram", Gornja Vratnica
emple", Gornja Vratnica

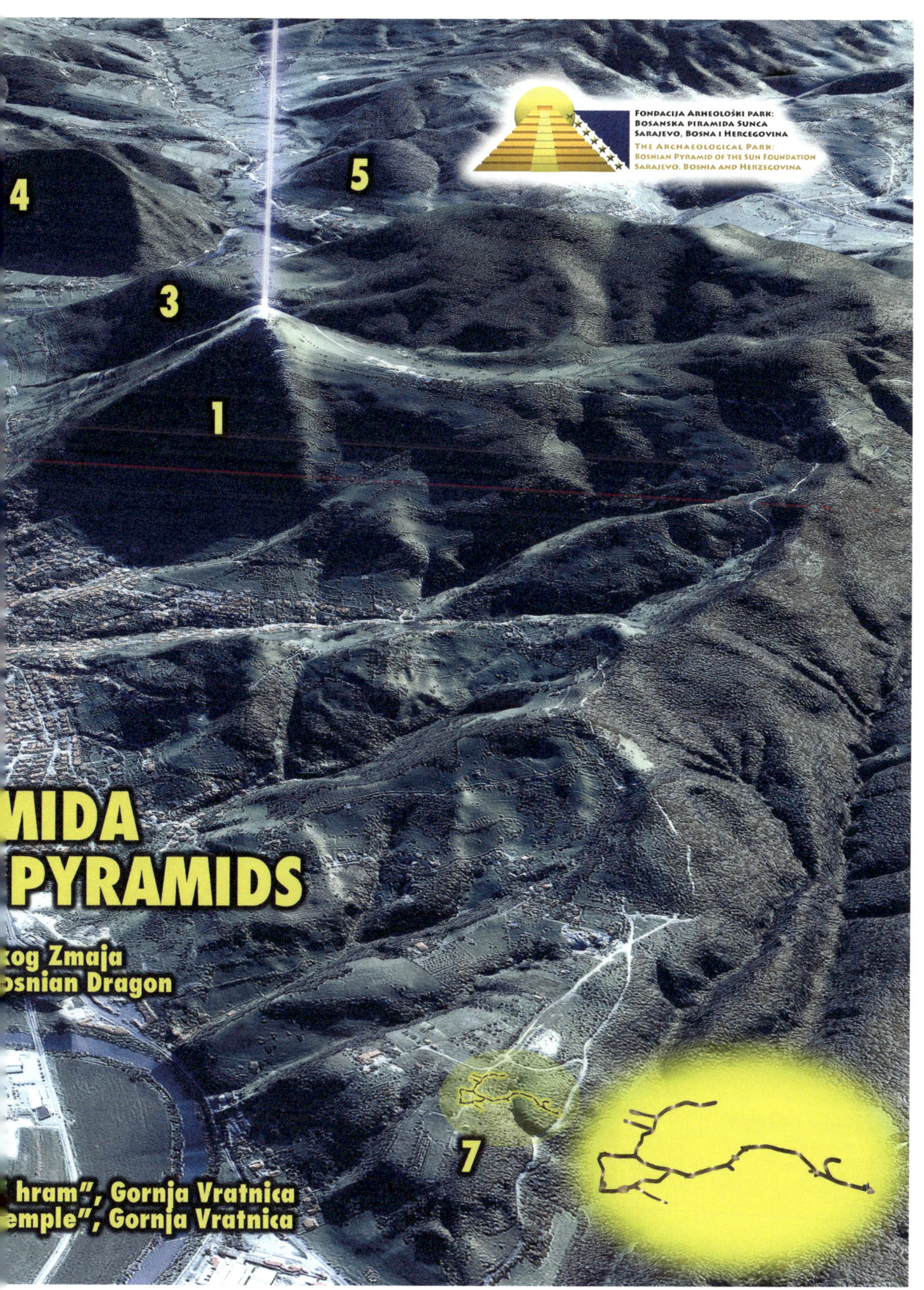

Plate LI

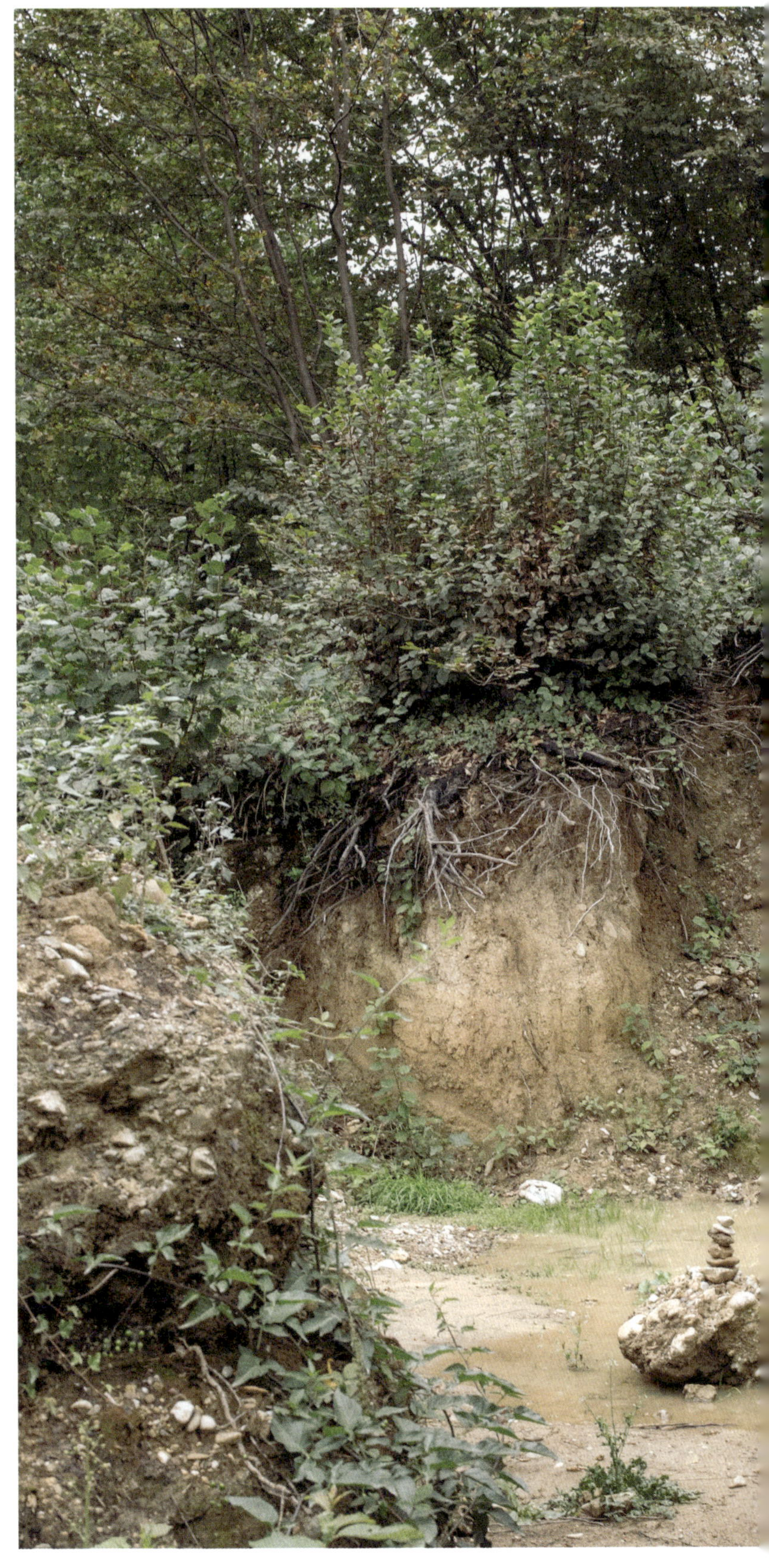

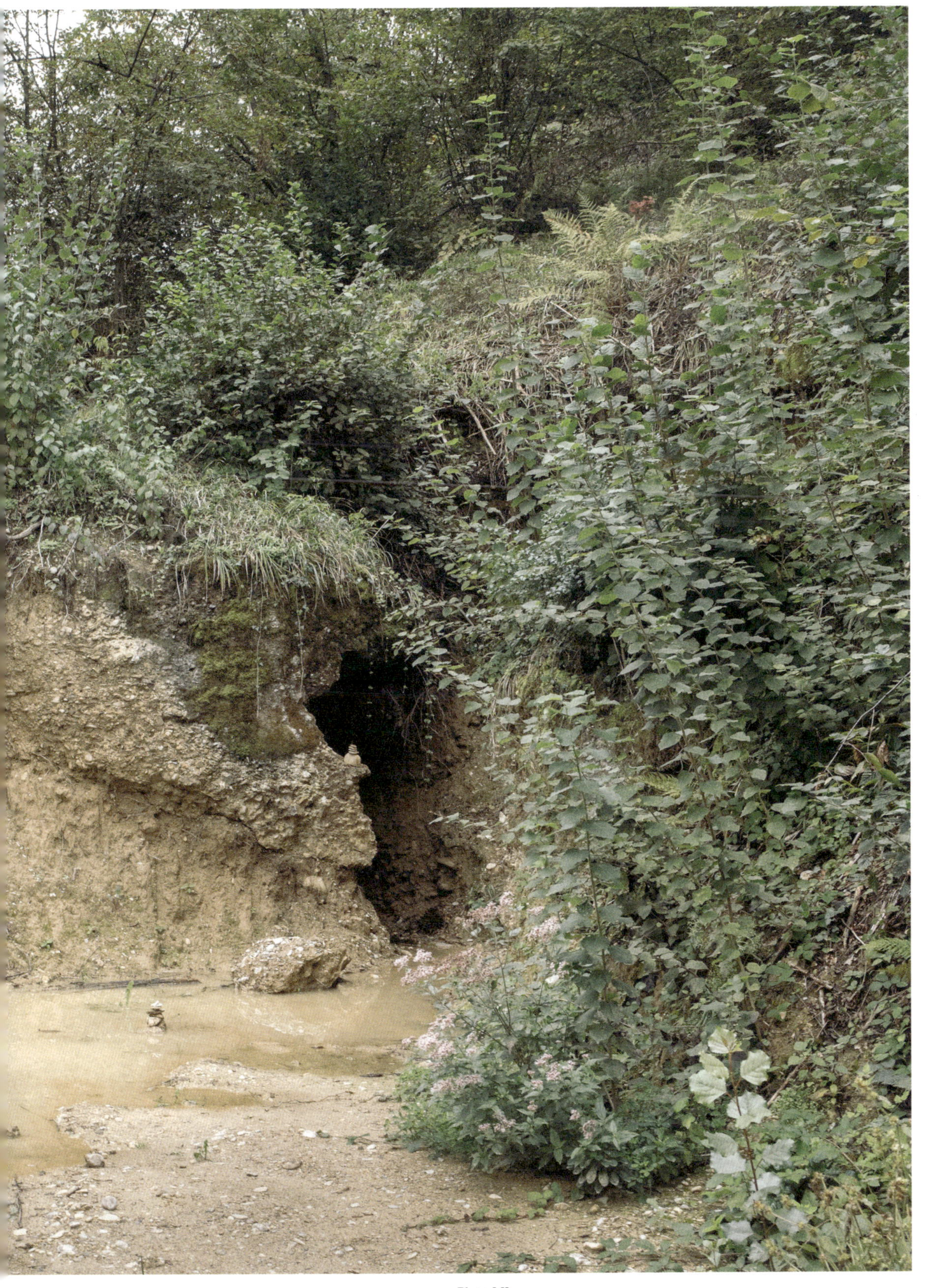

Plate LII

# Discussion

## DISCUSSION

During the month of December 2016 an online group debate was held between different individuals on the Bosnian Pyramid phenomenon. The aim was to broaden the discussion from its scientific debate towards the role of (pseudo)archaeology in a contemporary Bosnia-and-Herzegovina.

### PARTICIPANTS

Prof. Cornelius Holtorf (born 1968 in Sieglar, Germany) is lecturing Archaeology at Linnaeus University in Kalmar, Sweden. He is the director of the Graduate School in Contract Archaeology (GRASCA) and spokesperson for the Center for Applied Heritage at Linnaeus University. In his research he has an interest in the various meanings of archaeology, archaeological sites and the past in the present.

Andrew Lawler (born 1985 in Manchester, UK) is an Honorary Research Fellow at the School of History, Welsh History and Archaeology, Bangor University. He received his BA in Archaeology and Anthropology from the University of Cambridge in 2006, his MA in Archaeology from the Faculty of Arts, KU Leuven in 2010, and his M.Cons from the Raymond Lemaire International Centre for Conservation (RLICC), Faculty of Engineering Sciences, KU Leuven, in 2013. He has worked as a professional field archaeologist in the UK, Bosnia & Herzegovina and Belgium. He has written and presented extensively on the archaeological profession in Bosnia & Herzegovina, including two publications in the Discovering the Archaeologists of Europe series, as well as articles for journals and professional magazines such as Archaeologies: Journal of the World Archaeological Congress and The European Archaeologist.

Dr Danijel Dzino (born 1971 in Sarajevo, Bosnia and Herzegovina) is Lecturer at the Departments of Ancient History and International Studies (Croatian Studies) at Macquarie University, Sydney. He received PhD from Adelaide University in Australia in 2005 and moved to Macquarie University as recipient of Australian Research Council Discovery Project in 2010. Author of many scholarly publications including the books: Illyricum in Roman Politics 229BC-AD68 (Cambridge University Press: Cambridge, 2010), Becoming Slav, Becoming Croat: Identity Transformations in Post-Roman and Early Medieval Dalmatia (Brill Academic Publishers: Leiden and Boston, 2010) and Rimsko osvajanje Ilirika. Povijesni antinarativ (Školska knjiga: Zagreb: 2013) co-authored with Alka Domić Kunić. Participated in several research projects in Croatia, including Varvaria-Breberium-Bribir project of archaeological excavations on Bribirska glavica.

Sasha Buljevic is master student, currently finishing his studies in Archaeology at the University of Sarajevo. He participated in several researches that applied the ethnographic methodology in social research.

Irna is the pen name of a French geographer with a background in geomorphology and an interest, as an amateur, in archaeology. She writes a blog about pseudo-archaeology, and published a booklet about the Bosnian 'pyramids'.

—

**If you look to Bosnia-and-Herzegovina and the region today, how would you describe it in the context of the protests of 2014? Someone from Montenegro told me that in the region people don't know who to fight for. On the hand there is a greedy oligarchic political elite, on the other hand there is this mistrust towards a 'transition' to European membership. In the book 'Welcome to the desert of post-socialism', Igor Štiks and Srećko Horvat bring up the example of Croatia's accession towards the EU in where it exemplifies the semi-peripheral role of the post-socialist region: 'cheap and highly educated labour in proximity to the capitalist core, quasi-total economic dependence on the core and its multinational banks and corporations, and, finally, the accumulation of debt.'**

DZINO The protests of 2014 in B&H were combination of real popular dissatisfaction and more subtle political aims that appeared later during the protests, such as the push for centralization of the country. At the times some commentators indicated indirect involvement of US diplomacy in the "Bosnian spring" through different NGOs, but such a claim certainly needs to be researched in more detail. The protests failed to gain significant popular support in Republika Srpska and Croat- majority parts of Federation B&H, because it appears that the Serb and Croat public perceived the protests as internal Bosniak thing and could not identify with them.

The protests in 2014 failed outside of the Bosniak-majority areas because the situation in B&H is different from other post-communist countries in Eastern Europe (maybe FRY Macedonia and Ukraine are loosely comparable) as there is no general consensus how the country should look like. Lack of consensus about internal arrangement of B&H (unitary, federal, confederal/disintegrated) is capitalized by oligarchic political elites that profit from the status quo. However, it is important to keep the things in context – B&H was dominated by political networks established by oligarchic elites and family-clans in the communist times, so this kind of power-sharing is systemic atavism from the 1970s and 1980, rather than something which appears with the breakup of Yugoslavia. The only difference is that from 1992 B&H for a first time started to exist as political entity outside of larger political unit.

While I can partly agree with this statement of Štiks and Horvat (unfortunately, I did not read the book), it is important to notice that 'the desert of post-socialism' was also created by socialism itself. This is visible in survival of endemic corruption embedded into public service and economy, lack of economic competitiveness and maintenance of super-sized and inefficient public service. Post-Yugoslav countries, in contrast to many other ex-communist countries, never made political lustration, so sizeable proportion of post-Communist elites were recruited from the ranks of Communist elites who repositioned themselves in relation to new ideological discourse of nationalism as either its supporters or opponents. Mistrust towards the EU membership is relatively new phenomenon and has nothing to do with local situation in my opinion, it is general feeling within EU. In B&H the mistrust towards EU, at least on political level, is most noticeable amongst the Serbs and Bosniaks (whose political elites flirt with Russia and Turkey), while the Croats see EU membership as the way to connect more closely with Croatia without secession.

BULJEVIC I would say that protests in 2014 were reflection of dissatisfaction with government and local authorities. However most of the people that I spoke – and this is also my opinion – said that at least in case of Sarajevo and Tuzla there was a clear lack of response from the state police (SIPA) which was under the control of Fahrudin Radonččić at the time. He didn't want to act against protestors because he didn't want to lose political support of the people because although there was small proportion of population on the protests most of the people supported demonstrations. Regarding the choice between the oligarchic elite and EU membership, I would say that people in Bosnia and Herzegovina feel powerless when it comes to changing the current political situation. Mostly people except current condition as natural one, they support (ethno)nationalistic political parties for several reasons: job opportunities, mistrust towards other ethnic groups and fear of next conflict. Regarding the mistrust towards EU, I would agree with Danijel that it is product of recent political developments and the experience from other recently admitted countries that were part of Yugoslavia. In that regard people are starting to understand the price of entering the EU but in my opinion that are still favorable towards EU path since it means stability.

**Cornelius, you invited Semir Osmanagić at the Linnaeus University to give a lecture for your students. How was this invitation received by your colleagues? What were you aiming for?**

HOLTORFF When Semir Osmanagić lectured at Linnaeus University on 18 October 2011 there were some colleagues who were critical about him receiving this platform to voice ideas that are not generally accepted as academically legitimate. But for me the point was not to approve of his extraordinary suggestions about the "Bosnian pyramids" but rather to discuss this case as an interesting and very intriguing phenomenon in contemporary society. At the time, I used the following words to describe why I gave him the chance to speak at my University when he contacted me:

"We invited him not because we take his interpretations scientifically serious, but because we think we have to discuss his activities and its outcomes. The Bosnian pyramids have affected not only tourism and the perception of cultural heritage in Bosnia, but also how we see the cultural heritage in society more generally. Can invented heritage have the same (or greater) power than genuine cultural heritage? What are tourists really looking for when they visit cultural heritage sites? How does one present archaeology and heritage to the global media so that they will be covering it? How does Osmanagić himself see his critics among academic archaeologists and specifically among the archaeologists working in Bosnia?"

DZINO As a scholar, I understand the position of Prof. Holtorf, because the phenomenon of the 'pyramids' in Visoko should be researched in its social context. The lecture was presented accurately to local academic community, and it resulted with a very interesting forum discussion published in proper academic journal. However, personally I do not approve the idea of inviting Osmanagić to speak at (any) university, as it ultimately undermines authority of established academic institution and provides legitimacy to para-science. Taking students to the public lecture would be a much better idea, because such an occasion is perfectly suited for observing Osmanagić in his 'natural settings', as it presents the opportunity to see the ways his 'knowledge' is communicated to targeted consumers of that 'knowledge'.

LAWLER I understand the position of Prof. Holtorf for near-identical reasons. I don't, however have a view that a university is an 'improper' place for Osmanagić to speak (and to be held to account for his opinions through a public discussion). I think the choice of venue is largely dependent on what you want students to take away from the event – witnessing a phenomenon of pseudo-archaeology as anthropologists (where I believe Osmanagić's regular fare of community halls or conference centres may have been more appropriate), or critically assessing his approaches and conclusions, within the framework of a university-moderated discussion (where the approach taken is entirely acceptable, in my view).

It was interesting to read the following in the piece you've cited: "The lecture Osmanagić presented at Kalmar appeared to be his standard one. It consisted of the astonishing number of 201 PowerPoint slides. After more than an hour of presentation, when he was gently reminded to come to the end, it became clear that he had believed that the entire two-hour slot was for him to present."

To be honest, I wouldn't be surprised if Osmanagić was aware that his slot was only for 1 hour – this is something I have personally witnessed him do before, simply overrun his time allocation to prevent questioning. It seems to be a thing among his 'clique' that 'conferences' in the world of alternative history are not actually places to air new views and receive a constructive critiques, but instead seem to be social gatherings, with everyone meeting up, doing some form of trip or visit, presenting a paper (more seniority within the genre = more time), and going home until the next conference. I remember at ICBP 2008 there were two older women there, who someone (possibly Philip Coppens) pointed out to me, saying that they turn up to every alternative conference on every continent, and that they must spend tens of thousands of Euros per year on these events, even though they have never presented anything themselves. There's obviously a fair amount of money to be made in these events, and I guess it's considered common courtesy to 'not bite the hand that feeds you' by introducing some critical component. I think Osmanagić has become aware of this (although I don't believe he is motivated by personal financial gain in his hypothesis), and it's interesting to see how his 'volunteer experiences' are starting to shift further and further toward taking the form of conferences he presents at around the world.

**This bring us to the question on how archaeology should be presented to the public. In an article on archive.archeology.org, the writer G. Fagan states there is little doubt that presenting science (and archaeology) on television is a difficult business and only works when it tells a story where the human element is in the foreground. By focusing on the researcher's reasoning, the narrative becomes the most important element. This he would call the seduction of pseudo archaeology where the focus is rather on the narrative to be experienced by the viewer than on facts. Cornelius, In your book 'Archaeology is a brand' (Holtorf 2007) you write that "archaeologists are often rather clueless about the most important dimension of archaeology in popular culture: archaeo-appeal." Would you say, regarding the Bosnian Pyramid, Osmanagić is an exponent of this popularization of archaeology and how can institutional scientific research position itself towards this phenomenon of 'archaeology-appeal-consumerism'?**

CORNELIUS Indeed, I think Osmanagić uses archaeo-appeal to his advantage. He is very successful in making an impression on the audience, both through his appearance (see for example the images of him in the Arqueologia Publica Forum) and through the narrative he presents about the archaeologist-detective investigating an ancient civilization against considerable scholarly opposition. He is a gifted story-teller, and I think this is something professional archaeologists can get better at. I would argue that there is actually a lot to be learned from the example of the Bosnian pyramids. Delivery is one thing; popularity and perceived relevance in a post-factual world is another.

**Danijel, How would you opinionate that within this so called post-factual world, a possible threat of relativism towards 'genuine' historical research is at stake? In your writings you claim that archeology produces artifacts that then easily can be claimed as images or symbols for different contexts. How would you describe this regarding the Bosnian pyramids and its relation to the current context of Bosnia-and-Herzegovina? Are there any dangers or benefits?**

DANIJEL This calls for a bit longer response. The threat of relativism towards historical and archaeological research is problematic in B&H, because local academic community suffered significantly during the 1990s. Important authorities either retired, died or left the country and the existing scholars had no capability to maintain scholarly authority in public discourse when Osmanagić appeared in 2005. Today, the things are slightly better, but still far from how they should be.

The 'Bosnian Pyramids' continually produce images and symbols for different and sometimes unconnected groups: the people who believe in alternative history and conspiracy-theories, the groups interested in bio- and 'cosmic' energies, even the people from Visoko municipality who see the Visočica hill as new local landmark and the source of income. However, what interests me the most is the way the 'Pyramids' became the symbol exploited by Bosnian and Bosniak nationalisms in mid-2000s.

Bosnian and Bosniak nationalisms have different outward appearance. The first is inclusive and secular, the second exclusive and connected with Islam. However, they both share similar political aims such as unitarization of B&H and denial of group political rights for the Serbs and Croats. The beginnings of the 'Pyramid project' in 2005 coincided with the rise of these nationalisms in 2006, especially through election successes of Bosniak nationalist Haris Silajdžić and Bosnian nationalist Željko Komšić who was elected by overwhelmingly Bosniak votes as Croat representative in the B&H Presidency (collective Head of State). The 'Pyramids' at that time became embraced as 'sacred place', visited by numerous politicians from Bosniak and Bosnian political parties, Islamic religious leaders (Grand Mufti of Islamic community in B&H even prayed there), but also ordinary people who saw it as a place where they can experience (imagined) common past.

A frequently used phrase on different internet discussion-boards in the beginning was: "If the Croats can have Međugorje, why we (Bosnians/ Bosniaks) cannot have the Pyramids?" Međugorje in Herzegovina, the place of Mary's apparition in 1981, became important 'sacred place' for the Croats in Herzegovina and Bosnia, which reinvigorated common national and religious identity often suppressed by the Communist authorities. The comparison of two 'sacred places' very clearly shows significance of the 'Pyramids' as a potent symbol amongst the Bosnians and Bosniaks in B&H at that time – they were never accepted as a collective symbol on a level of public or political discourse amongst the Croats and Serbs in B&H. Flirt with these two nationalisms could also be seen on other levels. For example, the choice of name for the 'Pyramid of Bosnian Dragon' is interesting word-play that associates on 19th century political figure Hussein-bey Gradaščević, nicknamed 'The Dragon of Bosnia'. Osmanagić's Foundation also used to put strong emphasis on 'Bosnian patriotism' and role of the 'pyramids' in unification of the country in its public appearances, especially in the first years of the project.

I do not think that there are much dangers or benefits from the 'pyramids' as a symbol for these nationalisms today. Osmanagić is an opportunist and perhaps the person obsessed with his 'mission', but we most certainly cannot describe him as Bosnian/Bosniak ultranationalist as he shows no interest in capitalizing on the project to start political career in B&H. The failure of the project to present real archaeological evidence shifted its emphasis on 'cosmic energies', which is not useful motive for exploitation within national narratives. Thus, the link between the 'Pyramids' and Bosnian/Bosniak nationalism in my opinion is an unfinished political project. It will continue, but diminishing significance of the 'Pyramids' in local public discourse makes it less appealing for use as a symbol for these nationalisms, which will look for different and more usable symbols.

ANDREW Additionally, although Osmanagić claimed the names for the 'Pyramids' came to him through 'cosmic inspiration' (and variants thereof, depending on who he was addressing), he was also very quick to draw comparisons to the seal of a former Bosnian ruler on display in the National Museum, which depicts a dragon with a heart in its mouth, flanked by a sun and crescent moon.

DANIJEL If I remember it well, this is the mould discovered at Bobovac castle and is interpreted as a coat of the Gorjanski family (Dorotea, the wife of the king Tvrtko II Tvrtković came from this clan), it is not seal of the ruler. See P. Anđelić, 'Bosanska kraljica Dorotea Gorjanska' in Glasnik Zemaljskog muzeja u Sarajevu 27/28 (1973).

**Irna, Since the claim of the alleged pyramids you have developed an immense online database, trying to bring down the pyramid theory in Bosnia. What motivated you to do this and what were you aiming for? Did your work had any influence on the developments in Visoko?**

IRNA I began discussing the "pyramids" on various forums and newsgroups in the spring of 2006, and wrote my first articles on my blog during the summer of the same year. My interest in the subject was purely accidental at the beginning: I happen to understand more or less the Bosnian language, and to have a personal interest in both archaeology and geology/geomorphology. I started translating the published documents on the Bosnian Pyramid Foundation website, written by supporters of Osmanagić. Later I counteracted their statements by giving geological explanations for the various 'strange' characteristics of the hills.

I would never have dreamt, in the spring of 2006, that I would still be writing and talking about these "pyramids" ten years later! At that time I thought that the whole story would be very soon dismissed as a pure fantasy and forgotten after a few months. What decided me to write a blog on the subject was when I saw that Osmanagić was changing his claims from week to week, and that he was pretending to do actual science with various "reports" on geology, satellite imagery and so on.

I guess, now when I look back, that my motivations were quite complex. Firstly, I loved Bosnia and Herzegovina very much before the war; I traveled quite often there in the 80's (I lived one year in Yugoslavia at the end of the 70's and came back often, particularly in Sarajevo). I had been devastated by the effects of the war, and in a country where so much of the heritage was destroyed or at stake, the whole pyramid affair seemed to me a cruel joke.

Secondly, the professional archaeologists and geologists had given their opinion of the "pyramids" (for example in the EAA(The European Association of Archaeologists), but not in a way, it seemed to me, that was sufficiently pedagogic. I do not fault them for it, they have actual scientific work to do and, as we all know, never enough time nor credit to do everything that should be done. But I felt that, in order to convince laymen, some basic explanations were needed, like how a hill can have a triangular face, how nature can and do create regular forms and perfect spheres and so on.

Thirdly, In my opinion science is the best method we have to understand the world, and as a teacher I devoted my life to help young people understand science and use the scientific method. What is in my opinion the most dangerous is not beliefs, but false science, "bullshit masquerading as science", as John Oliver put it. And that's exactly what Osmanagić is doing, using a pretense of science with no respect to the rules of science. Or at least that's what he was doing in the first years, and what he does less and less: he has now almost abandoned any pretense of doing archaeology, and produces more and more some New Age gibberish.

As for the potential influence of my blog on the developments in Visoko, I have frankly no idea. I have been contacted from time to time by former volunteers, or ex-future volunteers, who told they had changed their minds after reading my blog; I have been in contact with quite a lot of people from Visoko or Sarajevo, including former members of the Foundation; and I know for sure that Osmanagić himself has read my blog at least once.

I think – but it's only my impression, with no objective elements to confirm it – that my work may have helped restrain the diffusion of Osmanagić's hypotheses in the Anglo-Saxon and French world, but I doubt that it had any serious influence in Bosnia itself. Except maybe on one point: one of my articles, the one on the geology of the "pyramids", has been copied almost verbatim by the Federal Institute for Geology in its 2007 report to the Minister of Culture.

**Cornelius, you defend the thesis that archaeology matters when its meta-stories matter. What exactly do you mean with that?**

CORNELIUS I have argued that archaeology matters in present-day society when it is part of larger stories, for example stories about the course of history or about how to gain new knowledge (Holtorf 2010). That does not mean that all stories are equally legitimate. In each case, we have to judge, based on ethical and political criteria, which stories we are happy with and which we are unhappy with and to what extent. Archaeology matters less when it is not linked to any such stories but simply presents historical facts or ancient artifacts as if they mattered in society somehow in their own right.

I respect Irna's views of science – I think it is fair to say that this is the view of the Enlightenment which has been very significant, especially for the natural sciences and technology. Where I perhaps differ is concerning the role of science in society. I don't necessarily think that it is appropriate to promote scientific thinking according to the enlightenment ideals as if it was some kind of ideology or even religion that necessarily and in all circumstances helps making the world a better place (Holtorf 2005). I think we need to accept that a field like archaeology can – and more often than not does – have benefits in society that are not based on the achievements of scientific method and scientific reasoning.

Judging the research of Osmanagić by the standards of science is to miss pretty much everything his project is about. Ironically, this is something which Osmanagić himself disagreed with on many occasions including when he was with us: at least back then he very much presented his work in terms of science. I agree with Irna that this position is misleading. I would also say that this claim is somewhat unfortunate in his case. But I would not call him a pretender, accusing him of practizing "false science", and describe his approach as "gibberish" – as if science must be every researcher's ideal and was the only valid standard for knowledge claims.

Generally, I think we should judge people in terms of who they are and what they do, rather than in terms of who they are not and what they do not do. Clearly, Osmanagić has achieved an awful lot, even though it may not be scientific. In my perspective, we should focus on that, critically of course.

IRNA I'm curious to what exactly Osmanagić has achieved in your opinion. An economic boom? an awareness of the heritage?

CORNELIUS I think Osmanagić has been very successful in the way he has been engaging and mobilizing people, in Bosnia and beyond. The Bosnian pyramids have been inspiring people in meaningful ways beyond everyday life, traditional politics, and the aftermath of war. Osmanagić has managed to make many people reflect on the Bosnian heritage, the potential of research (strictly scientific or not), and ultimately even the meaning of life as it were. All this is significant. It has had economic benefits in the region, too. In addition, Osmanagić put Bosnia internationally on the map again, and for other things than conflicts, hardship and destruction. Tera Pruitt (2009, 2012) has been investigating these benefits in more detail. She cites sources that quote residents in Visoko stating that even if there weren't any real pyramids they should be created for the benefits they had for people in the region.

ANDREW I'd counteract this with a few points. First, archaeology as a profession and a part of cultural heritage was on the cusp of revival in Bosnia & Herzegovina when Osmanagić decided to promote his hypothesis. A generation of new, young archaeologists had been educated abroad (particularly in Zadar and Zagreb), and a small number of archaeologists who had left during the war decided to return. Cultural heritage NGOs were starting to stabilize (after a period of undertaking emergency restoration/reconstruction activities) and become an identifiable part of the civil society landscape. The Mostar and Visegrad bridges were inscribed onto the UNESCO World Heritage List in 2005 and 2007 respectively. The Commission to Preserve National Monuments (in spite of its numerous drawbacks as a functioning agency of the State) had started working and inscribing sites as National Monuments, increasing their visibility (in particular rural sites and stećak necropolises). Osmanagić essentially rode in on the crest of a wave, and then drowned out much of the discourse on archaeology with his presentational tactics. Unfortunately, these 'tactics' were something that the academic community was unfamiliar with, and he used his business acumen (from his background in the scrap metal industry) to his advantage, being able to present archaeologists as 'stuck in their ways' and 'talking down to the little man', something which appealed to his followers, and fed into his later idea that the denial of the pyramids was part of a 'great conspiracy' by the 'academic elite'.

While Cornelius may see this as a positive in and of itself, I see the fact that academia in BiH was (and still is, in many ways) unprepared (both in terms of tactics and attitude) to counter-act his arguments 'at his level' as having been a huge error in this respect. Osmanagić's rhetoric fed into anti-intellectualism and encouraged a lack of critical thinking, and, unfortunately, the other side of the debate simply was not there. Many young archaeologists were afraid of speaking out, and discussion on the 'Pyramids' was essentially banned by professors (there was an incident in Mostar in 2005 or 2006 where the entire cohort failed an exam because the professor overheard students discussing the goings-on in Visoko prior to entering the examination room). To me, there was no 'engagement' of people by Osmanagić and his ideas, it was simply 'instruction' of people.

Furthermore, the idea of the 'pyramids' did nothing to 'inspire people in meaningful ways beyond everyday life, traditional politics, and the aftermath of war'. As already discussed above, the Pyramid idea soon found its place within the country's ethno-nationalistic constructs.

While Osmanagić might have managed to make many people reflect on the Bosnian heritage, the potential of research (strictly scientific or not) and the negatives of his methods far outweighed the positives, in my opinion. The television program Pozitivna Geografija (2001-09), presented by Nisvet Džanko, among others, had already made a huge impact in terms of making people aware of their surroundings and cultural heritage. Like I said above, a new wave of archaeologists educated abroad were just entering the profession, with a wave of graduates from Mostar and Sarajevo soon to follow (Although Sarajevo's archaeology academic program only started in the 2008-09 academic year (Lawler, 2014b), the idea had already been proposed in March 1993 (Kaljanac, 2014 p.241), and the department formed in June 2007 (ibid., p.248). Whether the program's formation was hastened by Osmanagić's ideas and activities is open to debate.There was also a generation of ethnologists who came out of Banja Luka University at some time after the war, but prior to 2005. These people (as well as initiatives and organizations highlighted above) should/would have had this exact effect, while at the same time providing a grounded framework for dialogue.

DANIJEL This is an interesting question which invokes discussion about the nature of and transmission of knowledge in contemporary scholarship and public discourse. Although relying a lot on different fields of natural sciences, it is beyond any doubt that archaeology belongs to the humanities. This means that interpretation of the evidence will always remain subjective and driven by the things such as education of the scholar who interprets the evidence, his/hers cultural habitus, political views, personal experiences, etc. The archaeologists engage with each other, but also with society around them which – let's be honest – pays their salaries through tax or student fees. This society is supplied with interpretation of the past from legitimate scholarly authorities, who act as interpreters of social reality. So, on this level I agree with professor Holtorf. The research of pseudo-archaeology is legitimate and necessary, because pseudo-archaeology is a social phenomenon and it is important to understand why a certain part of society accepts this kind of 'alternative knowledge', which circumvents official networks of academic authority.

Osmanagić had success in Bosniak-majority parts of Bosnia and Herzegovina, but failed to attract public attention in neighbouring Croatia, although he 'saw' pyramids and prehistoric 'wonders' over there as for example megalithic Iron Age walls on Bribirska glavica near Skradin where I have been involved in excavations for the past three years. Why did he fail there? Because academic networks in Croatia function more-less properly and maintain scholarly authority in public discourse, unlike B&H where those networks were destroyed by armed conflict and their rebuilding took long time.

This brings us to the question of authority and dispersion of knowledge. While contemporary scholars communicate with each other in post-modern meta-language (or even meta-modern, as some researchers claim that post-modernism is finished, e.g. Vermeulen & van der Akker 2010), the public discourse is very much rooted into modernistic discourse, which sees research of the past as a search for 'historical truth'. If academic meta-language with good reason acknowledges that the past can be interpreted in different ways, or that we will never be able to fully uncover 'historical truth', it is important not to oversimplify things and say that everyone has the right to interpret the past. For that reason, it is important to keep in mind that scholars must maintain authority in the wider community. So, I agree fully here with Irna – Osmanagić's project must be first labelled as gibberish and false science because it does not follow the established ways in research and interpretation of evidence. Only when this is clearly established as a fact, we can move to a post-modern (or meta-modern) approach and observe his project in different perspectives of contemporary politics, identity-construction, pseudo-archaeological discourse, etc.

CORNELIUS I am interested to hear from Danijel about the different reception of Osmanagić's efforts in Croatia. When you assert that this is because "academic networks in Croatia function more-less properly and maintain scholarly authority in public discourse" I wonder whether you mean – as this sounds – that this is ultimately a question of power. This would raise a few questions to pursue further. Is the success of alternative archaeology mainly reliant on the degree to which 'scholarly authority' has been maintained in the public domain? Are scholars, like the police or the military, in the business of maintaining authority? Are academic networks functioning "properly" when they contribute to maintaining scholarly power in society? By the same token, does that mean that people who are sceptical about the Bosnian pyramids hold this position because their minds are taken over by scholars, partly as a result of well functioning academic networks? And does that mean also that the followers of Osmanagić have liberated themselves from this kind of intellectual occupation? Ironically, Osmanagić himself might actually agree with such an assessment. In some way he is presenting himself as the people's archaeologist, taking on the academic establishment and its authorities.

DANIJEL I guess it is not the question of power over knowledge, but rather qualifications to do certain job, in the same way that for example medical professionals are qualified to interpret the issues of health, architects are qualified to construct buildings, or plumbers take care of plumbing. I am not questioning the work of doctors, architects or plumbers taken as a groups, because I know they are trained to do that job. The success of alternative forms of knowledge in my opinion is indeed connected with the influence (or lack of it) of academic/professional networks in particular society. I disagree with the term 'intellectual occupation' – academic training and participation in academic networks qualifies individuals to uphold or challenge and change established paradigms and discourses. The function of police and military in non-totalitarian regimes is not to maintain authority but to keep order. In the same way I see social role of academic community as group of professionals trained to interpret (in this case) the past for the wider audience. The membership in this group is limited only by successful completion of training, therefore by individual capabilities to interpret the past judged by people who are already have credentials to judge. I am not saying that interpretation of the past is free of its zeitgeist – on the contrary – it is influenced by it. Nevertheless, we are not talking here about interpretation of historical events (which are indeed open for discussion), but by hard facts which are easy to determine – whether Visočica is a hill or a pyramid. The whole story about 'intellectual occupation' is part of rhetorics used by 'alternative' science that cannot offer coherent arguments about the issues in which it challenges 'official' science.

CORNELIUS I do not think the role of archaeologists in society is to "keep order" as to people's interpretations of the past (Holtorf 2005, 2007). I think our responsibility in society is larger than providing people with hard facts about the past, and possibly a few somewhat softer interpretations too. There is value in the process of investigating the past as such. The past is also political: whatever we present as facts or interpretations has consequences in society. In my view, we need to look at what archaeology does in – and indeed for – society. From this perspective, I would say that maybe there were no pyramids in Bosnia for thousands of years but in a way they are there now. So the key question for me is not whether they exist but what they do.

REFERENCES


- Dzino, Danijel (2012) *Archaeology and (De)Construction of Bosnian identity*, Archaeological Review from Cambridge 27(2), 179-188.
- Holtorf, Cornelius (2005) *Beyond crusades: how (not) to engage with alternative archaeologies.* World Archaeology 37, 544-551.
- Holtorf, Cornelius (2007) *Archaeology is a Brand! The Meaning of Archaeology in Contemporary Popular Culture.* Illustrated by Quentin Drew. Oxford: Archaeopress. In North America, Walnut Creek: Left Coast Press.
- Holtorf, Cornelius (2010) *Meta-stories of archaeology.* World Archaeology 42(3), 381-393.
- Holtorf, Cornelius and Jacob Hilton (2012) *Learning about the past from the Bosnian pyramids? A final response. Forum: The limits of collaboration.* Osmanagić in the campus Arqueologia Publica: Online Journal in Public Archaeology 2, 44-51. Available via www.arqueologiapublica.es
- Horvat, Srećko and Igor Štiks (2015) *Welcome to the Desert of Post-Socialism: Radical Politics After Yugoslavia.* Verso: London, 30
- Kaljanac, Adnan (2014) *Historija arheologije: u potrazi za prošlošću.* Sarajevo: University of Sarajevo.
- Lawler, Andrew. (2014a) "Preliminary results of the Discovering the Archaeologists of Europe Project (Bosnia & Herzegovina)". Radovi sa konferencije i radionica projekta BIHERIT. Ljubljana: Univerza v Ljubljani, Filozofska fakulteta. pp.67-73.
- Lawler, Andrew. (2014b) *Perceptions of Ethnicity, Religion and Language Within the Archaeological Community of Bosnia and Herzegovina.* Archaeologies, 10(3), 232-247.
- Okey, Robin (2007) *Taming Balkan Nationalism: The Habsburg 'Civilising Mission' in Bosnia*, 1878-1914. Oxford: Oxford University Press.
- Pruitt, Tera C. (2009) *Contextualising alternative archaeology: socio-politics and approaches.* Archaeological Review from Cambridge, 24(1): 55–75.
- Pruitt, Tera C. (2012) *Pyramids, Performance and Pseudoscience in Visoko, Bosnia.* Arqueologia Publica: Online Journal in Public Archaeology 2, 26-34. Available via www.arqueologiapublica.es
- Vermeulen, Timotheus and Robin van den Akker (2010), *Notes on Metamodernism*, Journal of Aesthetics and Culture 2 (2010), 1–14.

# K2 Megalith

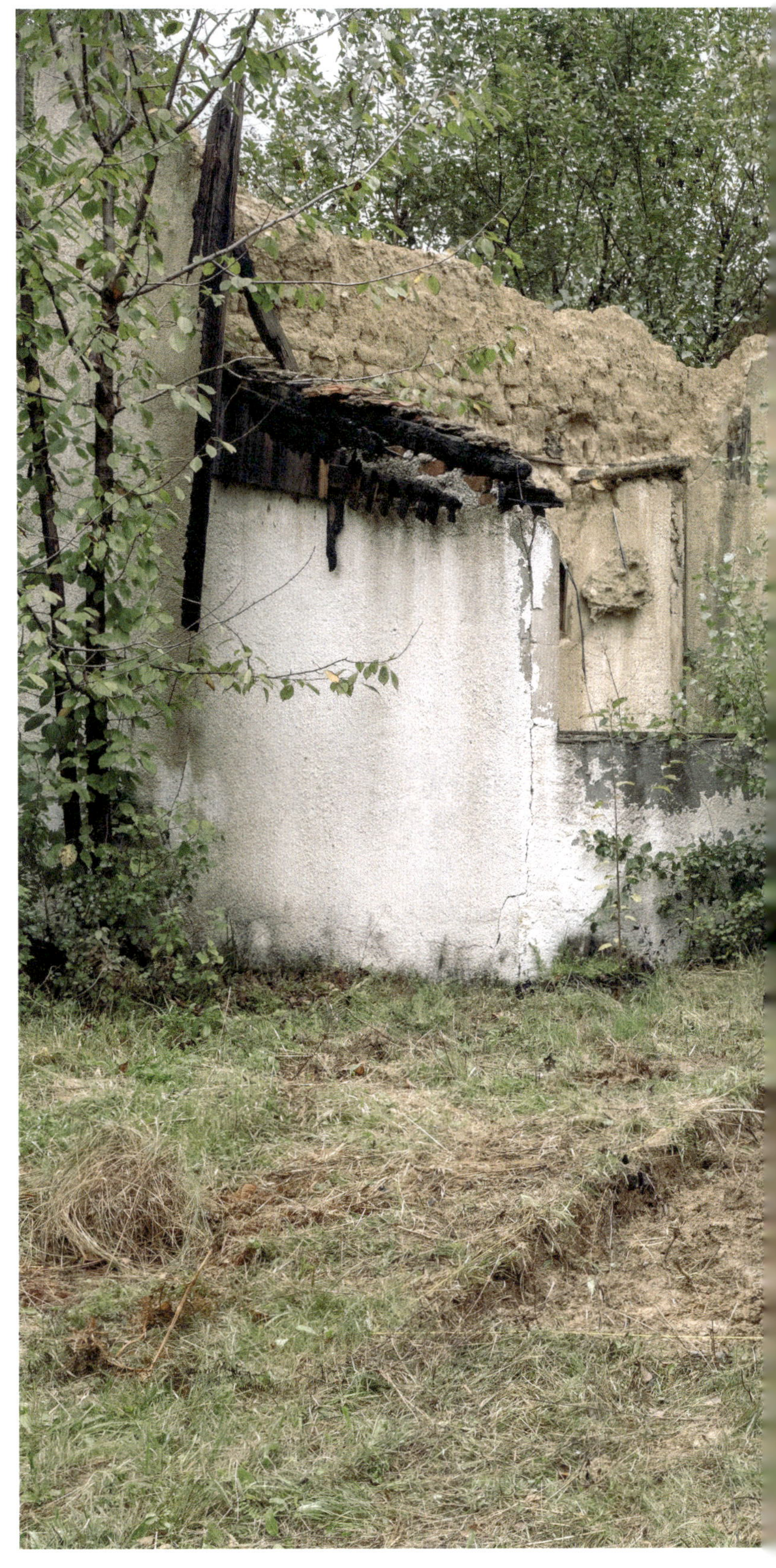

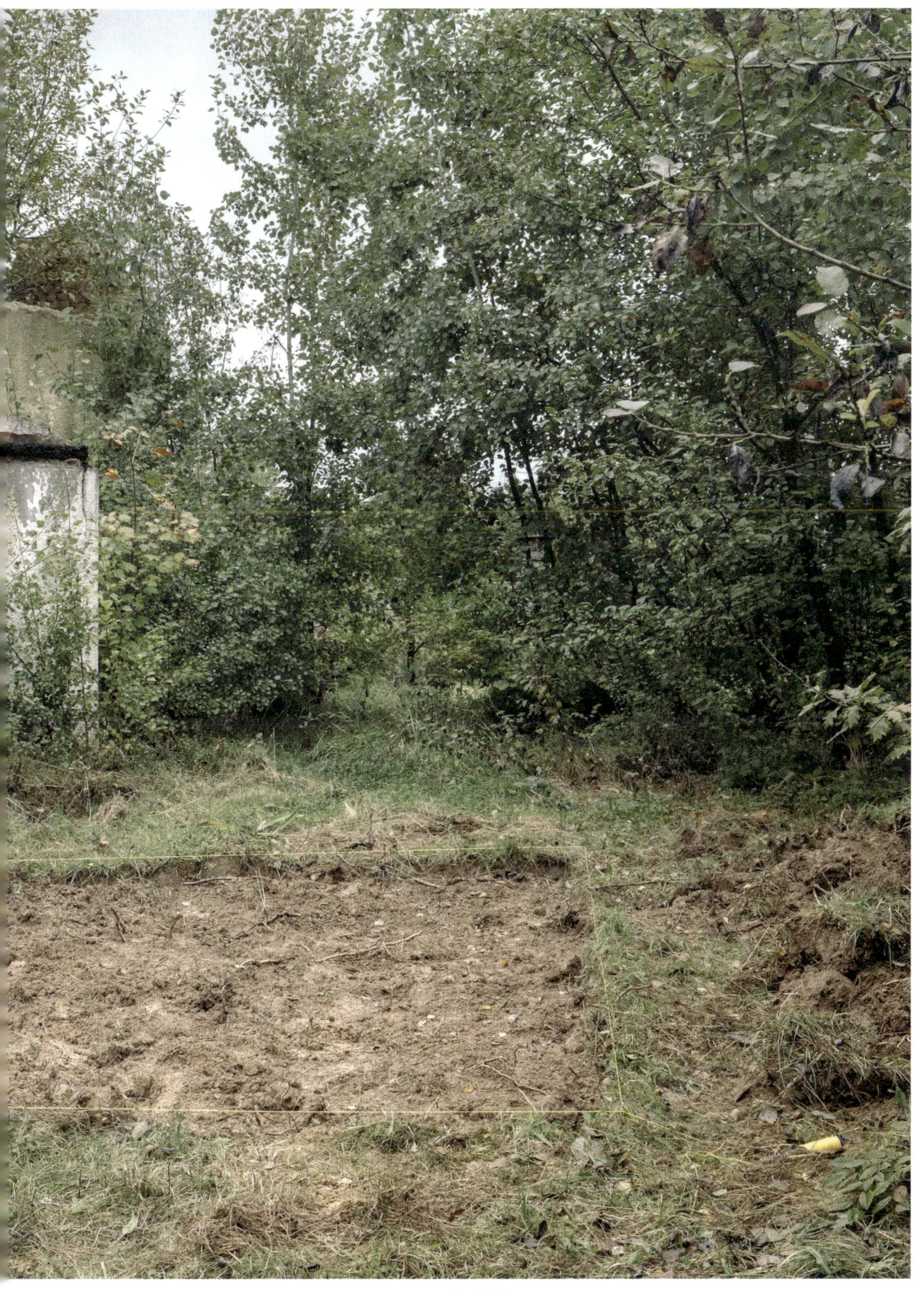

Plate LIII

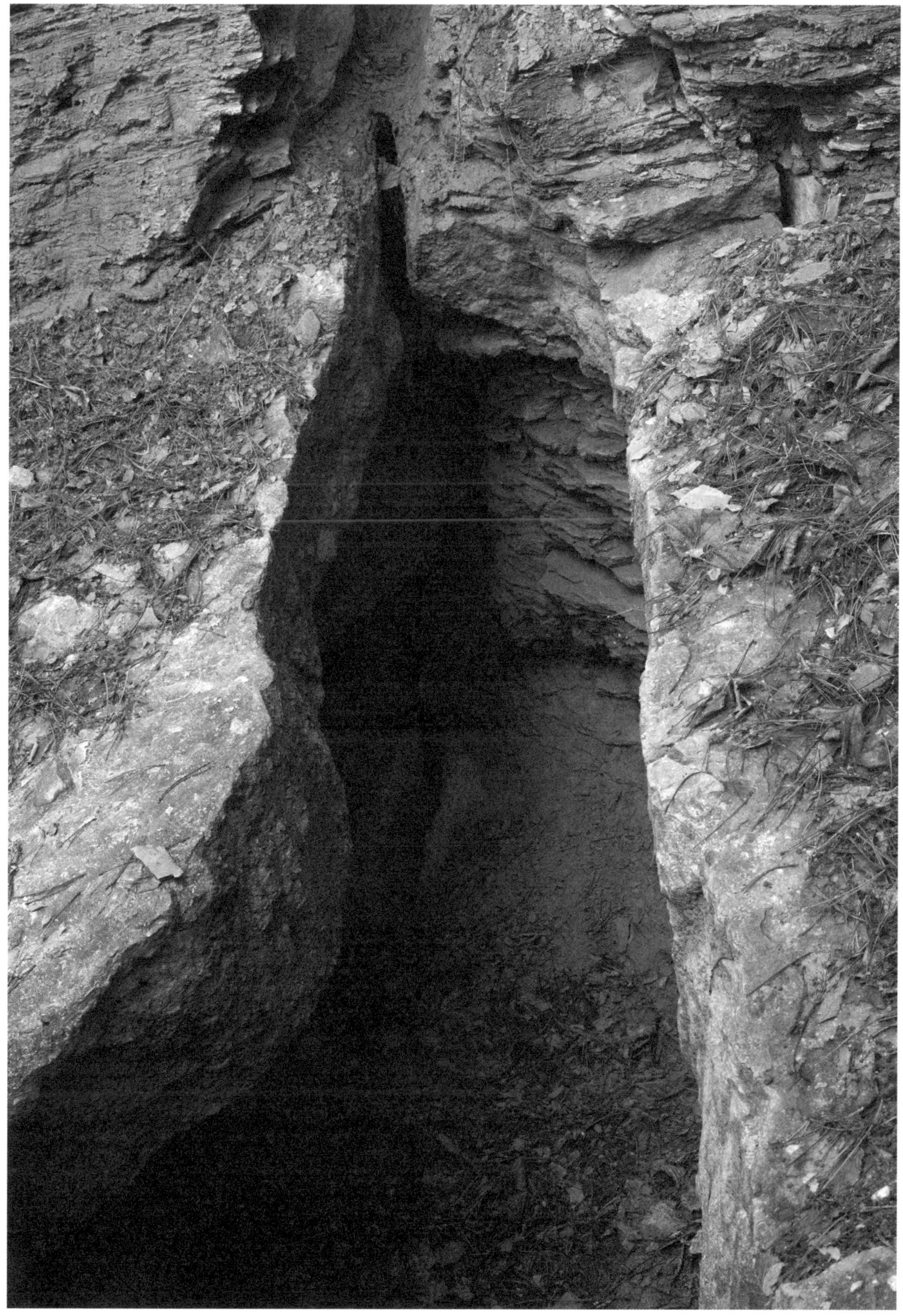

Plate LIV

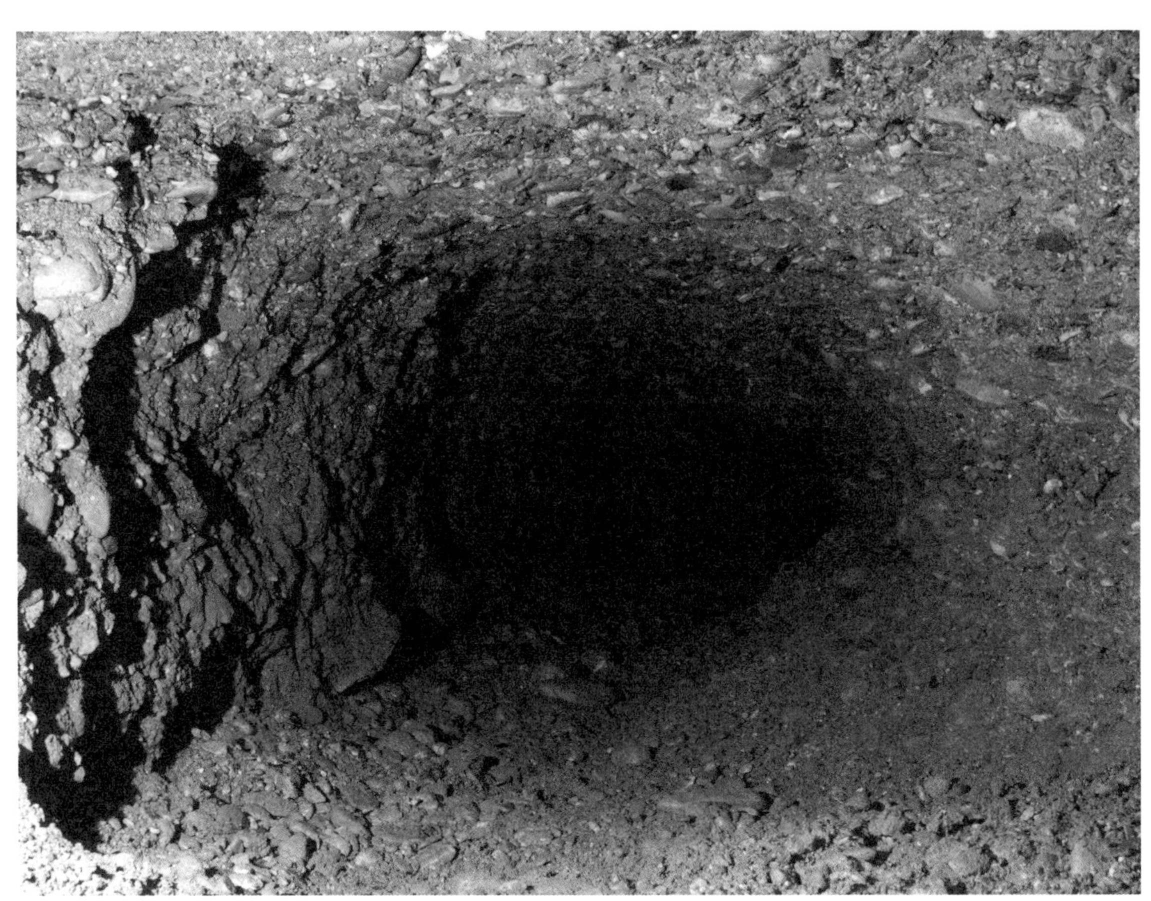

Plate LV

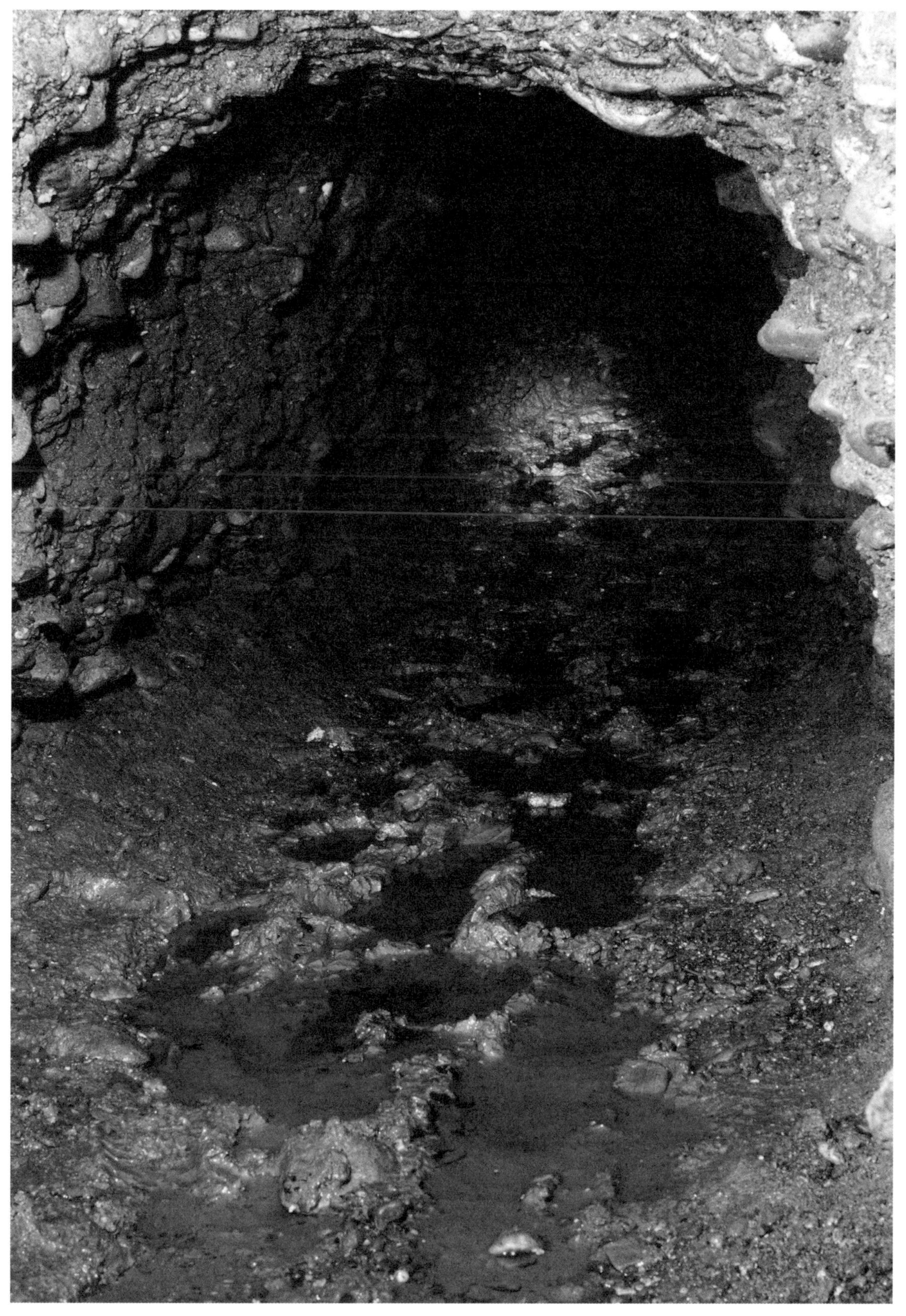

Plate LVI

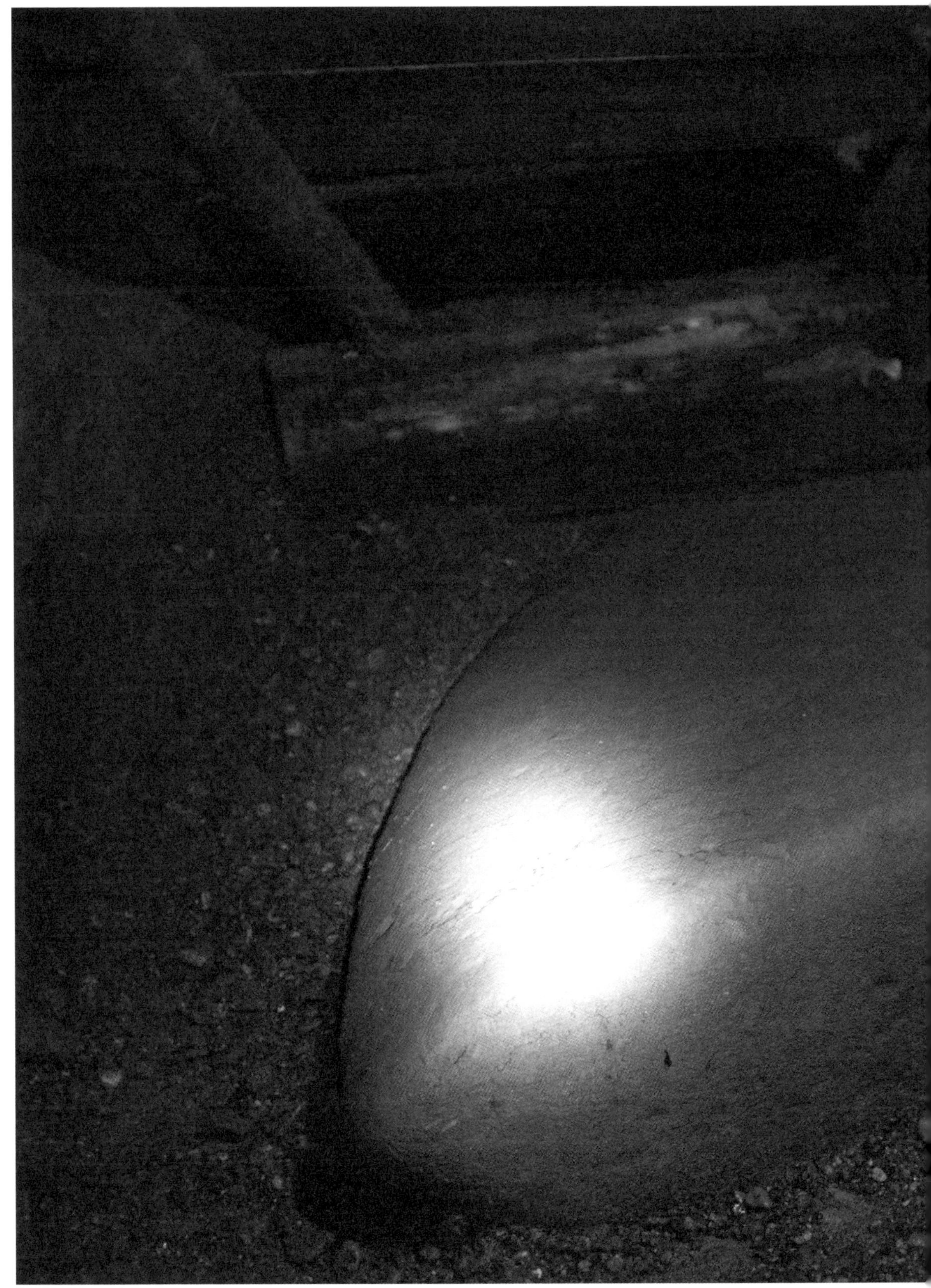

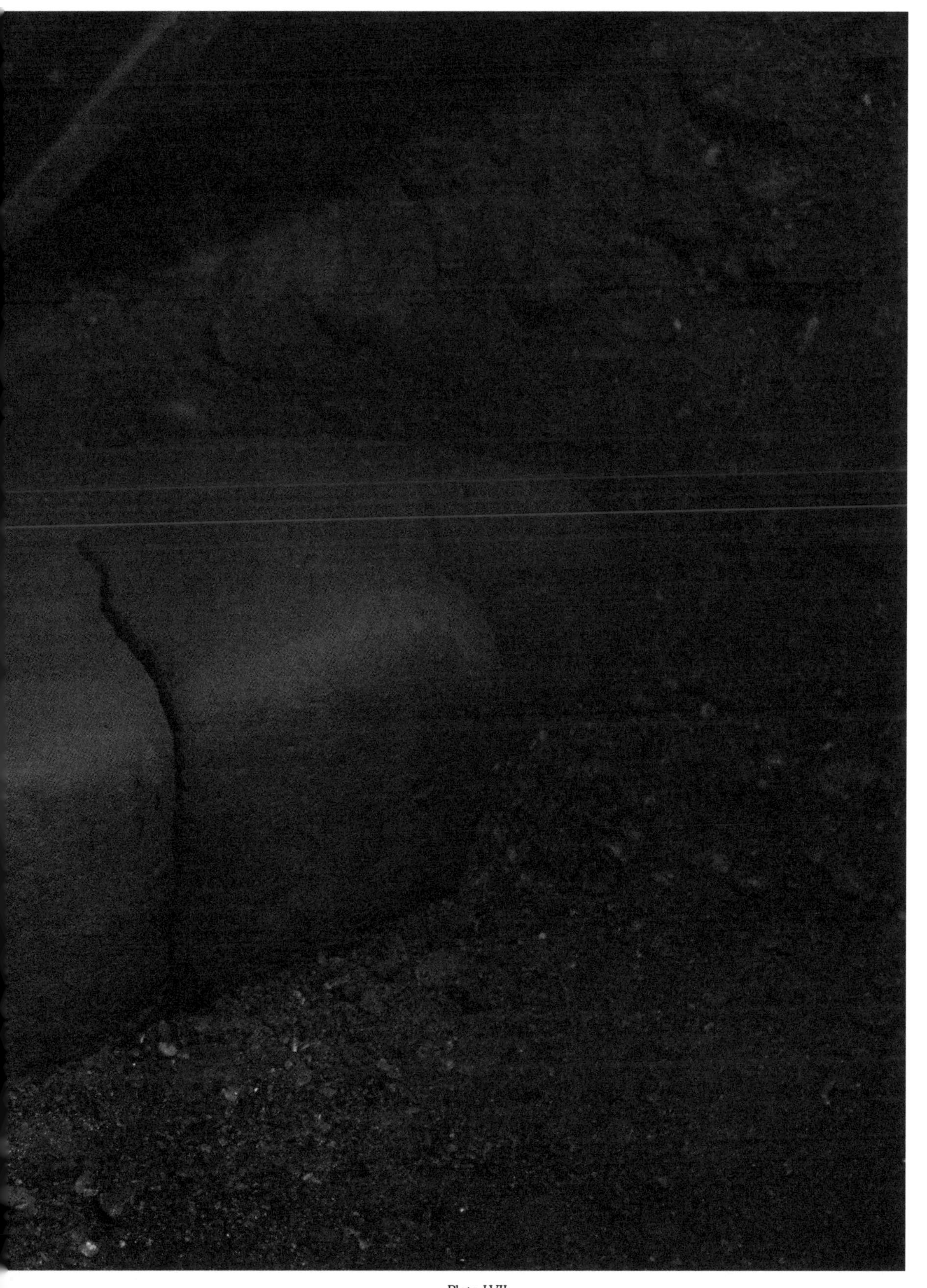

Plate LVII

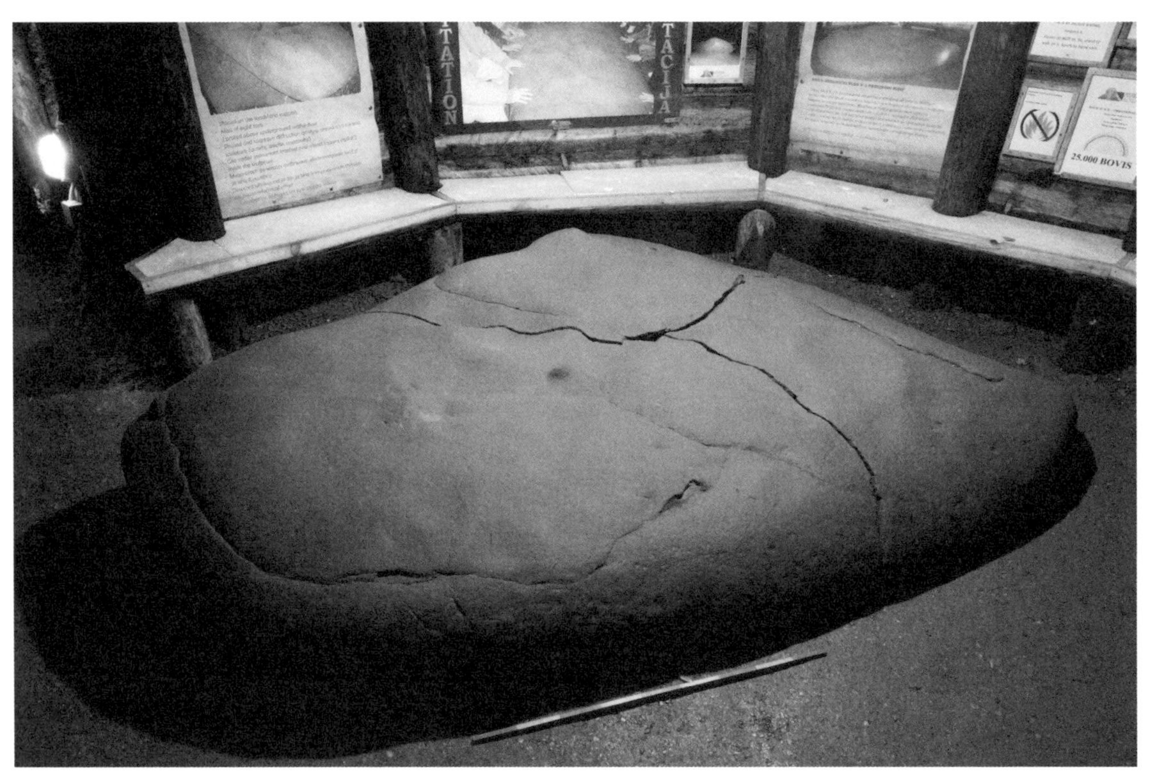
25.000 BOVIS

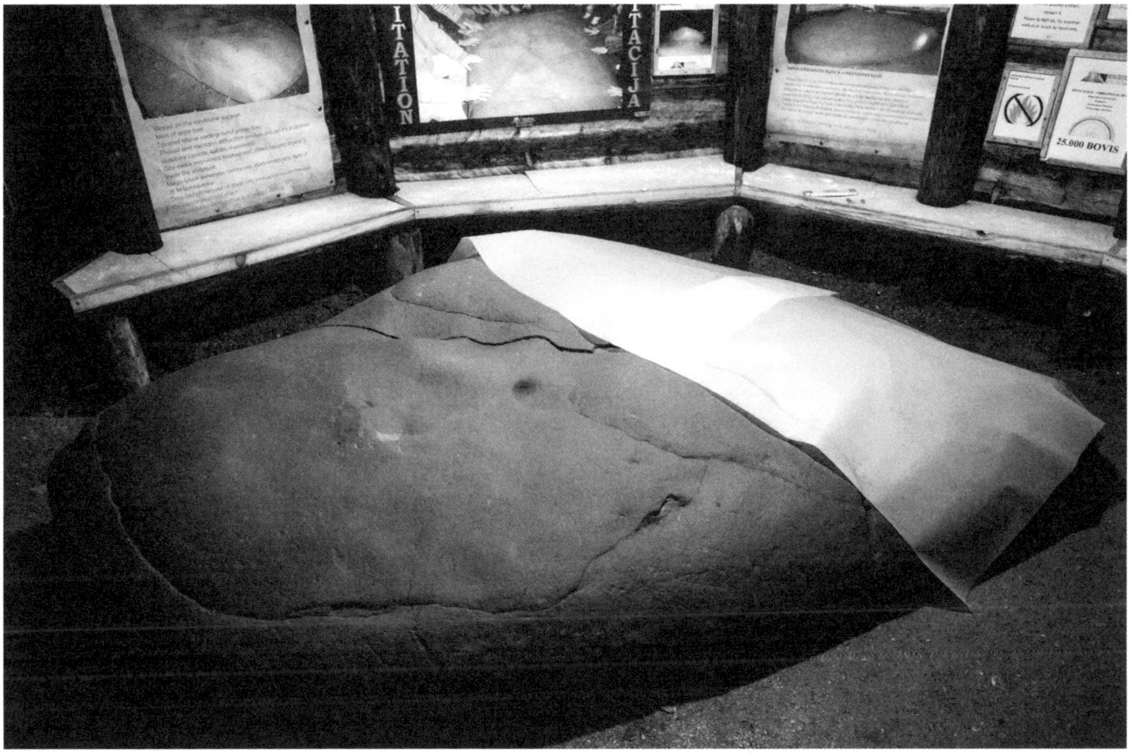

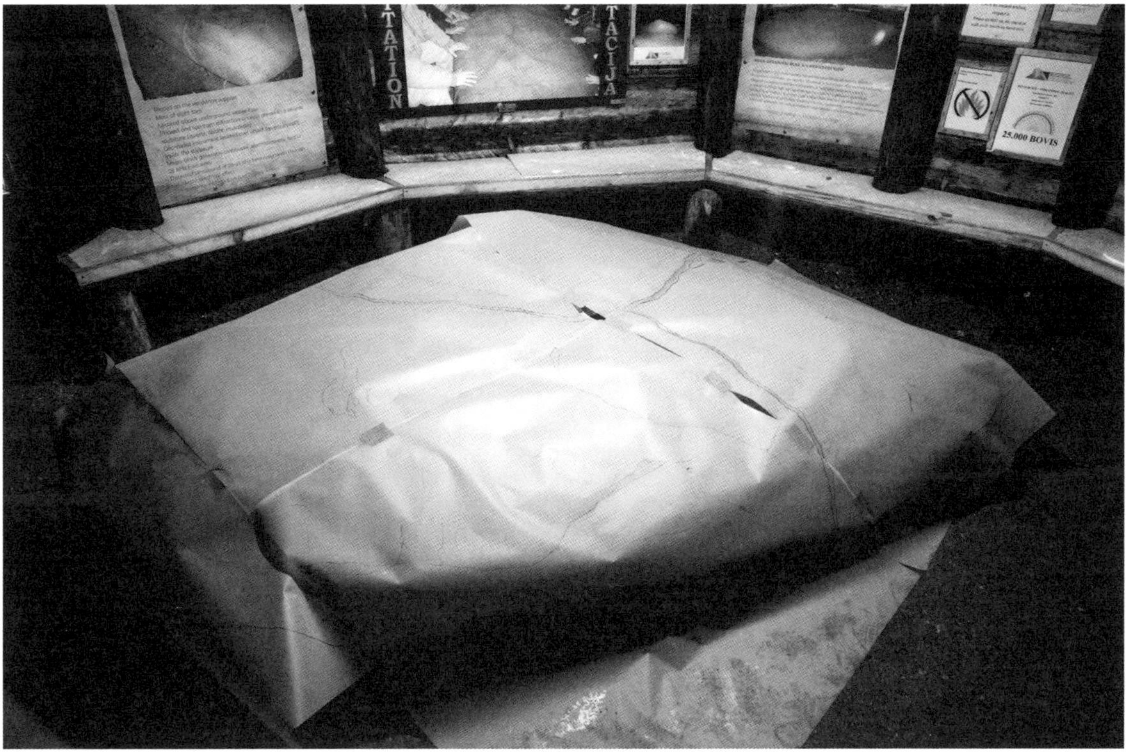

Plate LVIII

# A PROPOSAL TO EXTRACT K2 MEGALITH FROM THE RAVNE TUNNEL COMPLEX

DOCUMENTATION, ANALYSIS AND SUGGESTION

## 1. Ravne Tunnel Complex

The Ravne tunnel complex is located 2.5 km outside Visoko, not far from the Bosna river. It consists of a man-made underground network connecting the three pyramids and possibly 3.8 km long. In April 2006, first excavations were done by a group of mining specialists from Zenica and Semir Osmanagić. Since then, dry walls and various interesting artifacts were discovered. Some people say that the Archeological Foundation is making these tunnels themselves. I would like to stress that this cannot be true as many researchers report the complexity of this labyrinth and the different materials that are used.

The artifact is a yellow-brown stone, located about 18 meters under the ground. It has a length of 3 meters and a width of 2.5 meters at its widest point. The significance of this is that the stone is much wider than the tunnel itself which makes it impossible to transport the stone outside.

## 2. Documentation K2 Megalith (06/2016)

The artifact is located under an area with a large amount of trees. Because it would take a lot effort (time, money, tools) to remove these trees before extracting the artifact, we decided in June to make a registration of the artifact instead of trying to find a possible way of extracting it from the tunnel complex.

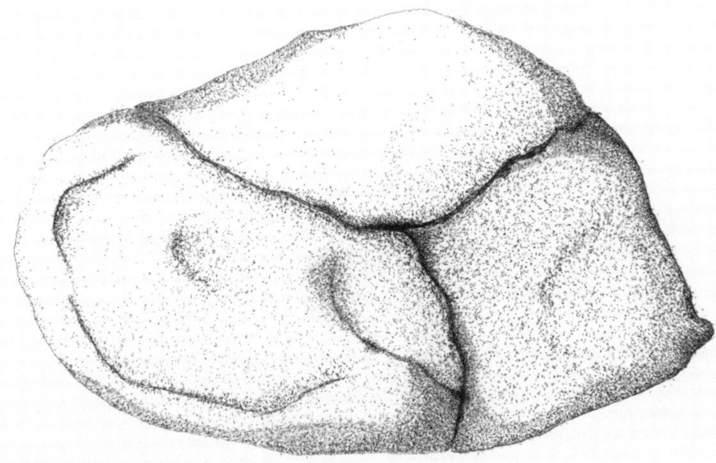

K2 Megalith, scaled drawing, 210 x 297 mm

What characterizes the K2 is a sort of crack in the middle of the artifact that creates three beautiful lines that go towards the contours of the artifact. This could be a kind of language map of the Visoko Valley, representing the two rivers Fojnica and Bosna.

## 4. Extraction Point K2 Megalith (09/2016)

In September we found a possible way to bring the artifact to the museum. On Google Maps, some 40 meters eastwards from the artifact, there is a white house near some farmland. In between this farmland and the house there is some green, 'unused' land that could be an excellent extraction point, if the tunnel would be extended around 50 meters.

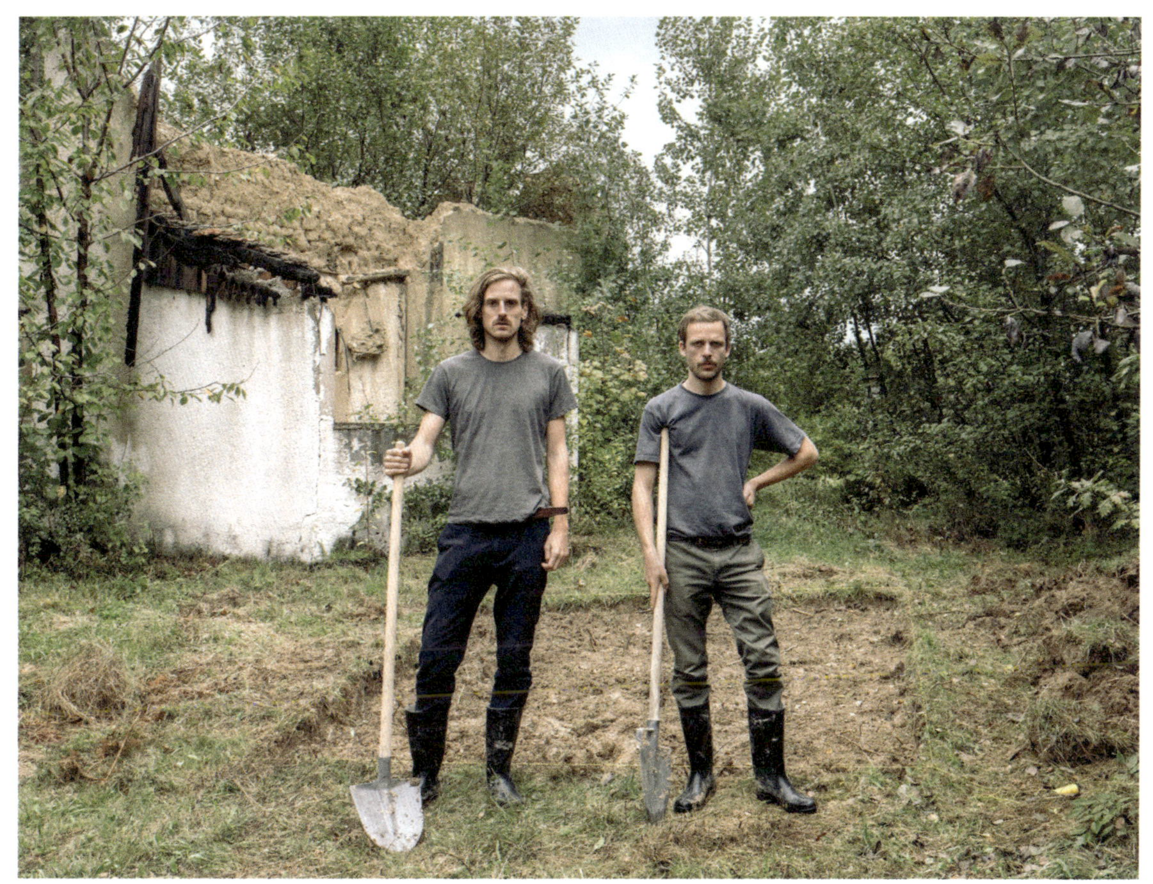

Plate LIX

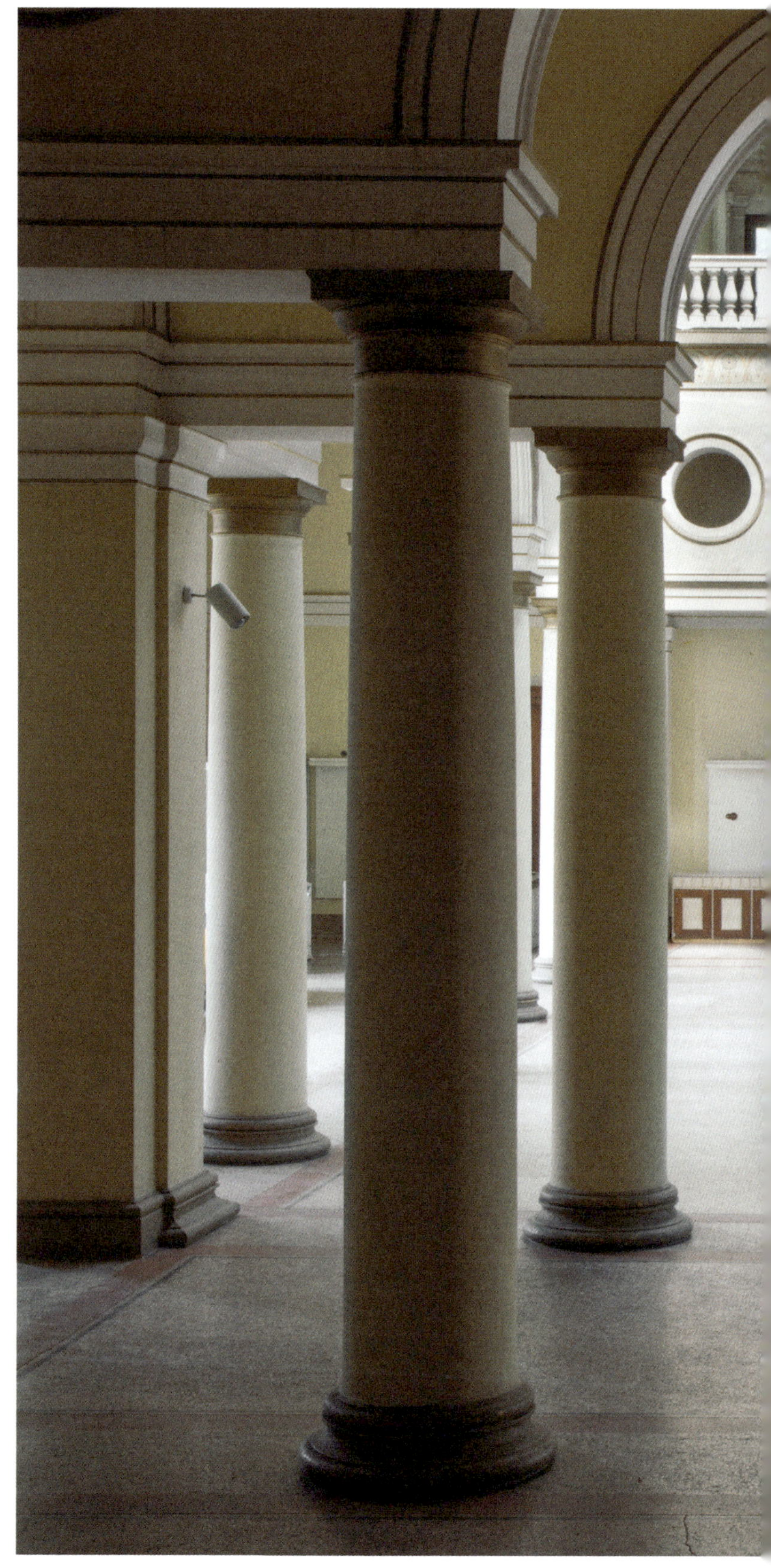

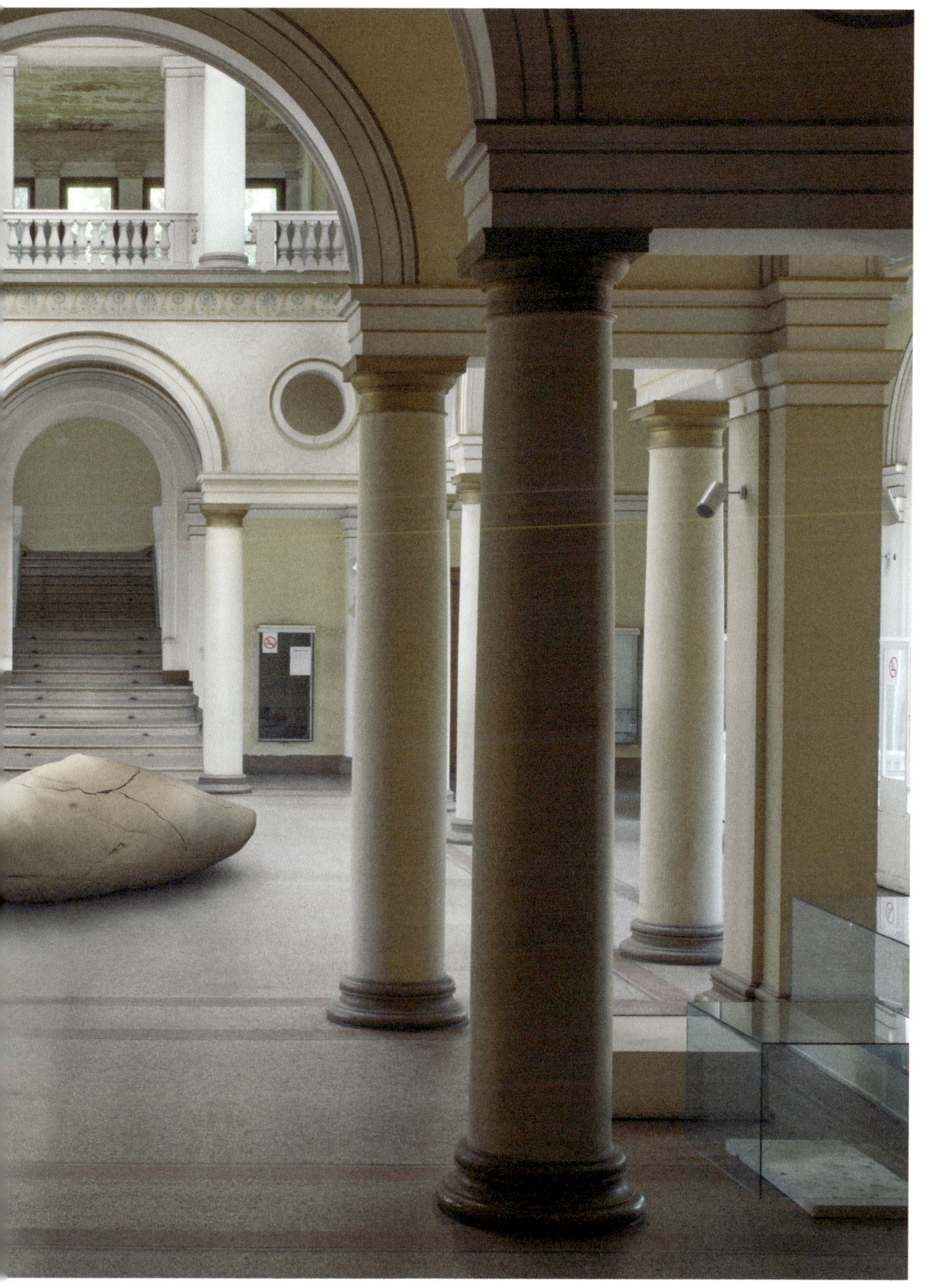

Plate LX

## BOSNIA'S NATIONAL MUSEUM IS LATEST VICTIM OF POLITICAL FUNDING CRISIS

Written by John Hooper, The Guardian, Wednesday 3 October 2012

The National Museum of Bosnia-Herzegovina will close on Thursday after 124 years – the victim of a political funding crisis that is devastating the divided nation's cultural institutions.

Bosnia has already lost its national art gallery this year. And international campaigners say at least five other cultural institutions are at risk. They include the National and University Library, which was attacked and reduced to rubble during the 1992-95 war.

Last month the library's electricity was cut off. On the same day the director of a projected national contemporary art museum announced his resignation saying he had nowhere to put a collection – including works by internationally renowned painters such as Jannis Kounellis – that was put together after the war by artists and benefactors.

The museum's deputy director, Marica Filipovic, said it had survived two world wars and the last one without ever closing totally. "But it seems it will not survive the peace," she said.

The museum's pride is the Sarajevo Haggadah, an illuminated 14th-century Jewish manuscript which has been valued at $700m. Other treasures include a 250,000-volume library, an extensive display of folk costumes, its renowned entomological collection and unique Neolithic ceramics from the internationally famous excavations at Butmir nearby.

"The explanation that is being given is budgetary, but the issue is political," said Azra Aksamija, a Sarajevo-born artist and academic who is assistant professor of art, culture and technology at the Massachusetts Institute of Technology (MIT).

The US-brokered Dayton accords, which stopped the fighting, entrusted Bosnia's leading cultural institutions to a state government whose powers and funding have since been eroded by the mutually antagonistic communities.

"The institutions were left in a legal vacuum and so it was unclear who should give them money," said Aksamija, a member of the editorial board of cultureshutdown.net, a website devoted to publicising the issue.

"The state of Bosnia-Herzegovina failed to transfer a single convertible mark (the Bosnian currency) into our account in 2011, while the federation terminated is financial support in 2012," said Ismet Ovcina, the director of the National and University Library.

The Vijecnica, the grand Moorish-revival building in which it was housed, is being rebuilt at a cost of €13m. But the library, which was rehoused in a former Austro-Hungarian army barracks, has managed to survive largely because of intermittent local authority handouts.

Its heating was turned off on 6 January. And after the electricity went on 26 September, Ovcina announced he was suing the state. “We have no other choice,” he said in a statement.

Day-to-day power in Bosnia is exercised not by the state, but at the level of its so-called entities: one for the Serbs; the other a federation of often mutually suspicious Croats and Bosniaks (predominantly Muslims). The entity administrations have been keen to promote ethnically or religiously defined cultural bodies of their own.

As a report commissioned by the Council of Europe noted: “After the war the different cultural groups, who define themselves as nations, have all wanted their own national cultural institutions with the Croats and Serbs asserting that the existing institutions, all of which are based in Sarajevo, increasingly represent Bosniaks.”

On the contrary, said Aksamija, institutions like the National Museum were “witness to the fact that cultural cross-fertilisation can work and be fruitful”. She called the neglect of state-level cultural institutions “the continuation of a sort of silent war against multicultural values”.

According to cultureshutdown.net, the institutions at risk of closure, apart from the National and University Library, include Bosnia’s Historical Museum, its National Film Archive, the Museum of Literature and Theatre Arts and the National Library for the Blind and Partially Sighted Persons.

Last year a conceptual artist, Damir Niksic, occupied the National Art Gallery in protest at its approaching closure. But, in general, the reaction to the gradual deterioration of Sarajevo’s cultural treasure houses has been one of indifference. On Tuesday a demonstration was called to protest against the imminent closure of its most important museum. Approximately 40 people took part.

| PLATE | DESCRIPTION |
|---|---|
| I | Jajce |
| I | Jajce |
| II | Lukavac |
| III | Luke |
| IV | Trebević |
| V | Sarajevo |
| VI | Child holding a gun |
| VII | Karstic cavern, Blagaj |
| VIII | Inside cavern, Blagaj |
| IX | Zalomska river valley |
| X | Farmer and goat |
| XI | View on Buna river, Blagaj |
| XII | Bosna river, Visoko |
| XIII | Bone near Bosna river, Visoko |
| XIV | Sarajevo citizens reading mural proclaiming the annexation, 1908 |
| XV | Austro-Hungarian Army passing through Visoko |
| XVI | Painting of Kravice Falls, Sami bar, Sarajevo |
| XVII | Artifact factory in the Zalomska Valley |
| XVIII | Carrying stone spheres to the mouth of the cavern, stones sphere pipeline, workman at rest |
| XIX | Biggest stone sphere in Europe |
| XX | Local people and tourists measuring the stone sphere |
| XXI | Map showing the locations of stone spheres in Bosnia |
| XXII | Lunch table, Donji Junuzovići (Zavidovići) |
| XXIII | Souvenir shop #1, Donji Junuzovići (Zavidovići) |
| XXIV | Stone Spheres Park, Donji Junuzovići (Zavidovići) |
| XXV | Sentinel-1A satellite image mapping the floods in Bosnia and Herzegovina |
| XXVI | Megalithic city, Daorson |
| XXVII | Tourist holding dowsing tool, Daorson |
| XXVIII | Osmanagić measuring stones, Daorson |
| XXIX | Stećci |
| XXX | Rented horse near gravestone, Arnautovići (Visoko) |
| XXXI | Rented horse near gravestone #2, Arnautovići (Visoko) |
| XXXII | National Museum of Bosnia and Herzegovina |
| XXXIII | Top of Vratnica Stone Temple, Vratnica |
| XXXIV | View on Bosna and Fojnica river, Visoko |
| XXXV | Megalithic block, Vratnica |
| XXXVI | Tourists at Pyramid of the Sun, Visoko |
| XXXVII | Valley of the Bosnian Pyramids |
| XXXVIII | Spring Equinox Conference, Vogošća |
| XXXIX | Child pointing a gun at the photographer |
| XL | Painting of Visoko municipality |
| XLI | Archaeological site, Bosnian Pyramid of the Sun, Visoko |
| XLII | Concrete blocks #1, Pyramid of the Sun, Visoko |
| XLIII | Concrete blocks #2, Pyramid of the Sun, Visoko |
| XLIV | Tourists at Pyramid of the Sun #2, Visoko |
| XLV | Souvenir shop #2, Visoko |
| XLVI | Child kneeling in front of small pyramid, Visoko |
| XLVII | Vratnica Stone Temple, Vratnica |
| XLVIII | The Pyramid of Amenemhat I at Lisht, Egypt |
| XLIX | The Pyramid of Senusret II at El-Lahun, Egypt |
| L | Souvenir shop #3, Visoko |
| LI | Map, Bosnian Valley of the Pyramids |
| LII | Near Ravne 2 tunnel complex, Visoko |
| LIII | K2 Megalith extraction point, Visoko |
| LIV | Entrance to inner chambre, Pyramid of the Sun, Visoko |
| LV | Ravne tunnel complex #1 Visoko |
| LVI | Ravne tunnel complex #2, Visoko |
| LVII | Megalith, Ravne tunnel complex, Visoko |
| LVIII | Drawing, documenting the K2 Megalith, Ravne tunnel complex, Visoko |
| LIX | Thomas Nolf and Gauthier Oushoorn near extraction point, Visoko |
| LX | K2 Megalith in the National Museum, Visoko |

NEOBIČNI ARTEFAKTI U BOSNI I HERCEGOVINI
imaginarna izložba

Thomas Nolf



Dragi Thomase,

Zahvaljujem se na poslanom mailu.

Ideja o izložbi zvuči interesantno, ali iskreno, plašim se da si odabrao jedino pogrešno mjesto za njezino održavanje. Pozivajući se na svoje široko znanje o ovoj oblasti, mogu ti reći da postavljanje izložbe u Zemaljski muzej (osobito u još prazno predistorijsko krilo) moglo bi biti pogrešno shvaćeno od strane "lokalaca" kao potvrda da piramide doista postoje, nevezano za očigledno drugačiji pristup izložbe. Ti polaziš od postmoderne (ili čak meta moderne) perspektive kao posjetitelj koji dolazi sa Zapada sa samo djelimičnim shvatanjem koje bi moglo ozbiljno naštetiti autoritetu Zemaljskog muzeja. Bilo je i drugih incijativa Zapadnjaka koji su željeli pomoći, ali nisu uspjeli usljed svog neznanja o lokalnim prilikama.

Nadam se da si razgovarao o ovome sa dr. Mirsadom Sijarićem, direktorom Muzej koji jedini ima istinsku moć da odluči hoće li se izložba održati ili ne (osim ako nije povezan sa aferama Ministarstva civilnih poslova koje trenutno kontroliraju Bošnjaci ili lokalni nevladin mafijaški sektor). Ipak, nemam ništa protiv da sudjelujem u intervjuu, premda nije baš najjasnija svrha samog intervjua.

Fotografije na web stranici su prilično dobre, tvoja namjera da promatraš ovo kao socijalni fenomen je očigledna. iako su neki naslovi fotografija prilično čudni i neprihvatljivi, kao što je recimo fotografija srećka Nekropola Radimlja, naslovljena kao crtež bosanskog nadgrobnog spomenika koji se referira na Bosanske piramide. Također, spomenuo si ponovno pisanje plana Zemaljskog Muzeja, autora Gauthiera Oushoorna, čija je svrha meni potpuno nejasna.

Nadam se da ćeš mi razjasniti ova pitanja i radujem se intervjuu.

—-

strana 21
TRANZIT

Rijeka Buna navodno je nastavak Zalomske rijeke, koja nekih trinaestak kilometara istočno od Blagaja ponire u planinskom procjepu. Kao dokaz zabilježena je sljedeća priča:

Jednoga dana čobanin iz Nevesinja baci svoju batinu u Zalomsku rijeku, a njegov otac, mlinar iz Blagaja, slučajno je pronađe u Buni. Otac i sin riješiše onda da unosno iskoriste svoje otkriće. Svakoga dana, čobanin bi ubio po jednu ovcu i bacio je u rijeku, a otac bi je vadio iz Bune. Kada bi ga što pitali o zagonetnom smanjivanju njegova stada, čobanin bi uvijek optuživao vukove, no poslije nekog vremena gazda postade sumnjičav, te riješi da ga kriomice prati. Jednoga dana otkri čobanina kako baca ovcu u rijeku, a sljedećeg jutra mlinar u Blagaju umjesto da, kao i obično izvadi ovcu, izvadi iz Bune mrtvo tijelo svoga sina.

—-

strana 35

PUTUJUCE KUGLE

Nakon što su arheolozi sa Zapada u zemlji otkrili zagonetno geometrijsko kamenje i brojne tumule (10. slika), "čobaninova priča" je inspirisala Austrougarsko carstvo da zavlada zemljom i pretvori je u Arheološki park, gdje bi budući turisti mogli otkrivati ogroman broj jedinstvenih artefakata.

U tu svrhu, država je svoje planove najavila građanima velikim plakatima okačenim po sarajevskim zidovima, obavještavajući ih da se fabrike artefakata već grade širom zemlje. Iako mnoge Sarajlije nisu bile pismene, ljudi su bili sretni da mogu raditi i zaraditi.

U dolini Zalomske rijeke položeni su cjevovodi iz novosagrađene fabrike (3. slika) sve do ulaza u pećinu. Kroz te cjevovode prolazile su oblikovane kugle sve do bivšeg korita Neretve (9. slika) i njenih pritoka.

—-

strana 42

Pronalazak artefakata i antikviteta širom zemlje uskoro je doveo do hipoteze da je u Bosni, prije nekoliko hiljada godina, postojala razvijena civilizacija.

Dok se u Beču razrađivala ova teorija, stanovnicima varoši Zadovići bilo je poručeno da treba širiti priču kako su se početkom 19. vijeka, poslije žestoke oluje, pojavile velike čudnovate kamene kugle. Nakon što se rijeka izlila, voda je stvorila omanju vododerinu, u kojoj su se pojavile ove kamene kugle od 0.6 do 1.6 m, a onda se skotrljale niz brijeg. S obzirom na to da se one i danas nalaze u koritu malog potoka, prilično je vjerovatno da je ova legenda zasnovana na činjenicama.

Međutim, rodila se i druga, maštovitija legenda, koja pripovijeda o sudaru svatova. Tvrdi se da su se na mjestu gdje su sad kamene kugle sukobili gosti dvaju svatova koji su se gađali medjusobno kamenovima, sve dok se i sami nisu pretvorili u kamene sfere. Ovo objašnjenje i nije baš tako vjerovatno, ali se u njemu mogu nazreti tragovi legendi iz drugih krajeva – na primjer iz francuskog Karnaka (Carnac) – o tome kako su megaliti, zapravo, okamenjeni ljudi.

—-

strana 79

ARHEOLOGIJA I DEKONSTRUKCIJA BOSANSKOG IDENTITETA

Danijel Džino

Ocjenjivanje odnosa između prošlosti i njezine interpretacije pobuđuje sve veći interes i postaje sve popularnijim među arheolozima. Utjecaj ideologije, kolonijalizma i nacionalizma na arheološka istraživanja i interpretaciju materijalnih nalaza možda je najprivlačniji i najpopularniji aspekt tog procesa (Díaz-Andreu 2007, Díaz-Andreu - Champion 1996, Fawcett - Kohl 1995; Galaty 2004). Između arheologije i projekata izgradnje nacija postoji čvrsta veza. Arheologija i stvaranje nacija nastaju približno u isto vrijeme – koncem osamnaestog i u devetnaestom stoljeću. Nacionalizam je bio stvaralački projekt intelektualnih elita na Zapadu koje su počele stvarati 'imaginarne zajednice' zasnovane na percepciji zajedničkog podrijetla, povijesti, tradicije i sudbine (Anderson 1991). Ti projekti na početku su bili internog karaktera rezultirajući stvaranjem zapadnih nacionalnih država. Iskustvo projekata stvaranja nacija pokazalo se vrlo korisnim i u doba europske kolonijalne ekspanzije u devetnaestom stoljeću, kao sredstvo imperijalne dominacije nad koloniziranim narodima, primjerice, u funkciji kolonijalne konstrukcije afričkih nacija (Young 1994).

Nacionalizmu je bila potrebna povijest – za 'biografije' tih imaginarnih zajednica, opisivanje njihova 'rođenja' i pripovijedanje pripovijesti o njihovu razvitku. Arheologija, koja se u 19. st. počela razvijati kao akademska disciplina, u početku je korištena kao pomoćna disciplina koja je artefaktima ilustrirala povijesne narative pisanih vrela. Povijesni artefakti, ali i spomenici, krajobrazi i lokaliteti, odvojeni od njihova povijesnog konteksta, pretvaraju se u slike i simbole koji široj javnosti pomažu vizualizirati prošlost. Te slike i simboli proizvode iskustvo prošlosti koje se može percipirati kao autentično i istinito jer javnost dovodi u izravan dodir s 'precima' i 'prošlošću' (Russell 2006). Takvi konstrukti nacionalnih 'biografija' učinkovito se prezentiraju u muzejima, gdje se slike prošlosti selektivno stavljaju u konkretan, čvrsto definiran redoslijed, kao ilustracija povijesnog narativa, pripovijesti o nacijama (Kaplan 1994). Osim putem muzeja, ideje o nacijama kao zajednicama prenose se i putem povijesnih lokaliteta, krajobraza i spomenika, novih mjesta hodočašća, koja članovima imaginarne zajednice omogućuju opipljivo zajedničko iskustvo prošlosti. Primjeri odnosa između projekata stvaranja nacija i arheologije vrlo su raznovrsni, ne samo s obzirom na povijesni i regionalni kontekst, nego i ovisno o tome je li nacionalni identitet konstruiran izvana ili u lokalnom kontekstu. Kako bih ilustrirao tu raznovrsnost, ukratko ću se osvrnuti na korištenje arheologije u pokušajima konstrukcije bosanskog identiteta u dva različita povijesna perioda, što će pomoći osvijetliti neke šire probleme povezane s odnosom između arheologije i konstrukcije nacija.

Teritorij moderne Bosne i Hercegovine formirao se u 18. stoljeću, na ostatcima osmanske provincije (ajaleta) Bosne. Naziv Bosna potječe od srednjovjekovne kraljevine Bosne (ne s istim teritorijem), koju je 1463. osvojio osmanski sultan Mehmed II. Berlinskim ugovorom iz 1878. Austro-Ugarskoj, kojom vladaju Habsburzi, daje se pravo zaposjedanja i uprave nad Bosnom i Hercegovinom, iako i jedna i druga nominalno ostaju pod vlašću sultana.Godine 1908. Habsburška monarhija anektira Bosnu i Hercegovinu kao posebnu upravnu jedinicu pod zajedničkom upravom Austrije i Mađarske. Stanovništvo Bosne i Hercegovine čine tri različite etničke grupe: pravoslavni Srbi, katolički Hrvati i Bosanski Muslimani koji govore slavenskim jezikom (godine 1993. ova nacija mijenja naziv u Bošnjaci). Prije 19. stoljeća, na bosanski identitet pozivale su se različite skupine, u različitim povijesnim kontekstima, uglavnom muslimani, ali nije postojala čvrsto definirana nacionalna skupina niti zajednički identitetski diskurs koji bi – osim u smislu regionalne pripadnosti – povezivao sve tri skupine (Džaja 1984).

Habsburšku vladavinu nad Bosnom i Hercegovinom značajno je obilježio Benjamin von Kállay (Béni Kállay de Nagy-Kálló), ministar financija Austro-Ugarske Monarhije mađarskoga podrijetla, i upravitelj Bosne i Hercegovine imenovan 1882., koji tu dužnost obnaša sve do svoje smrti 1903. godine. Njegovim osobnim djelovanjem i utjecajem habsburški se kolonijalni poduhvat oblikuje kao „civilizacijska misija“, slično suvremenim „civilizacijskim misijama“ europskih imperijalnih sila u Africi.

Dakako, Bosna i Hercegovina bila je poseban slučaj, jer se nije radilo o prekomorskom teritoriju već o graničnom području Monarhije. Tijekom osamdesetih i devedesetih godina 19. stoljeća Kállay je iz razumljivih političkih razloga provodio ideju troreligijskog bosanskog identiteta. Habsburška uprava plašila se politiziranja srpskoga i hrvatskoga identiteta u Bosni i Hercegovini pod utjecajem Srba u susjednoj kneževini (kasnije kraljevini) Srbiji, te Hrvata u Austro-Ugarskoj monarhiji. No takav se politički program ne može ocijeniti kao jasno definirano represivno nametanje bosanskoga identiteta, niti simplificirati kao održavanje kontinuiteta srednjovjekovnoga bosanskoga kraljevstva. Kállayeva politika vođena je ciljem izgradnje novoga bosanskoga identiteta kao višereligijskoga i nadnacionalnoga identiteta unutar imperijalnog ideološkoga okvira lojalnog Monarhiji, a motiviranoga što bezbolnijom tranzicijom ove provincije u Austro-Ugarsku (Kraljačić 1987; Okey 2007: 55–143, 253–255).

Razvitak arheologije u Bosni i Hercegovini mora se, dakle, promatrati u tom političkome i ideološkome kontekstu. Dok se u razdoblju osmanske vlasti ne može govoriti o postojanju organizirane arheologije, austro-ugarska vladavina odlikovala se značajnim ulaganjima i rezultatima u tom području. Arheologija se razvijala kao kolonijalni pothvat, dio habsburške „civilizacijske misije", što je razlikuje razvitak arheologije u Bosni i Hercegovini u usporedbi sa susjednim državama. Razvitak i institucionaliziranje arheologije, iskapanja, osnutak Zemaljskoga muzeja u Sarajevu kao nadležne ustanove – što su sve bile Kállayeve ideje i njegovu srcu vrlo prirasli projekti – zahtijevali su značajna materijalna ulaganja koja su se lako osiguravala putem političkih struktura Monarhije (Novaković 2011: 402–404). Najznačajniji arheološki rad i otkrića ostvarena su za periode željeznog doba i rimske vladavine, te kasne antike. Posebno mjesto u tom kolonijalnom pothvatu imala je srednjovjekovna povijest, a habsburška uprava uložila je veliki trud u oblikovanje narativa o srednjovjekovnoj prošlosti Bosne. Stećci, srednjovjekovni nadgrobni spomenici s karakterističnim estetikom, dovedeni su u izravnu vezu sa srednjovjekovnim heretičkim pokretom Bogumila. Bogumili su bili vrlo pogodni kao 'preci' nove bosanske 'nacije' jer se nisu mogli povezati ni s katoličkim Hrvatima ni s pravoslavnim Srbima. Arheologija srednjovjekovnoga perioda prvenstveno je bila usmjerena na stećke, a mnogo manje na ostale srednjovjekovne građevine, s iznimkom utvrda, dok je postojanje kršćanskih crkava od 12. stoljeća nadalje uglavnom poricano (Truhelka 1914: 227–252). Organiziranjem lapidarija sa stećcima unutar novoizgrađenoga muzejskoga kompleksa u Sarajevu (otvorenog 1913.) naglašena je njihova važnost kao suvremenih simbola (Truhelka 1914: 249-252). Stećci su postavljeni u botanički vrt između arheološkoga i etnološkoga paviljona Muzeja u kojima je izložena prošlost i sadašnjost Bosne i Hercegovine. To je bio način da se srednjovjekovno bosansko kraljevstvo i humsko vojvodstvo (Hercegovina) izravno povežu s austro-ugarskom sadašnjošću, ignorirajući gotovo četiri stoljeća osmanske vladavine koja nije bila zastupljena ni u jednoj muzejskoj zbirci (cf. Novaković 2012: 57). Povrh toga, kad je Karlo Pač ispod jednog stećka u Arnautovićima otkrio grob muškarca iz visokoga staleža, grob je pripisan srednjovjekovnome bosanskome kralju Tvrtku I, ali njihovo otkriće nije bilo nigdje objavljeno (Wenzel 1999; Zadro 2004). Nevolja s tim otkrićem sastojala se u tome što se grob nalazio u neposrednoj blizini crkve – a tadašnji interpretacijski okviri inzistirali su na tome da se Bogumili ne mogu povezivati s crkvama. Otkriće groba sasvim je prešućeno, a crkva sv. Nikole iz 14. st. svrstana je u starokršćanski period, tj. u 5./6. stoljeće, sudeći po jednom suvremenom pregledu srednjovjekovne povijesti ove provincije (Truhelka 1914: 226). Nemoguće je ustvrditi je li to otkriće zaista bilo skriveno iz ideoloških razloga, kako uvjerljivo obrazlaže Wenzel (1999: 175–180), što bi se dobro uklapalo u kolonijalni kontekst toga vremena.

Stoljeće poslije toga, arheologija se – u vrlo različitim povijesnim okolnostima – ponovno koristi u funkciji jedinstvenoga bosanskoga identiteta. Godine 1992. Bosna i Hercegovina postaje samostalnom državom, ali odmah potom i poprištem oružanog sukoba. Jedan od najvažnijih, među mnogim uzrocima ovog sukoba, neslaganje je triju nacija o političkom ustrojstvu zemlje. Srpska i hrvatska politička opcija u Bosni i Hercegovini zalagale su se za visok nivo političke decentralizacije i/ili razjedinjenje zemlje, dok su se Bošnjaci, najbrojnija od ovih nacija, zalagali za centraliziranu državu. Godine 2006. Semir Osmanagić, arheolog-amater iz SAD-a rođen u Bosni i Hercegovini, lansirao je u javnost tvrdnju kako su Visočica i još neka susjedna brda oko Visokog ni manje ni više nego piramide stare 27.000 godina. Otkriće je pobudilo kratkotrajno zanimanje medija, ali su ga stručnjaci, i domaći i strani, uskoro jednoglasno odbacili i obrazloženo diskvalificirali kao još jedan slučaj pseudoarheologije (Harding 2007). Međutim, iskapanja 'piramida' su se nastavila. Cijeli projekt bio je koordiniran izvan akademskih institucija, vodila ga je Zaklada „Bosanska piramida Sunca" koju je osnovao Osmanagić, uspjevši i dalje dobivati izvjesnu javnu i moralnu podršku, te financijsku potporu (Foundation 2012). Tera Pruitt (2009) je u svojem radu rasvijetlila složenost značenja i važnost toga 'otkrića' s obzirom na različite lokalne ekonomske i političke kontekste, iako nije uspjela cijeli pothvat jasno pozicionirati unutar aktualnih političkih i identitetnih narativa prisutnih u poslijeratnoj Bosni i Hercegovini. S jedne strane, otkrivač piramida i Zaklada "Bosanska piramida Sunca" lokalitet su koristili za novi nadnacionalni diskurs o bosanskome – sekularnom i inkluzivnom – identitetu koji je kao takav naišao na prihvaćanje uglavnom u područjima s bošnjačkom većinom, i među malim brojem ne-Bošnjaka. To se najbolje vidi u zaštitnom znaku Zaklade koji sadrži novu državnu zastavu Bosne i Hercegovine. Trokut u zastavi ukomponiran je u simolični prikaz piramide. Bošnjaci su lokalitet odmah počeli smatrati svojim, na više različitih razina. Na razini javnoga diskursa, lokalitet se percepirao kao mjesto hodočašća, 'sveto' mjesto koje predstavlja skupno iskustvo identiteta. Za ljude iz tog kraja, golemom većinom Bošnjake, 'piramide' su nudile i mogućnost ekonomske koristi. Najzad, bošnjački politički i vjerski lideri 'piramide' su počeli koristiti i kao sredstvo vlastite promidžbe. Osmanagićevo 'otkriće' nije privuklo Srbe i Hrvate u Bosni i Hercegovini – obje nacije pokazale su upadljivu ravnodušnost prema 'piramidama' na razini javnoga diskursa. Nijedan politički ili vjerski lider Srba ili Hrvata iz Bosne i Hercegovine nije posjetio lokalitet, a piramide – osim kao zabavna tema – nisu pobudile značajniji interes u javnome i medijskome diskursu u većinski srpskim i hrvatskim područjima.

Dva primjera korištenja arheologije za izgradnju bosanskoga identiteta o kojima je ovdje bila riječ pokazatelji su širih pitanja povezanih s rekonstrukcijom i dekonstrukcijom nacija u arheologiji. Oni pokazuju kako isti identitet – stvaran ili izvana ili iznutra, u vrlo različitim povijesnim okolnostima – može biti korišten za političke ciljeve. Birokracija Austro-Ugarske Monarhije pokušala je nadnacionalni i multireligijski bosanski identitet izgraditi kao instrument imperijalne kontrole i kolonijalne dominacije nad Bosnom i Hercegovinom. Kako bi to ostvarila, imperijalna sila spoznala je potrebu za uspostavljanjem kontrole nad novostvorenim povijesnim narativima o Srednjemu vijeku. Arheologija je u tom projektu igrala važnu ulogu, fokusirajući institucionalno istraživanje na srednjovjekovne nadgrobne spomenike koji su postali prepoznatljivim simbolima povijesnoga 'utemeljenja' ovog identiteta. Stoljeće poslije toga, 'otkriće' drevnih 'piramida' od strane arheologa-amatera iskorišteno je za ponovni pokušaj da se u samostalnoj poslijeratnoj Bosni i Hercegovini konstruira nadnacionalni bosanski identitet. S tom razlikom da se arheologijom sada manipuliralo na lokalnoj razini. Pseudoarheologija je zaobišla institucionaliziranu arheologiju i stvorila mjesto hodočašća i simbol, povezujući ga s novim državnim simbolima i identitetskim narativima bosanstva – što je bilo u potpunosti prihvaćeno samo u većinski bošnjačkim područjima.

Oba su pokušaja naposljetku propala. Habsburška monarhija odustala je od širega projekta konstruiranja bosanskoga identiteta čak i prije nego se i sama raspala, zbog toga što tri nacionalne grupe nisu bile zainteresirane za stvaranje zajedničke imaginarne zajednice. Stoljeće poslije toga, 'piramide' su, na razini javnoga diskursa, prihvatili samo Bošnjaci, dok ih druge dvije nacije nisu prihvatile kao zajednički simbol. Uloga arheologije u oba je primjera bila proizvođenje prepoznatljive slike i simbola u okviru dva različita projekta s ciljem formiranja iste imaginarne zajednice. To nas dovodi do same suštine odnosa između arheologije i projekata stvaranja nacije. Arheologija osigurava artefakte koji se putem njihova predstavljanja i izlaganja javnosti lako pretvaraju u prepoznatljive slike i simboli. Simboli – kao što su primjerice državna himna ili zastava – nužno su potrebni kao čimbenik jedinstva imaginarnih zajednica, dok – u slučaju arheoloških artefakata i lokaliteta – služe kao poveznica s 'zajedničkom' prošlošću jer omogućuju zajedničko iskustvo te prošlosti. Arheologija tu nastupa kao važna disciplina jer otvara prozor u prošlost, služi kao svojevrstan 'obiteljski album' vizualizirajući 'biografije' imaginarnih zajednica, a u krajnjoj liniji predstavlja dokaz da se ta prošlost stvarno dogodila. Na izvjesnoj razini, arheologija 'dokazuje' da se nacija, taj fluidni i nestabilni društveni konstrukt, može gledati kao fiksna i nepromjenjiva zbilja.

—-

U decembru 2016. godine održana je online-debata o fenomenu bosanskih piramida. Cilj debate bio je da diskusija izađe iz usko naučnog konteksta i proširi se na ulogu (pseudo) arheologije u savremenoj Bosni i Hercegovini.

Učesnici

Prof. Cornelius Holtorf (rođen 1968. u Sieglaru, Njemačka), predavač arheologije na Univerzitetu Linnaeus u Kalmaru, Švedska. Direktor je Visoke škole za zaštitna arheološka istraživanja (GRASCA) i glasnogovornik Centra za upravljanje baštinom Univerziteta Linnaeus. Glavni interes njegovog istraživačkog rada su razna značenja arheologije i arheoloških lokaliteta u prošlosti i sadašnjosti.

Andrew Lawler (rođen 1985. u Manchesteru, Ujedinjena Kraljevina) honorarni je istraživač pri Školi za historiju te historiju i arheologiju Walesa Univerziteta Bangor. Diplomirao je arheologiju i antropologiju na Univerzitetu Cambridge (2006.), magistrirao arheologiju na Filozofskom fakultetu Univerziteta Louvain (Belgija, 2010.), te završio i napredni magisterij Međunarodnog centra za konzervatorstvo Raymond Lemaire Tehničkog fakulteta Univerziteta Louvain. 2013. godine. Kao terenski arheolog radio je u Ujedinjenoj Kraljevini, Bosni i Hercegovini i Belgiji. Autor je mnogih radova i prezentacija na stručnim skupovima o problematici arheologije kao struke u Bosni i Hercegovini, među kojima dviju publikacija u okviru serijala o evropskim arheolozima Discovering the Archaeologists of Europe, te više članaka objavljenih u časopisima kao što su Journal of the World Archaeological Congress i The European Archaeologist.

Dr. Danijel Džino (rođen 1971. u Sarajevu, Bosna i Hercegovina) predavač je na Odjelu za historiju starog vijeka i Odjelu za međunarodne studije (hrvatske studije) na Univerzitetu Macquarie u Sydneyu, Australija. Doktorirao je 2005. na Univerzitetu Adelaide, da bi 2010. prešao na Univerzitet Macquarie kao dobitnik konkursa Australian Research Council Discovery Project. Autor je mnogih stručnih publikacija. uključujući knjige Illyricum in Roman Politics 229 BC- AD 68 (Cambridge University Press, Cambridge, 2010.), Becoming Slav, Becoming Croat: Identity Transformations in Post-Roman and Early Medieval Dalmatia (Brill Academic Publishers, Leiden / Boston, 2010.) i, zajedno s Alkom Domić Kunić, Rimsko osvajanje Ilirika. Povijesni antinarativ (Školska knjiga, Zagreb, 2013.). Učestvovao je u nekoliko istraživačkih projekata u Hrvatskoj, npr. u projektu “Varvaria-Breberium-Bribir”, tj. u iskapanju na lokalitetu Bribirska glavica.

Irna je autorski pseudonim francuskog geografa i geomorfologa s interesom za arheologiju. Irna je autorka bloga o pseudoarheologji i knjižice o bosanskim “piramidama”.

**Ako posmatramo Bosnu i Hercegovinu i cijelu regiju danas, što možete o njoj da kažete u kontekstu demonstracija iz 2014. godine? Neko iz Crne Gore rekao mi je da ljudi ne znaju za koga da se bore.**
**S jedne strane, tu je pohlepna politička elita oligarha, a s druge, nepovjerenje u “prelazak” u članstvo Evropske unije.**
**U knjizi “Dobrodošli u pustinju postsocijalizma”, Igor Štiks i Srećko Horvat opisuju primjer hrvatskog pristupanja u članstvo Evropske unije, upozoravajući na izvore polu-periferne uloge postsocijalističkog regiona: jeftina i visokoobrazovana radna snaga u blizini kapitalističke jezgre, gotovo totalna ekonomska zavisnost o toj jezgri i njenim multinacionalnim bankama i korporacijama i, najzad, akumulacija dugova.**

DŽINO Demonstracije u BiH 2014. bile su kombinacija stvarnog nezadovoljstva naroda i suptilnijih političkih ciljeva koji su se pojavili kasnije tokom demonstracija, npr. zalaganja za centralizaciju zemlje. U to vrijeme, neki komentatori pominjali su indirektnu upletenost u “Bosansko proljeće” diplomacije SAD-a putem raznih nevladinih organizacija, no tu tvrdnju svakako treba detaljnije istražiti. Ti protesti nisu naišli na značajniju podršku u Republici Srpskoj i većinski hrvatskim dijelovima Federacije BiH, čini se da su srpska i hrvatska javnost te proteste doživjeli kao internu bošnjačku stvar s kojom nisu mogle da se poistovjete.

Protesti iz 2014. nisu se proširili van područja s bošnjačkom većinom jer se situacija u BiH razlikuje od situacije u drugim postkomunističkim zemljama Istočne Evrope (sličnosti se mogu eventualno naći samo u BJR Makedoniji i Ukrajini), naime, ne postoji opšti konsenzus o tome kako bi zemlja trebala da izgleda. Odsustvo konsenzusa o unutrašnjem uređenju BiH (unitarna, federalna ili konfederalna/neintegrisana država) išlo je na ruku oligarhijskim političkim elitama kojima pogoduje status quo. Međutim, stvari je važno posmatrati u kontekstu: u komunističkom periodu, u BiH je postojala dominacija političkih mreža uspostavljenih od strane oligarhijske elite i porodičnih klanova, dakle, takva raspodjela moći sistemski je atavizam iz sedamdesetih i osamdesetih godina, a ne nešto što se pojavilo nakon raspada Jugoslavije. Jedina razlika je to da je 1992. godine BiH prvi put počela postojati kao politički entitet van veće političke jedinice.

Iako se djelimično slažem s citiranom tvrdnjom Štiksa i Horvata (nažalost, nisam čitao njihovu knjigu), važno je da se napomene da je za “pustinju postsocijalizma” kriv i sam socijalizam. To se vidi po preživljavanju endemske korupcije ukorijenjene u državnim službama i privredi, u odsustvu ekonomske kompetitivnosti i održanju hipertrofiranog i neefikasnog upravnog aparata. Post-jugoslovenske države, za razliku od mnogih bivših komunističkih zemalja, nikad nisu izvršile političku lustraciju tako da se velik dio postkomunističkih elita regrutovao iz redova bivše komunističke elite koja se unutar novog ideološkog diskursa nacionalizma samo prepozicionirala podijelivši se na njegove zastupnike i protivnike. Po mojem mišljenju, nepovjerljivost prema članstvu u EU relativno je nova pojava i nema nikakve veze s lokalnom situacijom, odraz je opšteg raspoloženja u EU. Nepovjerenje prema EU u BiH, barem na političkom nivou, najvidljivije je među Srbima i Bošnjacima (čije političke elite flertuju s Rusijom i Turskom), dok Hrvati u članstvu u EU vide način da se bez otcjepljenja čvršće povežu s Hrvatskom.

**Cornelius, ti si Semira Osmanagića pozvao da održi predavanje za studente Univerziteta Linnaeus. Kako su tvoje kolege gledale na taj poziv? Što se tim pozivom namjeravalo postići?**

HOLTORFF Kad je Semir Osmanagić držao predavanje na Univerzitetu Linnaeus, 18. oktobra 2011., neke kolege bile su prema njemu kritički nastrojene jer su smatrale da mu je data prilika da govori o idejama koje generalno nisu prihvaćene kao akademski legitimne. Međutim, moja namjera nije bila da se da podrška njegovim neobičnim idejama o “bosanskim piramidama” nego da se taj slučaj prodiskutuje kao interesantan i vrlo intrigantan fenomen savremenog društva. Kada me Osmanagić kontaktirao, na ovaj sam način objasnio zašto mu dajem priliku da govori na mojem univerzitetu:

Nismo ga pozvali zato što bismo njegove interpretacije smatrali znanstveno ozbiljnima, nego zato što mislimo da se mora razgovarati o njegovom djelovanju i posljedicama tog djelovanja. Bosanske piramide imaju uticaja ne samo na turizam i percepciju kulturne baštine u Bosni, nego i, na opštem nivou, na naše shvatanje kulturne baštine u društvu. Da li izmišljena baština ima istu (ili veću) moć od autentične kulturne baštine? Šta turisti stvarno traže kad posjećuju lokalitete kulturne baštine? Kako arheologiju i baštinu treba prezentirati globalnim medijima, a da bi oni pratili tu tematiku? Kako sam Osmanagić gleda na svoje kritičare u akademskim arheološkim krugovima i, u užem smislu, na kritičare među arheolozima u Bosni?

DŽINO Kao čovjek koji se bavi naukom, razumijem stajalište prof. Holtorfa, slažem se s tim da bi fenomen “piramida” u Visokom trebalo istražiti u njegovom društvenom kontekstu. Predavanje je lokalnoj akademskoj zajednici prezentirano u takvom kontekstu, a rezultiralo je vrlo interesantnom diskusijom koje je poslije objavljena u ozbiljnom stručnom časopisu. Međutim, lično, ne odobravam ideju pozivanja Osmanagića da govori na (bilo kojem) univerzitetu jer se time u krajnjoj liniji narušava autoritet akademske ustanove i daje legitimitet para-znanosti. Pametnije bi bilo studente odvesti na javno predavanje – takav kontekst savršen je za posmatranje Osmanagića u njegovoj "prirodnoj sredini", upravo takav kontekst bi dao priliku da se vidi kako on svoje "znanje" komunicira ciljnim potrošačima toga "znanja".

LAWLER Razumijem stajalište prof. Holtorfa, iz gotovo identičnih razloga. Ipak, ne smatram da je univerzitet "neprimjereno" mjesto za omogućavanje Osmanagiću da govori (i da se on putem javne diskusije tretira odgovornim za svoja mišljenja). Mislim da izbor mjesta uglavnom zavisi od toga šta želimo da studenti s takvog događaja ponesu – da li želimo da oni kao antropolozi budu svjedoci fenomena pseudoarheologije (u kojem slučaju smatram da je kao forma adekvatnije, što Osmanagić najčešće i prakticira, gostovanje u društvenim domovima ili kulturnim centrima), ili da studenti kritički ocjenjuju njegov pristup i zaključke u okviru moderirane univerzitetske diskusije (u takvom slučaju, mislim, pristup koji smo usvojili sasvim je prihvatljiv).

U tekstu koji si citirao, bilo je zanimljivo pročitati i ovo: Predavanje koje je Osmanagić održao u Kalmaru izgledalo je kao njegova standardna predavanja. Sastojalo se od nevjerojatnih 201 stranica prezentacije u PowerPointu. Nakon više od jednog sata, kad su ga nježno upozorili da bi izlaganje trebalo da se privodi kraju, postalo je jasno da je on mislio da je cijeli dvosatni termin bio predviđen samo za njega.

Iskreno rečeno, ne bi me iznenadilo da je Osmanagić znao da na raspolaganju ima samo jednosatni termin – lično sam ga vidio kako to radi – no da se toga jednostavno ne drži kako bi onemogućio postavljanje pitanja. Čini mi se da je to za njega i njemu slične redovna pojava – izgleda da "predavanja" u svijetu alternativne historije nisu stvarno prilika da se diskutuje o novim mišljenjima i iznose konstruktivne kritike, naprotiv, reklo bi se da su to društveni skupovi za druženje, koji osim izlaganja teme uključuju i neko putovanje ili obilazak (izlagači višeg ranga u žanru dobijaju više vremena), nakon čega se svi raziđu kućama do sljedeće prilike. Sjećam se kako mi je neko (možda Philip Coppens) na ICBP 2008 pokazao dvije starije žene koje su rekle da idu na sve alternativne skupove, na svim kontinentima, da godišnje na to vjerojatno troše desetke hiljada eura, iako same nikad nisu imale prezentaciju. Na takvim skupovima očigledno se može zaraditi priličan novac, a smatra se elementarnom učtivošću "ne piliti granu na kojoj sjediš", tj. ne upuštati se u bilo kakvu kritiku. Mislim da je sve to naučio i Osmanagić (iako ne mislim da ga motivira lični finansijski dobitak) i interesantno je gledati kako se njegovo "volontiranje" sve češće ostvaruje u vidu predavanja koja drži širom svijeta.

**To nas dovodi do pitanja o tome kako bi se arheologija trebala prezentirati javnosti. U jednom članku na archive. archeology.org, autor G. Fagan kaže da prezentiranje nauke (i arheologije) na televiziji nesumnjivo nije lak posao i da je uspješno samo onda kad je u prvom planu priče ljudski faktor. Fokusiranjem na izlaganje od strane istraživača, najvažniji element postaje narativ. On to zove zavodničkom pseudoarheologijom – tu situaciju gdje je fokus u prvom redu na naraciji koja se nudi publici, a ne na činjenicama.**

**Cornelius, u knjizi Archaeology is a brand (Holtorf 2007) kažeš da su "arheolozi često uglavnom nesvjesni najvažnije dimenzije arheologije u popularnoj kulturi: njenog arhepila". Šta misliš, a u kontekstu bosanskih piramida, da li je Osmanagić eksponent tog tipa popularizacije arheologije i kako bi se institucionalno naučno istraživanje trebalo postaviti prema tom fenomenu "potrošačkog arhepila"?**

CORNELIUS Da, mislim da Osmanagić iskorištava upravo taj arhepil. On je vrlo uspješan u ostavljanju utiska na publiku, kako svojom pojavom (vidi npr. njegove fotografije u Arqueologia Publica Forum) tako i stilom naracije kojim sebe predstavlja kao arheologa-detektiva koji istražuje drevnu civilizaciju prkoseći moćnoj akademskoj opoziciji. On je veoma nadaren pripovjedač – ne bi bilo loše da profesionalni arheolozi malo porade na tome. Zapravo, rekao bih da se od primjera bosanskih piramida mnogo može naučiti. Jedno je stil prezentacije, a drugo popularnost i percipirana relevantnost u postfaktualnom svijetu.

**Danijel, kako bi ti branio tezu da se u tom tzv. postfaktualnom svijetu zapravo radi o mogućoj prijetnji relativizma "autentičnom" istraživanju historičara? Ti pišeš o tome da arheologija proizvodi artefakte koji se zatim lako mogu iskoristiti kao slike ili simboli za razne kontekste. Kako se to može primijeniti na bosanske piramide i kontekst sadašnje situacije u Bosni i Hercegovini? Može li se govoriti o opasnostima ili koristima s tim u vezi?**

DANIJEL Pitanje zahtijeva malo opširniji odgovor. Prijetnja relativizma u odnosu na historijska i arheološka istraživanja problem je zbog toga što je u BiH domaća akademska zajednica tokom devedesetih godina značajno stradala. Najveći autoriteti ili su se penzionisali, ili preminuli ili napustili zemlju, a preostali stručnjaci nisu bili sposobni da održe akademski autoritet u javnom diskursu kad se 2005. godine pojavio Osmanagić. Danas stvari stoje donekle bolje, ali još uvijek daleko od toga kako bi trebalo da bude. "Bosanske piramide" stalan su izvor slika i simbola za razne i ponekad međusobno sasvim nepovezane grupacije: za ljude koji vjeruju u alternativnu historiju i teorije zavjere, za grupe koje se interesuju za bio- i "kozmičke energije", kao i za ljude iz opštine Visoko koji brdo Visočica sada vide kao novi lokalni zaštitni znak i izvor prihoda. Međutim, ono što me najviše zanima je način na koji su "piramide" sredinom 2000-tih godina postale simbol koji iskorištava i bosanski i bošnjački nacionalizam.

Izvana, bosanski i bošnjački nacionalizam ne izgledaju jednako. Prvi je inkluzivan i sekularan, a drugi ekskluzivan i povezan s islamom. Međutim, i jedan i drugi imaju slične političke ciljeve, npr. unitarizaciju BiH i nepriznavanje političkih prava Srbima i Hrvatima. Počeci "Projekta piramide" 2005. koincidirali su s usponom tih dvaju nacionalizama 2006. godine, posebno zahvaljujući izbornom uspjehu bošnjačkog nacionaliste Harisa Silajdžića i bosanskog nacionaliste Željka Komšića (izabranog pretežnim brojem bošnjačkih glasova za hrvatskog predstavnika u Predsjedništvu BiH). "Piramide" su tada postale sveto mjesto koje su počeli da obilaze mnogi političari bošnjačkih i bosanskih političkih stranaka, muslimanski vjerski lideri (veliki muftija Islamske zajednice BiH čak je tamo održao obred), ali i obični ljudi koji su tu vidjeli mjesto na kojem mogu da dožive (imaginarnu) zajedničku prošlost.

Česta fraza u raznim diskusijama na internetu u početku je bilo ovo: "Ako Hrvati mogu da imaju Međugorje, zašto mi (Bosanci/Bošnjaci) ne bismo imali piramide?" Međugorje u Hercegovini, mjesto gdje se 1981. ukazala Gospa, postalo je važno "sveto mjesto" za Hrvate u Hercegovini i Bosni uopšte, koje je ulilo novu snagu njihovom nacionalnom i vjerskom identitetu suzbijanom od strane komunističkih vlasti. Usporedba tih dvaju "svetih mjesta" veoma jasno pokazuje značenje "piramida" kao moćnog simbola za Bosance i Bošnjake u BiH u to vrijeme – piramide nikad nisu bile prihvaćene kao kolektivni simbol na nivou javnog ili političkog diskursa među Hrvatima i Srbima u BiH. Flertovanje s ta dva nacionalizma moglo je da se vidi i na drugim nivoima. Na primjer, izbor naziva "Piramida Zmaja od Bosne" interesantna je igra riječi koja asocira na Husein-bega Gradaščevića, političku ličnost iz 19. vijeka, Zmaj od Bosne bio je njegov nadimak. U prvim godinama projekta, Osmanagićeva fondacija je u svojim javnim nastupima također snažno naglašavala "bosanski patriotizam" i ulogu "piramida" u ujedinjavanju zemlje. Mislim da "piramide" kao simbol tih nacionalizama danas ne predstavljaju neku veću opasnost, a niti korist. Osmanagić je oportunist, možda osoba opsjednuta svojom "misijom", no sasvim je sigurno da ne možemo da ga okvalifikujemo kao bosanskog/ bošnjačkog ultranacionalistu jer on ne pokazuje nikakav interes za kapitaliziranje tog projekta u funkciji ostvarivanja političke karijere u BiH. Nakon što nije uspio u tome da prezentira prave arheološke nalaze, projekt je naglasak prebacio na "kozmičke energije" koje nisu tako iskoristive za eksploataciju unutar nacionalnih narativa. Dakle, po mojem mišljenju, veza između "piramida" i bosanskog/bošnjačkog nacionalizma nedovršen je politički projekat. Projekat će biti nastavljen, ali, padanjem važnosti "piramida" u domaćem javnom diskursu on kao simbol tim nacionalizmima postaje manje privlačan za eksploataciju, te će oni potražiti drugačije, upotrebljivije simbole.

ANDREW Pored toga, iako tvrdi da mu je naziv "piramide" došao putem "kozmičke inspiracije" (ili neke slične varijante, zavisno od toga kome se obraća), Osmanagić nije propustio da upozori na sličnost pečata jednog starog bosanskog vladara, izloženog u Zemaljskom muzeju, koji sadrži zmaja koji u raljama drži srce, a pored njega su sunce i polumjesec.

DANIJEL Ako me sjećanje dobro služi, to je odliv nađen u dvorcu Bobovac i tumači se da je posrijedi grb porodice Gorjanski (klana iz kojeg potiče Dorotea, supruga kralja Tvrtka II Tvrtkovića), a ne pečat vladara. Vidi P. Anđelić, "Bosanska kraljica Dorotea Gorjanska", članak u Glasniku Zemaljskog muzeja u Sarajevu 27/28 (1973.).

**Irna, otkad se u javnosti počelo govoriti o navodnim piramidama, ti si stvorila ogromnu online-bazu podataka koja bi trebala da pomogne rušenju teorije o piramidama u Bosni. Šta te navelo da to učiniš i šta ti je bilo cilj? Da li tvojr rad ima bilo kakav uticaj na tok događaja u Visokom?**

IRNA O "piramidama" sam počela da govorim na raznim forumima i grupama u proljeće 2006., a u ljetu iste godine napisala sam i prve članke na mojem blogu. Moj interes za tu temu bio je u početku sasvim slučajan: recimo da više-manje razumijem bosanski jezik, a imam i lični interes za arheologiju i geologiju/geomorfologiju. Počela sam da prevodim dokumente u vezi s bosanskim piramidama objavljene na sajtu Fondacije za bosanske piramide, koje su pisale Osmanagićeve pristaše. Kasnije sam počela da polemišem s njihovim izjavama dajući geološka objašnjenja za razne "neobične" karakteristike dotičnih brda.

U proljeće 2006. nisam mogla ni sanjati da ću deset godina kasnije još uvijek pisati i pričati o tim "piramidama"! U to vrijeme mislila sam da će se ta priča ugasiti kao puka fantazija i pasti u zaborav nakon nekoliko mjeseci. Blog o toj temi počela sam pisati kada sam vidjela da Osmanagić iz sedmice u sedmicu mijenja svoju priču, a pretendira na bavljenje "pravom" naukom pozivajući se na raznorazne geološke "nalaze", satelitske fotografije i slično.

Pretpostavljam – kad se osvrnem unazad – da je moja motivacija bila prilično kompleksna. Prvo, veoma sam voljela Bosnu i Hercegovinu prije rata. Osamdesetih godina često sam onamo putovala (krajem sedamdesetih cijelu godinu sam živjela u Jugoslaviji i poslije se često u nju vraćala, osobito u Sarajevo). Bila sam užasnuta posljedicama rata, u zemlji je bio uništen ili ugrožen tako velik dio kulturne baštine da mi je cijela ta stvar s piramidama izgledala kao okrutna šala.

Drugo, profesionalni arheolozi i geolozi dali su svoje mišljenje o "piramidama" (npr. EAA, Evropska asocijacija arheologa), ali, kako mi se činilo, ne na način koji bi bio dovoljno pedagoški. Ne krivim za to njih, imali su preča posla baveći se svojim pravim naučnim radom i, kako znamo, nikad dovoljno vremena ni novaca da naprave sve što se mora napraviti. Zato sam mislila, kako bi se informirali nestručnjaci, potrebno je dati neka bazična objašnjenja, npr. zašto brdo prirodno može imati trokutaste stranice, kako priroda može i zaista stvara pravilne oblike, savršene kugle itd.

Treće, mislim da je nauka najbolja metoda za razumijevanje svijeta kojom raspolažemo, a kao nastavnik, posvetila sam život tome da pomognem mladim ljudima da razumiju nauku i služe se naučnom metodom. Po mojem mišljenju, najveća opasnost nisu ubjeđenja nego lažna nauka, "bapske priče prerušene u nauku", kako to kaže John Oliver. A Osmanagić radi upravo to, služeći se prividom nauke i ne poštujući njena pravila. Odnosno, barem je to radio prvih godina, a sada to radi sve manje: sada je gotovo sasvim odustao i od privida da se bavi arheologijom, sve što proizvodi samo su sve gora New Age naklapanja.

Što se tiče mogućeg uticaja mojeg bloga na razvoj događaja u Visokom, o tome stvarno ne znam ništa. S vremena na vrijeme kontaktirali su me bivši volonteri ili budući bivši volonteri, koji bi mi rekli da su promijenili mišljenje nakon što su pročitali moj blog. Imala sam kontakte s prilično mnogo ljudi iz Visokog i Sarajeva, uključujući i bivše članove Fondacije, a sigurna sam da je i sam Osmanagić barem jednom čitao moj blog. Mislim – ali to je samo moj utisak, ne raspolažem nikakvim objektivnim elementima koji bi to mogli potvrditi – da je moj rad možda pomogao da se obuzda širenje Osmanagićevih hipoteza u anglosaksonskom i frankofonom svijetu, no sumnjam da je to imalo bilo kakav ozbiljniji uticaj u samoj Bosni. Osim možda u jednome: jedan od mojih članaka, onaj o geologiji "piramida", gotovo je doslovce prenijet u izvještaju koji je 2007. Federalni zavod za geologiju podnio ministru kulture.

**Cornelius, ti smatraš da je arheologija važna onda kada su važne njene meta-pripovijesti. Šta tačno podrazumijevaš pod tim?**

CORNELIUS Ja zastupam tezu da je arheologija za današnje društvo važna onda kad je dio širih pripovijesti, naprimjer, pripovijesti o toku historije ili o tome kako steći nova znanja (Holtorf 2010). To ne znači da su sve pripovijesti jednako legitimne. Za svaki pojedinačni slučaj moramo, na osnovu etičkih ili političkih kriterijuma, posebno prosuditi koja nas pripovijest zadovoljava, a koja ne, i u kojoj mjeri. Arheologija gubi na važnosti ako se ne nadovezuje na neku od takvih pripovijesti i ako historijske činjenice i stare artefakte naprosto prezentira kao da su oni sami po sebi važni za društvo

Poštujem Irnine nazore na nauku – mislim da se može reći da je to prosvjetiteljski nazor, koji je bio veoma značajan naročito za prirodne nauke i tehnologiju. No ja imam donekle različito mišljenje u pogledu uloge nauke u društvu. Ne mislim nužno da je primjereno da se naučni način mišljenja promoviše u skladu s prosvjetiteljskim idealima kao da se radi o svojevrsnoj ideologiji ili čak religiji koja nužno i bez obzira na okolnosti pomaže da svijet učinimo boljim (Holtorf 2005). Mislim da moramo prihvatiti da oblast poput arheologije može biti – i stvarno jeste – korisna za društvo, odnosno, koristi koje ona donosi nisu zasnovane na postignućima naučne metode i naučne misli.

Sudeći o Osmanagićevom istraživanju prema standardima koji vrijede za nauku značilo bi promašiti gotovo sve što je suština njegovog projekta. Ironija je u tome da se upravo u tome Osmanagić s tim nije složio u mnogim prilikama, uključujući i onu kad je bio kod nas: tada je svoj rad još uvijek predstavljao uglavnom u naučnom kontekstu. Slažem se s Irnom da nas ta pozicija zavodi na krivi put. Također bih rekao da je ta tvrdnja u njegovom slučaju donekle neodgovarajuća. Ali, ne bih ga nazvao šarlatanom, ne bih ga optužio da se bavi "lažnom naukom", ne bih njegov pristup opisao kao "bapsku priču" – kao da nauka mora biti ideal za svakog istraživača i kao da je ona jedini važeći standard za znanje.

Opšte govoreći, mislim da bismo o ljudima morali da sudimo na osnovu toga ko su i šta rade, a ne na osnovi toga šta nisu i šta ne rade. Osmanagić je očigledno postigao jako mnogo, iako to možda nisu naučna postignuća. Iz moje perspektive, trebalo bi da se koncentrišemo na to, naravno, kritički

IRNA Stvarno bi me zanimalo što je tačno po tvojem mišljenu Osmanagić postigao. Ekonomski bum? Rast svijesti o važnosti baštine?

CORNELIUS Smatram da je Osmanagić bio veoma uspješan u načinu na koji je angažovao i mobilisao ljude u Bosni i šire. Bosanske piramide inspiracija su za ljude, koja ima značenje koje nadmašuje horizont svakodnevnog života, tradicionalne politike i poslijerаća. Osmanagić je uspio navesti mnoge ljude da razmišljaju o bosanskoj baštini, o istraživačkim potencijalima (bili oni naučni ili ne), a u krajnjoj liniji čak i o smislu života. Sve je to značajno. Njegov rad donio je i ekonomsku korist toj regiji. Osim toga, Osmanagić je zaslužan da se o Bosni u svijetu opet govori, i to ne u kontekstu rata, teških uslova života ili razaranja. Tera Pruitt (2009, 2012) je detaljnije istraživala te koristi i citirala izvore prema kojima stanovnici Visokog smatraju da, ako njihove piramide nisu prave, trebalo bi ih napraviti jer donose korist ljudima te regije.

ANDREW Mislim da se ipak moram polemički osvrnuti na neke od ovih momenata.

Prvo, arheologija kao struka i dio kulturne baštine u Bosni i Hercegovini upravo su počeli da se oporavljaju kad je Osmanagić odlučio da promoviše svoju hipotezu. Genercija novih mladih arheologa obrazovana u inostranstvu (naročito u Zadru i Zagrebu), te izvjestan dio arheologa koji su za vrijeme rata otišli iz zemlje, odlučili su da se vrate. Nevladine organizacije koje se bave kulturnom baštinom počele su da se stabilizuju (nakon perioda u kojem je najhitniji zadatak bio rad na restauraciji/ rekonstrukciji) i postale su prepoznatljivo lice na sceni građanskog društva. Mostovi u Mostaru i Višegradu, godine 2005. odnosno 2007. uvršteni su na UNESCO-ov spisak svjetske baštine. Komisija za očuvanje nacionalnih spomenika (unatoč mnogobrojnim hendikepima koji proističu iz činjenice da se radi o državnom tijelu) počela je da radi na popisivanju lokaliteta koji se smatraju nacionalnim spomenicima, čineći ih tako vidljivijima (to se osobito odnosi na lokalitete u ruralnim sredinama i nekropole stećaka). Osmanagić se u biti ukrcao u taj voz, ali bazirajući prezentacijsku taktiku na uglavnom arheološkom diskursu. Na nesreću, ta njegova "taktika" bila je nešto što nije bilo blisko akademskoj zajednici. Koristeći svoj smisao za biznis (iskustvo iz vremena kad se bavio recikliranjem metala), uspio je da arheologe prikaže kao "zaparožene u svoje metode", "koji s visoka gledaju na običnog čovjeka", što se veoma dopalo njegovim sljedbenicima, a njemu je kasnije zgodno poslužilo da ubaci ideju da je osporavanje piramida dio "zavjere akademske elite".

Iako Cornelius to možda vidi kao samo za sebe i samo po sebi pozitivnu stvar, ja u tome vidim činjenicu da je akademska zajednica u BiH bila (i u višestrukom smislu još uvijek jeste) nepripremljena za takvo šta. Osmanagićeva retorika iskoristila je antiintelektualizam i ohrabrivala nekritičko mišljenje, tako da se u debatu o piramidama struka naprosto nije uključila. Mnogi mladi arheolozi bojali su se o njima javno govoriti, a profesori su diskusiju o "piramidama" u suštini zabranili (2005. ili 2006. u Mostaru je čak došlo do incidenta, odnosno, cijela grupa studenata oborena je na ispitu jer je dotični profesor u hodniku ispred prostorije u kojoj se održavao ispit čuo kako studenti razgovaraju o tome šta se događa u Visokom). Mislim da nije bilo nikakvog "regrutovanja" ljudi od strane Osmanagića, radilo se naprosto o "instruktaži".

Nadalje, ideja o "piramidama" ni u kom slučaju nije bila "inspiracija za ljude sa značenjem koje nadmašuje horizont svakodnevnog života, tradicionalne plitike i poslijeraća". Kako je već rečeno, ideja o piramidama ubrzo je našla prostor za sebe u etno-nacionalističkim konstruktima u zemlji.

Iako je Osmanagić možda stvarno mnoge ljude naveo na promišljanje o bosanskoj baštini, mislim da istraživački potencijal (bilo u strogo naučnom ili u nekom drugom smislu) i negativne strane njegove metode daleko pretežu nad onim što je u njoj bilo pozitivno. Televizijska serija Pozitivna geografija (2001. – 2009.), koju je, pored drugih, vodio Nisvet Džanko, već je izvršila jak uticaj u smislu da je među ljudima jačala svijest o vlastitoj sredini i kulturnoj baštini. Kako sam već rekao, novi val arheologa obrazovanih u inostranstvu tada je ulazio u struku, a za njima će uslijediti i val diplomiranih arheologa iz Mostara i Sarajeva: nastavni program iz arheologije na sarajevskom univerzitetu započe se ostvarivati tek u školskoj godini 2008./09. (Lawler, 2014b) iako je zamisao formirana kao prijedlog još u martu 1993. (Kaljanac, 2014, str. 241), a fakultetski odjel osnovan u junu 2007. godine (ibid., str. 248). Da li su Osmanagićeve ideje i aktivnosti ubrzale univerzitetski nastavni program stvar je za diskusiju. Postojala je i generacija etnologa s banjolučkog univerziteta koji su diplomirali neko vrijeme poslije rata, ali prije 2005. godine. Ti ljudi (kao i gorepomenute inicijative i organizacije) imale su, odnosno, trebale su da imaju upravo takav efekt i da istovremeno otvore prostor za dijalog.

DANIJEL Slažem se s Andrewom u glavnim tačkama. Radi se o zanimljivom pitanju koje navodi na diskusiju o prirodi i transmisiji znanja u savremenoj nauci i javnom diskursu. Iako se oslanja na razne oblasti prirodnih nauka, arheologija je van svake sumnje humanistička nauka. To znači da interpretacija nalaza uvijek ostaje subjektivna i pokretana aspektima kao što su npr. vrsta stručnog obrazovanja naučnika koji nalaze tumači, njegove/ njezine kulturne navike, politički nazori, lično iskustvo itd. Arheolozi egzistiraju u međusobnom kontaktu, ali su u kontaktu i s društvom koje ih okružuje i – budimo iskreni – od kojeg dobivaju plate ili stipendije. To društvo dobija interpretaciju prošlosti od zvaničnih naučnih autoriteta koji djeluju kao tumači društvene stvarnosti. Dakle, na tom nivou slažem se s prof. Holtorfom. No istraživanje pseudoarheologije takođe je legitimno i nužno jer je pseudoarheologija društveni fenomen, nije nevažno razumjeti zašto određeni dio društva prihvata tu vrstu "alternativnog znanja" koje egzistira van zvanične mreže naučnog autoriteta. Osmanagić je imao uspjeha u većinski bošnjačkim djelovima Bosne i Hercegovine, ali nije uspio da privuče pažnju javnosti u susjednoj Hrvatskoj, iako je i tamo "vidio" piramide i "čuda" prethistorije kao što su npr. megalitske zidine iz željeznog doba na Bribirskoj glavici kod Skradina, gdje tri posljednje godine učestvujem u iskapanjima. Zašto nije i tamo uspio? Zato što akademska mreža u Hrvatskoj funkcioniše više-manje normalno i akademski diskurs ima autoritet u javnosti, za razliku od BiH gdje je ta mreža uništena tokom oružanog sukoba, a za njenu je obnovu potrebno mnogo vremena.

To nas dovodi do pitanja autoriteta i širenja znanja. Iako savremeni naučnici međusobno komuniciraju postmodernim meta-jezikom (ili čak metamodernim, naime, neki istraživači tvrde da je postmodernizam mrtav, npr. Vermeulen & van der Akker 2010), javni diskus još uvijek je uvelike ukorijenjen u modernističkom diskursu koji istraživanje prošlosti sagledava kao potragu za "historijskom istinom". Mada akademski meta-jezik opravdano priznaje da se prošlost može tumačiti na različite načine, odnosno da nikad nećemo moći u potpunosti otkriti "historijsku istinu", treba izbjegavati pretjerane simplifikacije govoreći da svako ima pravo da interpretira prošlost. Iz tog razloga veoma je važno voditi računa o tome da nauka mora da održi svoj autoritet u široj zajednici. Dakle, u potpunosti se slažem s Irnom – Osmanagićev projekt prvo moramo da okvalifikujemo kao bapsku priču i lažnu nauku jer on ne slijedi etablirane načine istraživanja i interpretacije nalaza. Tek nakon što to utvrdimo kao činjenicu, možemo prijeći na postmoderni (ili metamoderni) pristup i njegov projekt osmotriti iz raznih perspektiva: iz perspektive savremene politike, konstrukcije identiteta, pseudoarheološkog diskursa itd.

CORNELIUS Jako bi me zanimalo da čujem od Danijela nešto o recepciji Osmanagićevih pokušaja u Hrvatskoj. Kad kažeš da "akademska mreža u Hrvatsko funkcioniše više-manje normalno i akademski diskurs ima autoritet u javnosti", pitam se da li to znači – barem tako zvuči – da se u krajnjoj liniji radi o pitanju moći. A to otvara više pitanja kojima bi se trebalo pozabaviti. Da li uspjeh alternativne arheologije uglavnom zavisi od stepena u kojem je održan "autoritet nauke" u javnoj domeni? Znači li to da se naučnici – poput policije ili vojske – bave održavanjem autoriteta? Da akademske mreže funkcioniraju "normalno" onda kada doprinose održavanju moći nauke u društvu? U tom kontekstu, da li to znači da oni koji su skeptični u odnosu na bosanske piramide tako misle zbog toga što njihovim umom vlada zvanična nauka, djelimično kao rezultat normalnog funkcioniranja akademskih mreža? Da li to ujedno znači da su Osmanagićevi sljedbenici oslobođeni od intelektualne okupacije te vrste? Ironija je u tome da bi se sam Osmanagić zapravo mogao složiti s takvom ocjenom. U nekom smislu, on sebe prezentira kao narodnog arheologa koji se bori s akademskim establišmentom i njegovim centrima moći.

DANIJEL Čini mi se da nije u pitanju odnos između moći i znanja nego kvalifikovanost za određeni posao, u istom smislu kako su medicinski stručnjaci kvalifikovani da tumače zdravstvene probleme, arhitekti da grade zgrade, odnosno vodoinstalateri da popravljaju vodovodne cijevi. Ne postavljam pitanje rada ljekara, arhitekata ili vodoinstalatera kao grupa jer znam da oni jesu stručno osposobljeni za taj posao. Uspjeh alternativnih oblika znanja po mojem je mišljenu zaista povezan s uticajem (ili odsustvom uticaja) akademskih/stručnih mreža u pojedinom društvu. Ne slažem se s terminom "intelektualna okupacija" – akademsko obrazovanje i učešće u akademskim mrežama pojedinca kvalifikuje da podržava ili osporava etablirane paradigme ili diskurse. Funkcija policije i vojske u netotalitarnim režimima nije da održavaju autoritet nego da održavaju red. Slično gledam i na društvenu ulogu akademske zajednice kao grupe profesionalaca stručno osposobljenih da interpretiraju (u ovom slučaju) prošlost za širu publiku. Pripadnost toj grupi uslovljena je samo uspješno završenim strukovnim obrazovanjem, dakle, individualnom osposobljenošću za tumačenje prošlosti, ovjerenom od strane ljudi koji imaju akreditive da o tome sude. Ne kažem da na interpretacije prošlosti ne utiče pripadni zeitgeist – naprotiv on itekako utiče. Međutim, ovdje ne govorimo o interpretaciji historijskih događaja (koji zaista uvijek podliježu diskusiji), nego o činjenicama koje je lako utvrditi – npr. da li je Visočica brdo ili piramida. A čitava priča o "intelektualnoj okupaciji" dio je retorike kojom se služi "alternativna" nauka koja nije sposobna da ponudi koherentne argumente o pitanjima u odnosu na koja osporava "zvaničnu" nauku.

CORNELIUS Ne, ne mislim da je uloga arheologa u društvu ta da "održavaju red" u pogledu raznih interpretacija prošlosti (Holtorf 2005, 2007). Mislim da je naša odgovornost u društvu više od pružanja ljudima činjenica o prošlosti, smatram da se ona po mogućnosti mora sastojati i u donekle mekšoj interpretaciji tih činjenica. Proces istraživanja prošlosti posjeduje vrijednost kao takav. A i prošlost ima politički karakter: što god prezentirali kao činjenice odnosno interpretacije, to će uvijek imati konzekvence u društvu. Po mojem mišljenju, potrebno je sagledati šta arheologija radi u društvu – i za to društvo. Iz te perspektive, rekao bih da u Bosni hiljadama godina nije bilo piramida, ali da ih sada na neki način ima. Dakle, ključno pitanje za mene nije da li one postoje, nego šta rade.

APE#086
Thomas Nolf
Peculiar Artifacts in Bosnia & Herzegovina
an imaginary exhibition

ISBN 9789490800642
www.artpapereditions.org

Graphic design:
Jurgen Maelfeyt, Jonas Temmerman (6'56")

Proofreading:
Victoria Gonzalez Figueras
Selma Kešetović

Translation to Bosnian:
Radmila Schneider
Selma Kešetović
Erwin van Horenbeeck

Text contribution:
Danijel Dzino

Printing: L.capitan, Ruddervoorde
International distribution: ideabooks.nl
Distribution Belgium: exhibitionsinternational.org

Thanks to my family, friends, funders and all the people who gave me their support over the past few years.

Special thanks to:
Dominique Somers, Johan Grimonprez, Max Pinckers, Maarten Devoldere, Anna Fernandez De Paco, Belgian Embassy: Diplomatic Office Sarajevo, Jusuf Hadžifejzović, Eleanor Rose, Pierre Courtin, Zlatan Hadžifejzović, Sandra Bradvic, Hannes Nolf, Gauthier Oushoorn, Sam Weerdmeester, Bence Bakkers, Victoria Gonzalez-Figueras, Alexis Gautier, Semir Osmanagić, Wouter Bouvijn, Hannes Nolf, Titus Simoens, Dino Hakalovic, Jan Desloover, DMV, Bieke Depoorter, Flor Declercq, Joke Berghmans, Pieter-Jan Vandromme, Andrea Copetti, KASK School of Arts, Alain Ayers, Katrien Reist, Semir Osmanagić, Andrew Lawler, Cornelius Holtorf, Danijel Dzino, Sasha Buljevic, Irna, Tatjana Sekulic, Kurt Bassuener, Tom Viaene, Hans Theys, Andrijana Pravidur, Rachel Monosov, Kahil Janssens, Lars Kwakkenbos, Laura Herman, Adela Jušić, Natasa Krsulj, Jock Doubleday

And all the crowdfunding contributors

Sources:

Nolf, Thomas (2013-2017)

Munro, Robert (1900) *Rambles and studies in Bosnia-Herzegovina and Dalmatia*, William Blackwood and Sons, Edinburg and London

Patsch, Carl (1911) *Bosnien und Herzegowina in Römischer Zeit*, B.-H. Instituts Für Balkanforschung, Bosn.-Herc. Landesdruckerei

Renner, Heinrich (1897) *Durch Bosnien und die Hercegovina*, Verlag von Dietrich Reimer, Berlin

Holbach, Maude (1910) *Bosnia and Herzegovina, some wayside wanderings,* J. Lane, London

Miller William (1898) *Travels and politics in the Near East*, Frederick A. Stokes, New York

European Space Agency, website

Miletić, Nada (1982) *Stećci*, Spektar, Zagreb

Milošević, Ante (1991) *Stećci i Vlasi*,Regionalni Zavod Za Zaštitu Spomenika Kulture, Split

Weerdmeester, Sam (2017)

Central Intelligence Agency (1995)

Werner von, Anton (1878) Congress of Berlin, 13 July 1878

Fondacija "Arheološki park: Bosanska piramida Sunca"

Dzino, Danijel, Commentary: *Archaeology and the (De)Construction of Bosnian Identity*, in: Archaeological Review from Cambridge, November 2012

Nolf, Thomas & Oushoorn, Gauthier (2016-2017)

With the support of:

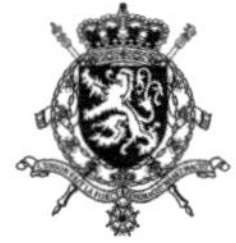

KINGDOM OF BELGIUM
Federal Public Service Foreign Affairs
Embassy of Belgium/
Diplomatic Office in Sarajevo